Global Governance and Its Effects on State and Law

Central and Eastern European Forum for Legal, Political, and Social Theory Yearbook

Edited by Jürgen Busch / Péter Cserne / Michael Hein /
Miklós Könczöl / Miodrag Jovanović / Marta Soniewicka

Volume 6

PL ACADEMIC RESEARCH

Martin Belov (ed.)

Global Governance and Its Effects on State and Law

PL ACADEMIC RESEARCH

Bibliographic Information published by the Deutsche Nationalbibliothek
The Deutsche Nationalbibliothek lists this publication in the Deutsche Nationalbibliografie; detailed bibliographic data is available in the internet at http://dnb.d-nb.de.

Library of Congress Cataloging-in-Publication Data
Names: Central and Eastern European Forum of Young Legal, Political, and Social Theorists (7th : 2015 : Sofia, Bulgaria) | Belov, Martin, editor.
Title: Global governance and its effects on state and law / Martin Belov (ed.).
Description: Frankfurt am Main : Peter Lang GmbH, 2016. | Series: Central and Eastern European Forum for Legal, Political and Social Theory yearbook, ISSN 2191-8317 ; volume 6
Identifiers: LCCN 2016000977 | ISBN 9783631673089
Subjects: LCSH: Law and globalization—Congresses. | International cooperation—Congresses.
Classification: LCC KZ1268 .C426 2015 | DDC 341—dc23 LC record available at http://lccn.loc.gov/2016000977

ISSN 2191-8317
ISBN 978-3-631-67308-9 (Print)
E-ISBN 978-3-653-06518-3 (E-Book)
DOI 10.3726/978-3-653-06518-3

PL Academic Research is an Imprint of Peter Lang GmbH.

Peter Lang – Frankfurt am Main · Bern · Bruxelles · New York · Oxford · Warszawa · Wien

This publication has been peer reviewed.

www.peterlang.com

Table of Contents

Introduction

Global governance is a threefold issue. It has theoretical, normative, and empirical dimensions. In combination they simultaneously reflect and form a new coordinated system for global policy making. Global governance is both multilayered with regard to the territorial aspect of the power structure and multidimensional with regards to the spheres of governance that it encompasses. Moreover global governance is accomplished through an extended set of actors which includes both bearers of public power (state, sub-state, local, and supranational institutions) and key veto players (see Tsebelis, 2002) with corporate and private background and structure that fulfil public functions or have influence over the public sphere and the public power (NGOs, transnational corporations, global religions, global professional and interest-based networks, different funds, rating agencies, stock and financial exchanges, banks, etc.).

The empirical aspect of global governance consists in the swirl of events that produce the current situation characterised by emerging supranational constitutionalisation with networks, hierarchic pyramids, transversally bordered spaces (see Sassen, 2013, 23), and symmetric or asymmetric chains forming the constitutional geometry of our time. Moreover it is a phenomenon with implications in different spheres of social relations – global, international and domestic, economic, financial, political, cultural, and constitutional.

There are different manifestations of the empirical dimension of global governance. Some of them produce reshaping of the institutional design of the systems or, vice versa, stem out of such remodelled institutional infrastructure. Others have projections in different policy fields. In any case they start to serve as important determinants of the political behaviour of the politicians, the citizens, the NGOs, the corporations, and all other actors of the socio-political process.

Thus the globalising processes related to the reshaping of constitutional geometry, reallocation of the power schemes, rescaling of the relations between the people, the public authority, and the territory produce the need for the legal institutionalisation of global governance. The multidimensional and multilayered socio-political process we are currently witnessing has to be democratically framed and based on rule of law in order to result in supranational constitutionalism and not to end up in expert led post-constitutionalism.

The normative dimension of global governance is nowadays not only a result of rational, centralised, and harmonised efforts for the establishment of a non-contradictory institutional system for public management of the socially important processes. It is polycentric and in many instances diachronic and asymmetric process of emergence of islands of governability of the increasingly complex and perplexed world. The "law's melody" (see Postema, 2003, pp. 227–241)[1] currently does not resemble the quasi-mathematical and well-ordered music of Mozart. Sometimes it is close to Schoenberg's dodecaphony of co-equal interrelated tones, in other instances, it is rather a jazz interpretation whereas there are also cases of recognisable authority and imperialism as in some of the Beethoven's works. To put it in the words of Martti Koskenniemi taken from his keynote speech at the IACL World Congress in Oslo in 2014 the current world resembles an institutional point of view very much like a Kandinsky painting.

Hence there are different approaches to the formation of the normative dimension of global governance. There are systematic efforts for establishing and reestablishing hierarchical or network public authority on different territorial and substantial domains. They are conscious and programmatic attempts at a rational (re)construction of the world and for regaining the dominance of the public authority over the private interest and thus for the maintenance of rational constitutionalism. In addition there are also negotiated and inductive forms of authority grounded on the reasonableness of the market logic and on the idea of interest based equilibrium (i.e. in the form of the Friedrich Hayek's catallaxy) blurring the boundaries between the public and the private. In parallel to these general models for normative institutionalisation of global governance there are also normative practices of key veto players usually playing "nested games" (see Tsebelis, 1990). They also are being reflected in the normative dimension of global governance.

We have witnessed a rising theoretical interest in global governance during the last decades. The interest is accelerated by the advance of globalisation and the need to find new concepts and paradigms to approach the structural and functional changes it produces in the legal system and in the social and political reality. The theory of global governance has its specific profile and own standing in the debates on supranational and multilevel policy making in the context of late modern and early postmodern society. However often it is intermingled with the globalisation scientific discourse.

The global governance theory is closely related to the theory of globalisation. However it has its own profile, range of conceptual, normative and practical issues, and analytical apparatus. The scope and substance of the global governance theory may be constructed in a twofold way. One possible approach for the construction

---

1 Here I borrow the term "law's melody" from Gerald Postema but I use it with a different meaning.

of a global governance discourse is to represent it as a continuation and mixture of several classical approaches to constitution-, policy- and law-making. Thus it will start to serve as an upgrade to theories, concepts, and paradigms that have already been developed with a view to different problems related to policy making in an increasingly pluralist setting, e.g. game theory, rational choice theory, supranational integration or supranational federalist theory, libertarianism, etc. Sometimes these discourses on which global governance is supposed to step upon are rather controversial and inconsistent with each other. Moreover global governance should not be tackled as a mere reproduction of theories with regard to new problems stemming out of the new realities that have emerged during the last decades.

Consequently a second approach is more plausible. It tackles global governance as an independent discourse that has to serve as a theoretical answer to the structural and functional changes of key concepts of legal, political, and constitutional theory. Core concepts such as power, authority, identity, state, society, territory, demos, nation, community, sovereignty, democracy, rights, jurisdiction, etc. are being put into question by several phenomena that have recently gained momentum. Here one can mention the information and communication revolution, globalisation, the crisis of territoriality, the new production modes, the structural changes in economy, finance and capitalism, and the global and trans-generational issues related to economy, ecology, public morality, and sustainable development.

The global governance theory is necessarily interrelated with the globalisation and modernisation discourses with regard to its ontology, teleology, axiology, and pragmatics. However it has its own standing. More precisely its analytical contributions regarding the conceptualisation and problematising of the structural, functional, and procedural changes in policy making and its legal and constitutional frame and infrastructure have to be welcomed and further elaborated.

This current book tries to address some of the above-mentioned issues. It is a conference volume of the 7th Central and Eastern European (CEE) Forum of Young Legal, Political, and Social Theorists which was held on March 27 and 28, 2015 at the University of Sofia "St. Kliment Ohridski," Bulgaria. It encompasses selected papers of participants in this conference that was devoted to global governance and its effects on state and law.

The book is based on the following logic. It begins with conceptual issues concerning the fundamental concepts of constitutional law science, political science, and the sociology of globalisation. It problematises the penetration and interrelation of legal orders and the structural changes of the law and state produced by the globalisation and global governance. Furthermore it continues with the influence of globalisation and global governance over substantial constitutional and philosophical issues such as human rights and trans-generational justice. Last but not least the emergence and development of new supranational forms of jurisprudence and their impact on the supranational and national legal order and institutional systems are analysed.

Thus the book tries to address some of the main issues and topics of research in the global governance discourse. On a structural level, the fluidisation of the demos, the enhanced importance of the global social communities, the crisis of territoriality, the reshaping of capitalism, and the relationship between the "public" and the "private" are discussed. The interrelations between legal orders, the monistic, dualistic or pluralistic architecture of the globalised legal space and the new institutional logic and dynamics of the governance are approached from legal, philosophical, political science, and sociological points of view. On the actors' level the increased influence of transnational corporations, global religions and supranational regimes, and jurisdictions is conceptualised and critically studied. On the substantive level new approaches towards human rights, sovereignty, identity, and future generations are presented. What follows is a brief overview of the main topics and aspects of the authors' contributions.

Part I is devoted to the paper of one of the keynote speakers of the conference. Professor (Prof.) Saskia Sassen analyses the current changes in global capitalism. She problematises the predominance of financial capitalism over politics and economy and the effects produced by the transnational activity of the global financial actors.

Sassen analyses the effects of the most advanced forms of capitalism on the global North and the global South. She believes that the global South has been forcefully integrated into the realm of global finance and world capitalism through several "disciplining mechanisms" – the increase of debt, the debt controlling instruments, and the appropriation of land by foreign public and private investors. According to Prof. Sassen, "The IMF, World Bank and other such programs establish the criteria and process these debts, thereby functioning as a global disciplining regime."

On the other hand, the global North was submerged from the logic of financial capitalism via systemic financial crises. Sassen believes that the global North is being disciplined through financial adjustment crises that launched a new financial era that started in the 1980's but accelerated after 1997.

To put it in Sassen's words, "What stands out in this phase that begins in the 1980's is that global and adjustment crises had the effect of securing the conditions for globally linked financial markets and the ascendance of a financial logic organising larger and larger sectors of the economy in the global North. In this process large components of the non-financial economy in these countries were ruined."

According to Sassen 'crisis' is a structural feature of deregulated, interconnected, and electronic financial markets. Moreover, "If crisis is a structural feature of current financial markets, then crisis becomes a feature of non-financial economic sectors through their financialising." Sassen believes that "The sharp growth of finance, partly based on the financialising of non-financial economic sectors," is leading "to overall extremely high financial deepening." Thus she introduces the concept of "financial deepening of economies."

Sassen suggests that "the new age of radical reshuffling of capitalism" introduces structural changes in the society, economics and systems of welfare, and solidarity mainly via two logics. "The first one is the systemic logic of economic and (de)regulatory policies of most countries. The second logic is the actual material development of growing areas of the world into extreme zones for the enactment of that systemic logic, that is, for these new or sharply expanded modes of profit extraction disregarding the side-effects and social consequences."

Sassen focuses on the capacity of key international institutions to impose particular logics across economic sectors and across the world. She does so through the lenses of several key normative concepts such as "corporate globalising," "financialising of more and more domains," which marks "the ascendance of a new organising logic in advanced capitalism," "geographic expansion and the systemic deepening of capitalism." Sassen believes that we are living in a "time of extreme financialisation" that is defined by the "expulsion of people and the destruction of the 'advanced' capitalisms of the mid-20th century."

Three main ideas launched in this paper reveal continuity with previous key themes in Sassen's work. Here she problematises the issue of territory through a specific angle. While analysing the land acquisition by foreign investors she emphasises "the shift of that acquired land from 'national sovereign territory' to the commodity 'land' for the global market. In other words, a weakening of a complex category that at its best brought with it a formal enabling of the state's authority and inhabitants' rights to make the state accountable." Thus a second key issue reemerges namely the structural transformation of capitalism into a territory detached phenomenon and its emancipation from the economic and political substantiality. The destructive effects of globalisation towards established modes of economic and social relations resulting in expulsions are the third cornerstone idea from Sassen's works around which her paper in this volume is organised.

If we continue the territory and foreign investment discourse initiated by Sassen, we can come to the conclusion that the buying of foreign land may serve as a device for the buying of sovereignty. The territory as an element of statehood in the terms of Georg Jellinek's theory is gradually challenged and even replaced by its status as a financialised commodity in the global financial markets. Common concerns can be raised by the phenomenon of sovereign funds buying sovereign debt of foreign states. This process again resembles acquisition of foreign sovereignty through market and more precisely financial market instruments.

There is an implicit dialogue in the book between the papers of Saskia Sassen and Christoph Good. Sassen highlights the "predatory logics" of the transnational corporations and their social irresponsibility. Good presents and analyses an emergent phenomenon – corporate human rights initiatives aimed at increasing or at least demonstrating some kind of corporate social responsibility.

The papers published in Part II have several common features. They discuss the effects of globalisation and global governance on the key constitutional principles and concepts. As well, Part II discusses some of the most important normative ideologies, concepts, and paradigms in legal and political philosophy. The crisis of territoriality, the changes in the territory's role as a normative reference for ascribing of authority, community, solidarity, and welfare are among the central problems that are part of the analysis of the papers framed by Part II.

The idea that "the rising of new categories of actors" and the "de-territorialisation of the [societal, political and economic] relations questions central fundamental principles of […] law" (see the paper of Christoph Good in this book) is also a common core of the papers of Saskia Sassen, Martin Belov, Mate Paksy, and Michele Saporiti. All three papers in Part II discuss directly or indirectly the issue of whether Georg Jellinek's traditional "three element theory" of the state is still valid under the conditions of globalisation and post-modern societal fragmentation and implicitly if the global governance paradigm provides an appropriate analytical framework.

In my paper I discuss the effects of globalisation and the crisis of territoriality on the constitutional principles (sovereignty, democracy, rule of law, and welfare state). I believe that three main phenomena – the information and communication revolution, the global fluidisation and dispersion of the demos, and the territorial irresponsibility of the financial capital deeply affect constitutional principles.

Sovereignty is usually perceived as a monolithic conception. Moreover the constitutionalism is tackled as a holistic and all-encompassing legal frame for public power and public decision making with predominantly political character. Classical constitutional law is functional upon more or less clear distinctions between the public and the private, the state and the society, the politics and the economy, and finance. In my paper I am trying to prove that the current phase of globalisation has led to the fragmentation of sovereignty, a substantial proliferation of constitutionalism, and a strategic redefinition of the demarcation lines between the private and the public.

I am exploring the increasing divergence and mismatch between the holders of supreme decision making power in the different fields of socio-political relations. Moreover I am analysing the influence of the global governance players on the concept and practice of sovereignty. I am presenting also the tension between the personal and territorial sovereignty of the states in the context of globalisation and crisis of territoriality. The investment of financial sovereignty through financial mechanisms and of personal sovereignty via migration in the sovereign domain of the territorial state is also explored.

Furthermore I am problematising the effects of territoriality crisis, global fluidity of the demos, and the transnational migration on the increasingly tensed relation between liberalism and democracy. I am presenting the impact of these phenomena on the erosion of the territory based democratic community. I am questioning the possibilities for democratic participation of the diasporic communities in the decision making of their state of origin as well as the eventual emergence of non-territorial and aterritorial democracy.

Moreover I am providing an analysis of the influence of globalisation and global governance on rule of law. I am trying to historically deconstruct the concept of rule of law and to provide evidence whether the determinants that have led to its emergence in Western Modernity are still available. I am presenting also several scenarios for the development of global or at least supranational rule of law.

Last but not least I am exploring the structural and functional changes of the welfare state in the current global context. I am presenting the challenges of the information and technology revolution, the current phase of capitalistic development, and the global fluidity of the demos to the constitutional principle of welfare state.

Mate Paksy is questioning whether the idea of the territorially based nation-state can still be sufficiently functional as a normative methodological construction. He presents different classical and more recent theories and approaches for territorial and non-territorial protection of minorities. According to Paksy "'in the field of social science, the expert should try to understand that a given territory is not simply a neutral geographical unity, but a particular space in which the political community lives and should live irrespectively of its ethnical composition."

Moreover he problematises the discrepancy between the universality and normativity of justice and the locality and factuality of the territory.

Mate Paksy presents two types of techniques for the preservation of the rights of national minorities – one based on the principle of territoriality and another based on the principle of personality. He believes that "the principle of territoriality will always preserve its priority over the principle of personality in general and, for the time being, there is no specific reason why the principle of territoriality should be limited geographically to Western multi-ethnic states."

Michele Saporiti's paper focuses on the possibility to conceptualise global religions as transnational nations. He analyses global religions as the new transnational nations with reference to the core idea of identity. According to Saporiti "sovereignty does not exclusively concern states" due to the "emergence of new international actors in the last few decades" such as the "financial and economic global players" as well as the "global religions." Saporiti insists that "globalisation has transformed the power phenomenology" and has led to the emergence of both new actor schemes as well as new levels of policy making. In fact this is a common denominator of several papers published in this volume (e.g. Sassen, Belov, and Good).

According to Saporiti the state-centred world relies on national, international, and supranational levels of power allocation and sovereignty conceptualisation. However a further level marks the age of globalisation: the transnational level, where global powers address their influence towards states. After delimiting different power types he puts an emphasis on the power relations on the transnational level of the power infrastructure. In conclusion Saporiti believes that the theory should reconsider the concept of exclusive state sovereignty in the light of the processes of deterritorialisation and deculturation. Thus according to Saporiti a reexamination of the power and identity relationship between the states and the global actors such as the global religions has to be done.

Part III is generally framed by two abstract theoretical phenomena – constitutional geometry and constitutional identity. Constitutional identity is a pressing issue in the current discourse in European, comparative, and national constitutional law as well as in legal theory and philosophy. It is widely discussed with regard to its capability of "drawing red lines" that should never be crossed in the context of European integration or with view to reasserting the concept of identity while making it not purely anthropological, sociological, or historical but also a constitutional and legal notion.

Constitutional geometry is the theoretical paradigm through which one can analyse the power relations scheme of the key constitutional and political institutions (see Belov, 2015, pp. 153–154). This scheme may simultaneously concern different spheres of public governance and government and different territorial levels of power allocation. It may be constructed as exclusively focused on the main decision making factors or as a wider and more inclusive model giving a broader view over the power architecture. Moreover the constitutional geometry may be perceived as part of the broader phenomenon of legal geometry – a theoretical approach that aims to explain the typical ordering of normative regulators and sources of law. Hence while the constitutional geometry is more institutionally than norm oriented, legal geometry is focused on the law, legal order, and the legal system.

The differing approaches to constitutional geometry in the context of an increasingly pluralist legal setting fostered by globalisation and global governance may produce different answers regarding the prevailing models of power allocation and decision making. Monocentrism competes with polycentrism, the pyramid and the hierarchy are challenged by the network. Two of the leading approaches for explaining the nature, system, and structure of the supranational constitutionalism are the multilevel governance and multilevel constitutionalism theory, on the one hand, and the constitutional pluralism, on the other, are in fact aspects and projections of the more general paradigm on the evolution of the constitutional geometry at the beginning of the XXI century.

The papers by Anna Kalisz and Monika Zalewska and Alexander Tsekov address the need to discuss and maybe rethink the currently floating and unstable legal relationship between the supranational and national legal orders and legal systems. Kalisz and Zalewska focus on the Kelsenian dilemmas regarding the interrelations between different legal orders, whereas Tsekov uses the concept of constitutional identity as a tool for the limitation of the constitutionalisation of the European integration.

The reflections of all three authors have common ground in that they take the law as the central instrument for constructing the relationship between multiple legal orders. Both papers are based on the normativist theory and methodology of law and state and make use of the dynamic concept of law in a normativist sense.

The paper by Anna Kalisz and Monika Zalewska is an attempt to clarify whether the theory of Hans Kelsen, which is usually associated with pyramid-like hierarchical legal and constitutional geometry, can still serve as an explanatory devise in the context of a multicentric and globalised legal world. According to Kalisz and Zalewska, the concept of a legal order is more appropriate than those of a legal system in the context of the multicentric world of global governance. This is due to the fact that the legal order contains also soft law as well as normative regulators produced by non-typical regulators.

Kalisz and Zalewska discuss whether one can apply "Kelsenian answers" to the multicentric legal reality. Thus their paper explores the uneasy relationship between the theory of multicentrism and the Kelsenian theory of state and law. Kalisz and Zalewska analyse the application of Kelsen's theory to global and European governances. They are initiating a discussion on the appropriateness of the distinction between monism and dualism from a Kelsenian point of view. Tsekov's paper also provides some arguments on the issue of the adequacy of the distinction between "monism" and "dualism" in the context of European and global governance from a legal positivist point of view.

Tsekov provides a formal understanding of the constitutional identity. According to him, the constitutional identity can be extracted only from the written constitution itself and cannot be traced to the ideal or factual constitutions (for these types of constitutions see Tanchev, 2003, 112). Tsekov criticises both the legal realist and meta-legal approaches to the issue of constitutional identity. He tries to provide a purely legal answer to the issue of whether the national constitutional identity can serve as a legal limit to the constitutionalisation of the European Union (EU) in several analytical steps. He defines the concepts of constitution and identity in order to be able to further differentiate between structural *ipse* and formal *idem* constitutional identity.

Tsekov believes that it is impossible to constitutionalise European integration by purely legal means. He emphasises that by rejecting both constitutional pluralism and constitutional globalism. Tsekov concludes that "the concept of sovereignty is not lost. It has been just renamed constitutional ipse identity." He finds that the ideal of a constitutionalised EU is based on factual assumptions rather than on legal arguments with a solid base in EU law and in the laws of the EU's member states.

Two parts of the book are devoted to human rights issues. The influence of globalisation and global governance on human rights is the analytical object of Part IV of the present volume. Trans-generational justice and the conceptualisation, preservation, and representation of the rights of future generations are discussed in Part V.

Global governance reshapes the institutional scheme of power as well as melts down the distinction between public and private. Many actors that institutionally were supposed to belong to the private sphere commence to accomplish public functions. Two of these actors – global religions and transnational corporations – are research objects of papers that are part of this book.

Christoph Good provides an analysis of the atypical role of transnational corporations as a standard setting for proactive actors in the human rights domain. He allocates his research in the context of the relationship between global and transnational business and the humanitarian standards in supranational and international law. Good explicitly aims at redefining "the corporate sector's role within the relevant norm-creating and norm-shaping process and the granting of regulative agency to corporations." Moreover he tries "to clarify the interdependent linkages between [the corporate human rights'] initiatives and the existing international human rights law framework," "to sketch current interdependencies of these governance driven corporate human rights standards with the classical legal human rights framework and to highlight synergies and challenges with respect to the legislative agency and the underlying dogmatic fundaments."

Good believes that individual and collective corporate human rights initiatives represent a new regulative type. Continuing the suggestions made by the author one can suppose that they are a phenomenon that is closely interrelated with globalisation, global governance, reshaping of the concept of public authority and power, as well as deterritorialisation. According to Good, the corporate human rights initiatives are a result of the "paradigmatic turn towards new polycentric governance approaches," and more precisely towards multistakeholderism.

Good's paper is part of the corporate social responsibility debate. Thus it is element of a more general trend of this volume, which aims at problematising the issue of territorial and social irresponsibility of the transnational capital. Different aspects of this problem are discussed also by the papers by Saskia Sassen and Martin Belov.

The paper by Axelle Reiter concerns the problem of state responsibility for private breaches of international law and the possibility for the horizontal application of human rights. Reiter analyses the horizontal application of international human rights standards in three aspects. First, she provides research of the direct effect of international norms in interpersonal conflicts before domestic courts. Second, she studies the indirect effect of international norms between private actors by invocation of states' international responsibility before international courts. Third, the author analyses the direct applicability of international norms to non-state actors in international trials or domestic trials based on universal jurisdiction.

Reiter stipulates that "universal rules have revolutionised the conception of normativity at the international level." In that respect she grounds her research on the suggestion that the emergence of community interests on international and supranational level has led to a shift from bilateralism. Thus she believes that the ideas of the international public order and core normative values start to have a formative role in the human rights domain. Reiter provides research devoted to the influence of global governance and multilevel constitutionalism in the horizontalisation of human rights.

The papers by both Szilárd Tattay and Miklós Könczöl are devoted to the rights of future generations. They have not only a common object of research but also try to specifically address the issue of future rights representation in general and in the context of globalisation and global governance.

Tattay provides a conceptualisation of rights for future generations from a philosophical and legal point of view. He questions whether future generations are capable to be holders of rights and provides a critical assessment of the different theories in that domain. More precisely Tattay presents the main theoretical approaches to future generations rights based on the concepts of "will," "choice," "interest," or "benefit" of the generations to come. Then he addresses some of the key philosophical problems, e.g. the non-existence of future people, the "non-identity problem" and the "will-interest controversy."

Könczöl problematises the very concept of future generations. According to him, the group of people denominated as future generations "is not simply too narrow or too broad: it is infinite and non-existent at the same time." He explores the origin and the content of the potential obligation of currently living people to protect the interests of their potential descendants and the "trans-generational character of human projects and, consequently, of communities."

Könczöl asks the question of "how to represent" future generations. He presents several possible models for the representation of the rights of future generations. He especially addresses the issue of representation of future generations on the supranational and EU level. Könczöl notes that "proposals for a democratic representation of future-related interests are usually meant to work within a nation-state context" and then admits that "decisions influencing the life circumstances of future people are not necessarily made at the national level." Hence he suggests an institutional model for supranational and even global discursive representation of future related interests.

Part VI addresses the procedural issues of global governance. It concerns the influence of global governance on law application and legal dispute resolution. Uroš Zdravković explores the multilateral system of rules centred on the World Trade Organization (WTO) and creating global trade order. He accomplishes an analysis of the WTO's role to provide security and predictability of the multilateral trading system. He does so with a view to the WTO's double nature as an intergovernmental international organisation and as a supranational regime.

According to Zdravković "the WTO strives to establish the universal regulatory framework for trade which should be the legal feature of economic globalisation." He considers that "the interdependent structure of the world's economy does not allow for the unilateral national decisions. In such conditions the WTO has become the regulator of governmental behaviour in international trade relations with a propensity to become the "world trade ministry."

Adam Szot's paper is devoted to the influence of global governance, international human rights standards, and the international court's jurisprudence over the internal separation of powers in the territorial state in general and the administrative discretion in particular. Szot explores the ways in which the jurisprudence of a supranational court – the European Court of Human Rights – determines the functioning of the activity of the administration of the member states of the Council of Europe. As Szot puts it "the question is in what manner and how 'deeply' and 'broadly' may the judicial decision influence the scope and manner of implementation of the discretionary power of the administration."

I would like to express my gratitude to the rector, the vice rectors, the rector's and university's administration and to the vice-deans and the members of the dean's office of the Law Faculty of the University of Sofia "St. Kliment Ohridski" for their organisational and financial support with regard to the realisation of the 7th CEE Forum "Global Governance and its Effects of State and Law" held on March 27 and 28, 2015 on the premises of the University in Sofia, Bulgaria and for the publication of this book. I would like to especially acknowledge the contribution of the dean of the Law Faculty of the University of Sofia "St. Kliment Ohridski" Prof. Dr. Sasho Penov who made possible the smooth carrying out of this project.

References

Belov, Martin. 2015. Can We Still Drive the State Machine the 'Old School' Way? Structural and Functional Deficits of the Modern State. In Law and State. Classical Paradigms and Novel Proposals, edited by Luka Burazin, Dorde Gardasevic and Alessio Sardo, 153–154. Frankfurt am Main: Peter Lang.

Postema, Gerald. 2003. Law's Melody: Time and the Normativity of Law. Associations. *Journal for Legal and Social Theory. Vol. 7, Number 1*: 227–241.

Sassen, Saskia. 2013. When Territory Deborders Territoriality. *Territory, Politics, Governance*. Vol. 1, Issue 1: 21–45.

Tanchev, Evgeni. 2003. Introduction in the Constitutional Law. Sofia: Sibi. (in Bulgarian)

Tsebelis, George. 1990. Nested Games. Rational Choice in Comparative Politics. Berkeley: University of California Press.

Tsebelis, George. 2002. Veto Players. How Political Institutions Work. Princeton and New York: Russell Sage Foundation/Princeton University Press.

Sofia, November 2015 Martin Belov

Part I. Global Governance and Transformation of Capitalism

Saskia Sassen

The Savage Sorting: Emergent Predatory Logics

Abstract

In the last two decades there has been a sharp growth in the numbers of people that have been "expelled," numbers far larger than the newly "incorporated" middle classes of countries such as India and China. I use the term "expulsion" to describe a diversity of conditions: the growing numbers of the abjectly poor, of the displaced in poor countries who are warehoused in formal and informal refugee camps, of the minoritised and persecuted in rich countries who are warehoused in prisons, of workers whose bodies are destroyed on the job and rendered useless at far too young an age, and able-bodied surplus populations warehoused in ghettoes and slums. A very different type of expulsion is the sharp increase in the amount of land bought by foreign governments and corporations, including financial firms. From 2006 to 2010, they acquired over 200 million hectares of land in Africa, Latin America, and Asia to grow food, to access underground water tables, and to access minerals, metals, and rare earths. Yet another type of expulsion is the massive destruction of the environment – bits of the biosphere herself expelled from their life space. My argument is that these diverse and many other kindred developments amount to a logic of expulsions, signalling a deeper systemic transformation in advanced capitalism. This transformation has been documented in bits and pieces by specialists of one or another element. I argue that we are confronting an overarching dynamic that is taking us into a new phase of global capitalism.

1. Introduction

Following a period of Keynesian-led relative redistribution in developed market economies, the United States (US) became the point actor for a radical reshuffling of capitalism. Today the shape of this reshuffling has become clear, particularly in its extreme visual orders. On the one hand, an expanded glamour zone of state of the art global city centres, high-tech research campuses, impressive engineering of state-of-the-art systems of all sorts. On the other, there is an expanded zone of devastations, losses, and miseries. In between these extremes there are the losses of the modest middle classes in most Western countries and the gains of the rural poor in China.

Two logics organise this reshuffling. One is systemic, and in the 1990's and onwards got wired into the economic and (de)regulatory policies of most countries. Eventually specific fiscal and monetary policies were implemented in most countries and came to affect key economic sectors, albeit with varying degrees of intensity. This opened up ground for new or sharply expanded modes of profit extraction even in unlikely places and through unlikely instruments. Examples are the financialising of even modest assets and debt in the global North and the sharp shift to extractive economies in the global South.

The second logic is the actual material development of growing areas of the world into extreme zones for the enactment of that systemic logic, that is, for these new or sharply expanded modes of profit extraction, no matter the cost in lives and the environment. The extreme forms are the proliferation of global cities, on the one hand, and on the other, extreme mining and work situations (for instance, workers who dismantle discarded ships in India, plantation workers exposed to poisonous inputs). These types of extreme settings have long been part of capitalism but today have expanded their domains to the global scale: they have become two strategic, thick local settings for global capitalism.

Critical to both these logics is the invention of extremely complex organisational and financial instruments to engage in what are, ultimately, new forms of primitive accumulation, albeit highly intermediated.

Many of the key components of the post-1989 global economy, already were present and under development in the early 1980's. The silent revolutions of 1989 are the iconic representation of a political process that had been building for a long time; the corporate globalising that took off in the late 1980's started many years earlier. But 1989 did make a major difference, most notably in giving these innovations the run of the world via the legitimatizing aura of market triumphalism. The outcome was the formation of a new kind of global economy.

Here I can only examine a few aspects of the dominant economic tendencies of the last decades and their deeply destructive character. The first section focuses on the capacity of key international institutions to impose particular logics across economic sectors and across the world. The equivalent of today's "austerity" policies in the global North began in the 1980's in the global South, weakening their economies and their governments. The financialising of more and more domains marks the ascendance of a new organising logic in advanced capitalism. This is not just a matter of the volume of finance, but, more importantly, of its getting wired into more and more economic sectors across the world.

2. A New Phase of Advanced Capitalism

The geographic expansion and systemic deepening of capitalist relations of production over the last 20 years have led to a brutal sorting of winners and losers. Since its origins and across its diverse phases, capitalism has been marked by violence, destruction, and appropriation – and it has engendered an enormous diversity of critical interpretations (e.g. see Galeano, 1997; Mignolo, 2007; Frank, 1998, 1971; Maldonado-Torres, 2007). It has also been partly shaped by the making of the regulatory state, a victory for the struggling working classes and the expanding middle classes.

Much attention has gone to the destruction of pre-capitalist economies via their incorporation into capitalist relations of production. The post-1980's period makes visible yet another variant of this appropriation via incorporation – the appropriation of traditional capitalisms to further the deepening of advanced capitalism. I use this term to capture a phase dominated by a financial logic. Built into this proposition is the fact of diverse phases of capitalist development and hence the possibility that in today's global phase the extension of capitalist relations has its own distinct mechanisms and that these need to be distinguished from older national and imperial phases.

One key mechanism is the capacity of today's financial system to financialise more and more components of economies. This has led to an appropriation of advanced capitalist economic sectors into a yet more advanced form of capitalism. It is this that I mean by the notion of new forms of primitive accumulation inside advanced capitalism itself, a thesis I develop at length elsewhere (see Sassen, 2008a, 2010, 2014).

Thus I find that the organising logic of this post-Keynesian period is now making legible its shape. An extreme component of this logic diverges sharply from the earlier systemic "valuing" of people as workers and as consumers. To put it starkly, it is a phase marked by the expulsion of people and the destruction of the "advanced" capitalisms of the mid-20th century in order to feed today's emergent forms of advanced capitalism shaped by the logics of high finance – its need to financialise more and more sectors, from used car loans to gold.

One of these instances is the structural adjustment project implemented by global regulatory institutions, notably the International Monetary Fund (IMF) and the World Bank starting in the 1980's, joined by the WTO in the 1990's. My argument here is that beyond the much-noted extraction of billions of dollars from global South countries in the form of debt servicing, the key is the work of systemic conditioning that took place. Debt servicing was the instrument for this disciplining; it weakened the governments of those countries by forcing them to pay growing shares of national revenue for interest on their debts rather than engaging in economic development. Further, it made them susceptible to signing unfavourable deals with global firms in extractive industries rather than furthering mass manufacturing by national firms.

The second instance is the sub-prime mortgage crisis that began in the early 2000's and exploded in 2007. Most of the attention has gone, and rightly so, to the massive losses for the individuals and families who were sold these mortgages, losses that will continue through 2014. In this case my argument is, again, that beyond the logics of extraction in the form of mortgage payments and mortgage agents' fees, also here we can detect a more foundational emergent dynamic: the use of a contract on a material asset (the mortgage) as one ingredient for making a complex investment instrument for high finance, with willingness to sacrifice the basic livelihood of what have become over ten million households in the US, and over two million (and growing) in Europe.

Central to my analysis is that inside capitalism itself we can characterise the relation of advanced to traditional capitalism as one marked by predatory dynamics rather than merely evolution, development, or progress. At its most extreme this can mean immiseration and exclusion of growing numbers of people who cease being of value as workers and consumers. It also means that traditional petty bourgeoisies and traditional national bourgeoisies cease being of value. I see the latter as part of the current systemic deepening of capitalist relations.

One brutal way of putting it is to say that the natural resources of much of Africa and good parts of Latin America count more than the people on those lands count as consumers and as workers. This is part of the systemic deepening of advanced capitalist relations of production. We have left behind the varieties of Keynesian periods that thrived on the accelerated expansion of prosperous working and middle classes – though not in today's emergent economies, especially in Asia. Keynesianism's valuing of people as workers and consumers was critical for the deepening of capitalism.

In what follows, the emphasis is on the making of capitalist relations of production, whether those of early or of advanced capitalism. In this paper, and in the larger projects on which these cases are based, I focus on two instances that are easily described as familiar resource-extraction. While extraction is indeed a major feature, which I describe, it is critical to go deeper so as to recover the making of a systemic transformation – how older forms of "advanced" capitalist economies are being destroyed or incorporated into the operational space of a new type of advanced capitalism. In brief, besides extraction, the two cases I describe are system-changing practices and projects.

3. Systemic Deepening: The Debt Nexus as a Logic of Extraction

The extraction of value from the global South and the implementation of restructuring programs at the hands of the IMF and the World Bank, have had the effect of "reconditioning" the terrain represented by these countries for an expansion of new forms of advanced capitalism. This includes its explicitly criminal forms.

The aspect that concerns me here is above all systemic deepening more so than extraction. Throughout the global South we see the rise of extremely rich elites along with the devastations of vast sectors of their economies and populations. More concretely, many of the poor countries subjected to this regime now have richer and larger elites than they used to have, along with larger shares of their populations in desperate poverty and less likely to enter the capitalist circuit via consumption than they did even 20 years ago. Many of the sub-Saharan countries had functioning health and education systems and economies, and less destitution than today.

Systemically governments have been weakened and corrupted; even resource-rich countries have had expanded shares of their people become destitute with Nigeria the most noted case. The dominant dynamic at work for these populations is, to a good extent, the opposite of the Keynesian period's valuing of people as workers and as consumers. This expelling has given expanded space to criminal networks, greater access to land and underground water resources to foreign buyers, whether firms or governments. Systemically, the role of rich donor countries has also shifted: overall they give less in foreign aid for development than 30 years ago. As a result, the remittances sent by low-income immigrants are larger than foreign aid. Philanthropies now enter the realm once almost exclusive to governments.

These systemic shifts contribute to explaining a complex difference that can be captured in a set of simple numbers. For much of the 1980's and onwards indebted poor countries were asked to pay a share of their export earnings toward debt service. This share tended to hover around 20%, which is far higher than that asked from other instances of country indebtedness. For instance, in 1953, the Allies cancelled 80% of Germany's war debt and only insisted on 3% to 5% of export earnings for debt service. They asked only 8% from Central European countries in the 1990's. In comparison, the debt service burdens on today's poor countries have wound up being extreme, as I discuss below. It does suggest that the aim regarding Germany was re-incorporation into the capitalist world economy of the time, and incorporation into today's advanced capitalism with regard to Central Europe.

In contrast, the aim vis-à-vis the global South countries in the 1980's and 1990's was more akin to a disciplining regime. It started with forced acceptance of restructuring programs and of loans from the international system – measures that helped large extractive firms enter these economies on favourable terms. After 20 years of this regime, it became clear that it did not deliver on the basic components for healthy development. The discipline of debt service payments was given strong priority over infrastructure, hospitals, schools, and other people-oriented development goals.

The primacy of this extractive logic became a mechanism for systemic transformation that went well beyond debt service payment. It included the devastation of large sectors of traditional economies, including small scale manufacturing, the destruction of a good part of the national bourgeoisie and petty bourgeoisie, the sharp impoverishment of the population and, in many cases, the impoverishment and thereby corruptibility of the state.

4. Debt as a Disciplining Regime

Debt and debt servicing problems have long been a systemic feature of the developing world. It is the particular features of the IMF negotiated debt rather than the fact of debt per se that concerns me here. The second feature that concerns me here is how this gradual destruction of traditional economies prepared the ground, literally, for some of the new needs of advanced capitalism, among which are the acquisitions of vast stretches of land – for agriculture, for underground water tables, and for mining. Precisely at a time of extreme financialisation and systemic crisis, the growing demand for those material resources has ascended in importance and visibility. The third aspect that concerns me here is the new survival economies of the impoverished middle classes and of the poor. While each one of these three components is familiar and has happened before, my argument is that they are now part of a new organising logic that changes their valence and their interaction; there is much contingency here, but also the shaping of such a new organising logic.

Even before the economic crises of the mid-1990's that hit a vast number of countries as they implemented neoliberal policies, the debt of poor countries in the South had grown from US$507 billion in 1980 to US$1.4 trillion in 1992. Debt service payments alone had increased to $1.6 trillion, more than the actual debt. From 1982 to 1998, indebted countries paid four times their original debts, and at the same time, their debt stocks went up by four times.

These countries had to use a significant share of their total revenues to service these debts. For instance, Africa's payments reached $5 billion in 1998, which means that for every $1 in aid, African countries paid $1.40 in debt service in 1998. Debt to Gross National Product (GNP) ratios were especially high in Africa, where they stood at 123% in the late 1990's com- pared with 42% in Latin America and 28% in Asia. By 2003, debt service as a share of exports only (not overall government revenue) ranged from extremely high levels for Zambia (29.6%) and Mauritania (27.7%) to significantly lowered levels compared with the 1990's for Uganda (down from 19.8% in 1995 to 7.1% in 2003) and Mozambique (down from 34.5% in 1995 to 6.9% in 2003). As of 2006, the poorest 49 countries (i.e. "low income countries" with less than $935 per capita annual income) had debts of $375 billion. If to these 49 poor countries we add the "developing countries," we would have a total of 144 countries with a debt of over $2.9 trillion and $573 billion paid to service debts in 2006 (see Jubilee Debt Campaign UK, 2013a, b).

The IMF, World Bank, and other such programs establish the criteria and process these debts, thereby functioning as a global disciplining regime. The Heavily indebted poor countries (HIPC) initiative was set up in 1996 by the World Bank and the IMF to assist countries with debts equivalent to more than one and a half times their annual export earnings and part of an IMF and World Bank program. In order to be eligible countries have to have been compliant to the IMF for at least three years. The HIPC process begins with a "decision point" document. This sets out eligibility requirements. Among these is the development of a Poverty Reduction Strategy Paper (PRSP) that replaces the earlier Structural Adjustment Programs (SAPs). PRSPs describe "the macroeconomic, structural, and social policies and programs" that a country is required to pursue in order to be eligible for debt relief (see IMF, 2009a; IMF 2009a,b; 2015a, b, c, e).

As of July 1 2009, 26 countries had completed the HIPC, and nine had "passed the decision point" (see IMF, 2009b). Finally, the Multilateral Debt Relief Initiative (MDRI) went into full force in July 2006. It was intended to address many of the critiques of the HIPC initiative. The MDRI promised cancellation of debts to the World Bank (incurred before 2003), the IMF (incurred before 2004), and the African Development Fund (incurred before 2004) for the countries that completed the HIPC initiative. According to one estimate, the major cancellation schemes (including the HIPC and the MDRI initiatives, and the Paris Club) have written off $88 billion so far (see Jubilee Debt Campaign UK, 2007; 2013 a, b).

The debt burden that built up in the 1980's, and especially the 1990's, has had substantial repercussions on state spending composition. Zambia, Ghana, and Uganda, three countries that global regulators (notably the World Bank and the IMF) saw as cooperative, responsible, and successful at implementing SAPs illustrate some of the issues even when held in high esteem by global regulators.

A few examples of expenditure levels paint a troubling picture about how they achieved this high esteem. At the height of these programs in the early to mid-1990's, Zambia's government paid $1.3 billion in debt but only $37 million for primary education; Ghana's social expenses, at $75 million, represented 20% of its debt service; and Uganda paid $9 per capita on its debt and only $1 for health care. In 1994 alone, these three countries remitted $2.7 billion to bankers in the North. When the new programs became an option, these three countries benefited from the HIPC and the MDRI programs and conceded to the attendant PRSP requirements. Thus, while in 1997 Zambia spent 18.3% of income on exports of goods and services on debt service, by 2007 this was reduced to 1.3% (see IAEG, 2009). For Ghana these figures are 27.1% and 3.1% respectively (see IAEG, 2009). For Uganda they are 19.7% and 1.2% (see IAEG, 2009).

Generally, the IMF's debt management policies from the 1980's onwards can be shown to have worsened the situation for the unemployed and poor (see United Nations Development Programme (UNDP), 2005, 2008). Much research on poor countries documents the link between hyper-indebted governments and cuts in social programs. These cuts tend to affect women and children in particular through cuts in education and health care, both investments necessary to ensuring a better future (for overviews of the data, see UNDP, 2005, 2008, 2015; World Bank, 2005, 2006, 2015a, b). There is by now a large literature in many different languages on this subject, including a vast number of limited circulation items produced by various activist and support organisations. An older literature on women and debt also documents the disproportionate burden that these programs put on women during the first generation of SAPs in the 1980's in several developing countries in response to growing government debt (see Beneria & Feldman, 1992; Bose & Acosta-Belen, 1995; Bradshaw et al., 1993; Tinker, 1990). Unemployment of women themselves but also, more generally, of the men in their households has added to the pressure on women to find ways to ensure household survival (see Buechler, 2007; Kyle & Koslowski, 2001; Lucas, 2005; Rahman, 1999; Safa, 1995). Subsistence food production, informal work, emigration, and prostitution have all become survival options for women and, by extension, often for their households. For instance, when there is a shortage of basic healthcare women usually take on the extra burden of caring for the sick. When school fees are introduced or spending is cut their sons education is prioritised over their daughters. Water privatisation can reduce access to water and increase the water-gathering burden placed on women. When families grow cash crops for export women's work produces money, which men usually control, rather than food (see Jubilee Debt Campaign UK, 2007).

One question concerns the option of not becoming part of the IMF debt servicing disciplining regime and foregoing the help it is meant to provide. The so-called adjustment programs of the 1980's and 1990's destroyed many traditional economies, leaving many countries only with major debts. At that point, becoming part of the debt cancellation program launched in 2006 has probably been preferable. The evidence suggests that once a country has been pushed into debt, cancellation can, in principle, help a country allocate more government revenue for general social and development questions. This has been the case with Ghana, Uganda, and a few others that have seen the growth of middle classes – along with continuing abject poverty. On the other hand, Angola which was not accepted for debt cancellation, spent 6.8% of their gross domestic product (GDP) on debt service payments and only 1.5% of their GDP on health in 2005; it continues to spend about $2.2 billion each year on external debt payments (see Jubilee Debt Campaign UK, 2007, 2013 a, b).

The Angola case also points to another combination of elements. Its elites have become wealthy on the vast mining resources, mostly for export, and this arrangement can now continue to do so without much interference. The vast poverty continues and so does the mining for export. One cannot help but ask, who are the other beneficiaries of this situation?

The above is part of a larger history in the making. In my reading it includes as one key element a repositioning of much of Africa and good parts of Latin America and Central Asia in a new massively restructured global economy. Weakened governments and the destruction of traditional economies have launched a new phase of extraction by powerful states and firms and a new phase of survival economies by the impoverished middle classes and the long-term poor. (For a more detailed analysis see Sassen, 2008a, b, c; 2014).

5. The Rise of Foreign Land Acquisitions: Expanding the Operational Space of Advanced Capitalism

The weakening and corrupting of global South governments described above enables the rapid and sharp increase in foreign land acquisitions that took off in 2006. While this can be seen merely as a continuation of an old practice, the available evidence points to significant change in the curve describing the size of overall acquisitions. From 2006 to 2011 over 200 million hectares of land in Africa, Latin America, and particular regions of Asia were acquired by foreign governments and foreign firms; this figure includes only acquisitions of a minimum 200 hectares.

What concerns me here is this sharp rise in the curve of acquisitions: it points to a new phase rather than the continuation of a centuries old practice going back to diverse imperial phases. In my interpretation, these diverse phases can be quite different, notably because of the fact that most territory in the world today is part of formally independent sovereign countries. Thus the recent sharp rise in land acquisitions might indicate a larger structural transformation in an old practice.

It is a well-known and generally accepted fact that the key reason for this growth is rapid development in several parts of the world that has generated a demand for industrial crops, food crops, wood, water, metals, and more (e.g. Land Matrix 2012, 2014). The larger context within which this growth takes place is characterised by changes in the global economy and in financial markets, and, at a deeper level, changes in the inter-state system, still the basic frame for cross-border transactions. Further, the financialising of commodities has brought new potentials for profit making to the primary sector, from food to minerals and metals, thus stimulating speculative investments in land.

The issue for me here is not one of nationalism versus globalism, but one of complexity. Where once there was a prospect of democratic decision making, now there is an expansion of opaque transnational networks that control the land. These massive foreign land acquisitions re-position that acquired land for their own aims. This also brings with it a shift of that acquired land from "national sovereign territory" to the commodity "land" for the global market. In other words, a weakening of a complex category that at its best brought with it a formal enabling of the state's authority and inhabitants' rights to make the state accountable (see Sassen, 2008a).

While the much-reported explosion in food demand and in its prices was certainly a key factor in this new phase of land acquisitions, it is bio-fuels that account for most of the acquisitions. Cross-referenced data from the Land Matrix show biofuel production accounts for 40% of land acquired. In comparison, food crops account for 25% of cross-referenced deals, followed by 3% for livestock production, and 5% for other non-food crops. Farming broadly understood accounts for 73% of cross-referenced acquisitions. The remaining 27% of land acquired is for forestry and carbon sequestration, mineral extraction, industry, and tourism (see Figure 1).

Figure 1: Land acquired by Foreign Governments and Firms by Sector (2006–2011).

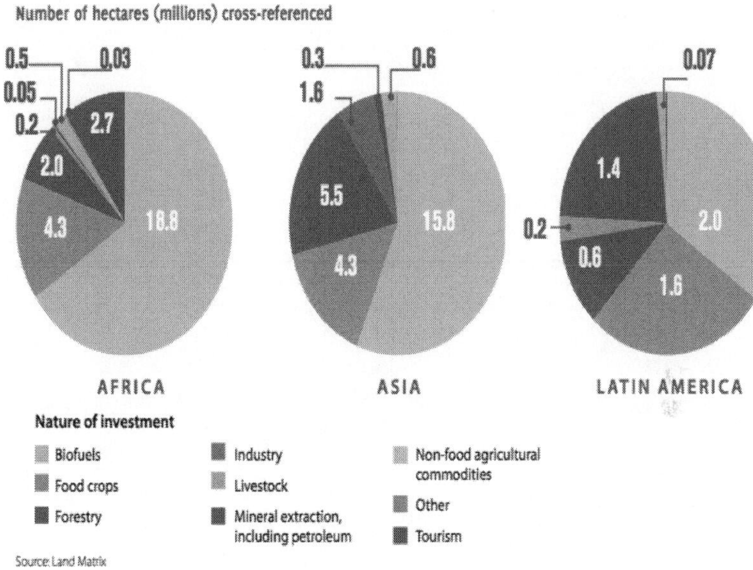

Source: Land Matrix 2014; minimum acquisition reported 200 hectares.

A second major pattern is the massive concentration of foreign acquisitions in Africa. Of the publicly reported deals, 948 land acquisitions totalling 134 million hectares are located in Africa; 34 million of these hectares have been cross-referenced. This compares with 43 million hectares reported for Asia (of which 29 million hectares have been cross-referenced) and 19 million hectares in Latin America (of which six million hectares have been cross-referenced). The remainder (5.4 million hectares reported and 1.6 million hectares cross-referenced) is in other regions, particularly Eastern Europe and Oceania (see Figure 2).

Figure 2: Land acquired by Foreign Governments and Firms (2006–2011).

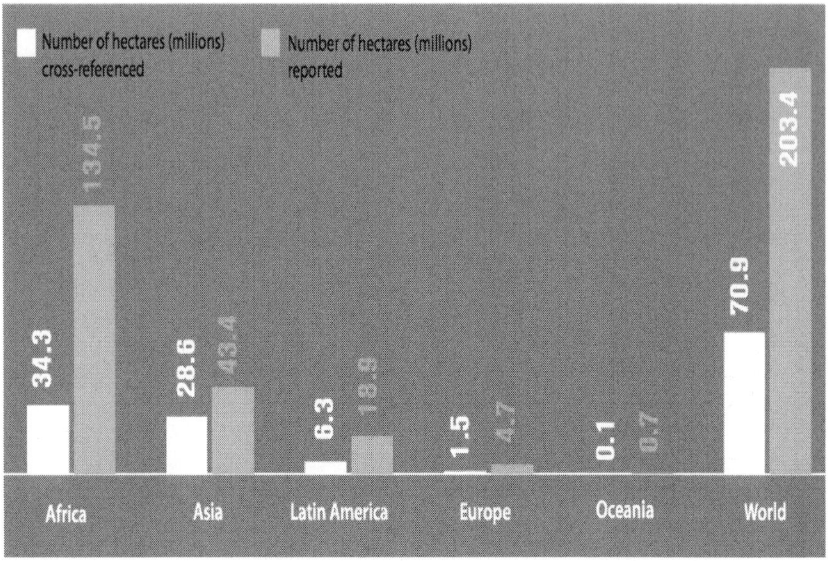

Source: Land Matrix 2014; minimum acquisition reported 200 hectares.

In an analysis of 180 large land acquisitions in Africa, Friis, and Reenberg (2010) categorise major investors into four main groups: 1) oil-rich Gulf States (Saudi Arabia, United Arab Emirates (UAE), Qatar, Bahrain, Oman, Kuwait and Jordan; 2) populous and capital-rich Asian countries such as China, South Korea, Japan and India; 3) Europe and the US; 4) private companies from around the world. Investors are mostly energy companies, agricultural investment companies, utility companies, finance and investment firms and technology companies. Just considering investment capital, three countries dominate: the US, United Kingdom (UK), and Saudi Arabia together, account for 25% of all investments in these six countries, and each has investments in four countries.

The top six African land sellers are Ethiopia, Madagascar, Sudan, Tanzania, Mali, and Mozambique – all Sub-Saharan, and all, except Mali, in East Africa. In all these countries both private investors and government agencies have acquired land. Overall Friis and Reenberg (2010) find a total of 47 different country origins among investors in these six countries. Among the countries with the most diverse group of investors by country of origin are Madagascar with 24 foreign investors from 15 countries, and Ethiopia with 26 investors from twelve countries. Asian countries (China, South Korea, India, and Japan) make up almost 20% of investors, as distinct from investments, in these six countries. Middle Eastern Countries (Saudi Arabia, UAE, Egypt, Jordan, Qatar, Lebanon, and Israel) account for almost 22% of investors. European countries (UK, Sweden, the Netherlands, Germany, Italy, Denmark, and France) account for 30% of investors. African countries (South Africa, Mauritius, Libya and Djibouti) account for about 10% of investors. The remaining investors are from Australia, Brazil and the US.

These investments in land have crowded out investments in mass manufacturing and other sectors that can generate good jobs and feed the growth of a middle class. The rise in such investments happened at a time when several countries of the global South were beginning to experience significant growth in mass manufacturing, and much foreign direct investment was in this sector (see Sassen, 2014: ch 2). This is the type of development that can contribute to the growth of a middle class and a strong working class. If we just consider Africa, for instance, the data shows a sharp decline in foreign direct investment in manufacturing. South Africa and Nigeria, Africa's top two foreign direct investment (FDI) recipients accounting for 37% of FDI stock in Africa by 2006, have both had a sharp rise in FDI in the primary sector and a sharp fall in the manufacturing sector. This is also the case in Nigeria, where foreign investment in oil has long been a major factor: the share of the primary sector in inward FDI stock stood at 75% in 2005, up from 43% in 1990. Other African countries have seen similar shifts. Even in Madagascar, one of the few (mostly small) countries where manufacturing FDI inflows began to increase as recently as the 1990's and onwards, this increase was well below that of the primary sector. Overall, the current phase of land acquisitions dwarfs investments in manufacturing.

6. The Launch of a New Financial Era: Debunking the Notion of the post-1997 "Global Stability"

The 1980's opened a new financial phase that became yet another disciplining mechanism, not through structural adjustment programs but through financial adjustment crises. Since the 1980's there have been several financial crises, some famous, such as the 1987 New York stock market crisis and the 1997 Asian crisis. Some obscure, such as the individual country financial crises that happened in over 70 countries in the 1980's and 1990's, as they deregulated their financial systems. This was mostly under pressure from global regulators aiming at facilitating the globalising of financial markets.

Conventional data show the post-1997 financial crisis period to be a fairly stable one, until the 2008 crisis explodes. One element in this picture is that after a country goes through an "adjustment" crisis, "stability" (and prosperity!) follows.

This then produces a representation of considerable financial stability, except for a few major global crises, such as the dot-com crisis. A much mentioned fact regarding the current 2007–2008 crisis intended to show that the system is fine, is that in 2006 and 2007, 124 countries had a GDP growth rate of 4% a year or more, which is much higher than that of previous decades. The suggestion is then that the 2007–2008 crisis is precisely that – an acute momentary event, but that the system is fine.

Behind this post-1997 supposed stability lies a making of winners and losers, and the fact that it is easier to track winners than to track the slow sinking of households, small firms, and government agencies (such as health and education) that are not part of the new glamour sectors (finance and trade). The miseries these adjustment crises brought to the middle sectors in each country and the destruction of often well-functioning economic sectors is largely an invisible history to the global eye. These individual country adjustment crises only intersected with global concerns and interests when there were strong financial links, as was the case with the 1994 Mexico crisis and the 2001 Argentine crisis. Further, when these miseries became visible, as when members of the traditional middle class in Argentina went on food riots in Buenos Aires (and elsewhere) in the mid-1990's – after adjustment! – something unheard of in Argentina, and which took many by surprise.

Besides the very partial character of post-adjustment stability and the new "prosperity" much praised by global regulators and global media, there is the deeper fact that "crisis" is a structural feature of deregulated, interconnected, and electronic financial markets. These same features also fed the sharp growth of finance, partly based on the financialising of non-financial economic sectors, leading to overall extremely high financial deepening. The financial deepening of economies has become one of the major dynamics characterising advanced economies. The number of countries where financial assets exceed the value of their GNP more than doubled from 33 in 1990 to 72 in 2006 (see McKinsey, 2008). Securitising a broad range of types of debt is a key vehicle for this financial deepening. The extension of securitisation into consumer debt, including mortgages, took off in the 1980's in the US.

Thus, if crisis is a structural feature of current financial markets, then crisis becomes a feature of non-financial economic sectors through their financialising, a subject I have developed elsewhere (see Sassen, 2008b, 2008a, pp. 355–365). The overall outcome is extreme potentials for instability even in strong and healthy (capitalist) economic sectors, particularly in countries with highly developed financial systems and high levels of financialisation, such as the US and the UK.

What stands out in this phase that begins in the 1980's is that global and adjustment crises had the effect of securing the conditions for globally linked financial markets and the ascendance of a financial logic organising larger and larger sectors of the economy in the global North. In this process large components of the non-financial economy in these countries were ruined. Against this background, the 2007–2008 financial crisis is yet another step in this trajectory. One question is whether it spells the exhaustion of this trajectory, or rather the beginning of its decay.

7. The Global North has its own Versions of Extraction: A New Frontier for Finance

In what follows I argue that the specific way of using the sub-prime mortgage in the 2001–2007 period makes it a dangerous instrument that is likely to be used worldwide over the next decade. It is a mistake to see this instrument as having to do with providing modest income households with housing. It has rather to do with a structural condition of high finance marked by the combination of a growing demand for asset-backed securities given extremely high levels of speculative investments. This structural condition is at the heart of the actual event that momentarily brought the system to a (partial) standstill – the credit-default swap crisis of September 2008 – which in turn suggests an even keener interest in asset-backed securities, and hence in the speculative use of sub-prime mortgages. I see this as one of the new global frontiers for finance, specifically, the billions modest-income households worldwide. The effect could be yet another brutal sorting, with expulsions from more traditional economies, not unlike the consequences of the structural adjustment crises in the global South discussed in the first half of this paper.

Much has been made, especially in the US media, of the sub-prime mortgage crisis as a source of the larger crisis. These modest-income families unable to pay their mortgage were often represented as irresponsible for having taken on these mortgages. The facts show another pattern. The overall value of the sub-prime mortgage loss was too small to bring this powerful financial system down. What triggered the crisis was a far more complex financial innovation. The key was the growing demand for asset-backed securities by investors, in a market where the outstanding value of derivatives was $630 trillion, or 14 times the value of global GDP. The total value of financial assets (which is a form of debt, but unlike derivatives represents actual money) in the US stood at almost five times (450%) the value of its GDP in 2006, before the crisis was evident. The UK, Japan, the Netherlands, all had a similar ratio (see McKinsey & Company, 2008, 11). From

2005 to 2006 the total value of the world's financial assets grew by 17% (in nominal terms, 13% at constant exchange rates) reaching $167 trillion. This is not only an all-time high value; it also reflects a higher growth rate in 2006 than the annual average of 9.1% since 1980. This points to growing financial deepening. The total value of financial assets stood at $12 trillion in 1980, $94 trillion in 2000, and $142 trillion in 2005 (For full details and sources see Sassen op cit. Expulsions).

This is the context within which the demand for asset-backed securities became acute. To address this demand, even sub-prime mortgage debt could be used as an asset. Sellers of these mortgages needed vast quantities of them to make it work for high finance: 500 such sub-prime mortgages was a minimum. As the demand for asset-backed securities grew, so did the push by sub-prime mortgage sellers to have buyers sign on, regardless of capacity to pay the mortgage. This combination of demand and increasingly low-quality assets meant mixing slices of poor quality mortgages with high-grade debt. Out came an enormously complex instrument that was also enormously opaque: nobody could trace what all was there. When the millions of foreclosures came beginning in 2006 (see Table below for numbers based on the US Federal Reserve data base), investors had a crisis of confidence: it was impossible to tell what was the toxic component in their investments. According to the Federal Reserve over 14 million households lost their homes by 2014.

U.S. Home Foreclosures, 2006–2014
2006: 1.2 million foreclosures, up 42% from 2005. This is: One in every 92 U.S. households
2007: 2.2 million foreclosures, up 75% from 2006
2008: 3.1 million, up 81% from 2007
2009: 3.9 million (or 1 in 45 US households)
(From 2007 to 2009: 120% increase in foreclosures)
2010: 2.9 million (2006–2010: total 14.2 mil)
Source: RealtyTrac 2007, 2008, 2009, 2010;

Sub-prime mortgages can be valuable instruments to enable modest-income households to buy a house. But what happened in the US over the last few years was an abuse of the concept. The small savings or future earnings of modest-income households were used to develop a financial instrument that could make profits for investors even if those households in the end could not pay the mortgages and thereby lost both their home and whatever savings and future earnings they had put into it—a catastrophic and life-changing event for millions of these households. This becomes clear in the microcosm that is New York City (NYC). Whites in NYC, who have a far higher average income than all the other groups in NYC, were far less likely to have sub-prime mortgages than all other groups. Thus

9.1% of all whites that got mortgages in 2006 got a sub-prime mortgage, compared with 13.6% of Asians, 28.6% of Hispanics, and 40.7% of blacks. If we consider the most acute period, 2003 to 2005, it more than doubled for whites, it basically tripled for Asians and Hispanics, and quadrupled for blacks. A big majority of those who sub-prime mortgages went into foreclosure and lost their homes eventually.

Rate of Subprime Lending by Race in New York City, 2002–2006

	2002	2003	2004	2005	2006
White	4.6%	6.2%	7.2%	11.2%	9.1%
Black	13.4%	20.5%	35.2%	47.1%	40.7%
Hispanic	11.9%	18.1%	27.6%	39.3%	28.6%
Asian	4.2%	6.2%	9.4%	18.3%	13.6%

Source: Furman Center for Real Estate & Urban Policy, 2007. [http://furmancenter.nyu.edu/documents/FurmanCenterHMDAAnalysis.pdf] Retrieved 26 July 2008.

There were, then, two very separate crises: the crisis of the people who had gotten these mortgages and the crisis of confidence in the investor community. The millions of home foreclosures were a signal that something was wrong, but in itself, it could not have brought down the financial system. There is a profound irony in this crisis of confidence: the brilliance of those who make these financial instruments became the undoing of a large number of investors (besides the undoing of the modest-income families who had been sold these mortgages). The toxic link was that for these mortgages to work as assets for investors, vast numbers of mortgages were sold regardless of whether these homebuyers could pay their monthly fee. The faster these mortgages could be sold, the faster they could be bundled into investment instruments and sold off to investors as an asset-backed security. Overall, sub-prime mortgages more than tripled from 2000 to 2006, and accounted for 20% of all mortgages in the US in 2006. This premium on speed also secured the fees for the sub-prime mortgage sellers and reduced the effects of mortgage default on the profits of the sub-prime sellers. In fact, those sub-prime sellers that did not sell off these mortgages as part of investment instruments went bankrupt eventually, but not before having secured fees.

In brief, the financial sector invented some of its most complicated financial instruments to extract the meagre savings of modest households in order to produce an "asset" – the mortgage on a house.

The complexity of the financial innovation was a series of products that de-linked sub-prime sellers and investors' profits from the creditworthiness of consumer home mortgage buyers. Whether the mortgage is paid matters less than securing a certain number of loans that can be bundled up into "investment products." The crisis of homebuyers was not a crisis for financial investors, even though millions of middle and working class families now live in tents in the US. For finance it was a crisis of confidence, but it showed the importance of the systems of trust that make possible the speed and orders of magnitude of this financial system. The crisis of homeowners (valued at a few hundred billion dollars) was the little tail that dented the enormous dog of trust in the financial system. In other words, this type of financial system has more of the social in it than is suggested by the technical complexity of its instruments and electronic platforms (see Sassen, 2008a, pp. 355–365).

The critical component that brought the financial system to a momentary standstill was more of an old-fashioned speculation gone wrong: the $62 trillion dollar credit-default swap crisis that exploded on the scene in September 2008, a full year after the sub-prime mortgage of August 2007. This was more than the combined domestic product of all countries in the world, $54 trillion. These credit-default swaps grew from about 1 trillion in 2001 to $62 trillion by 2007; this is an extremely sharp growth over an extremely short period of time.

Credit-default swaps could not have grown so fast and reached such extreme values if they had been sold as insurance, which would have been the lawful way. None of the financial firms had the capital reserves they would have needed to back $60 trillion in insurance. Because they were recoded as derivatives, they could have an almost vertical growth curve beginning as recently as 2001. While much attention has gone to sub-prime mortgages as causes of the financial crisis, the $62 trillion in swaps in mid-2008 is what really got the financial crisis going. Declining house prices, high foreclosure rates, declining global trade, rising unemployment, all alerted investors that something was not right. This, in turn, led those who had bought credit-default swaps as a sort of "insurance" to want to cash in. But the sellers of these swaps had not expected this downturn or the demand to cash in from those whom they had sold these credit-swaps. They were not ready, and this catapulted much of the financial sector into crisis. Not everybody lost. Among the winners are also those who "shorted" sub-prime mortgage securities: once again, Soros is the emblematic actor in this parallel circuit, making well over $3 billion on the sub-prime mortgage crisis, just as he did on the British pound's fallout from the European Exchange Rate Mechanism (ERM).

These credit-default swaps are part of what has come to be referred to as the shadow banking system. According to some analysts this shadow banking system accounted for 70% of banking at the time that the crisis explodes. The shadow banking system is not informal, illegal, or clandestine. Not at all: it is in the open, but it has thrived on the opaqueness of the investment instruments. The complexity of many financial instruments is such that nobody can actually trace what all is bundled up in some of these financial instruments. Eventually this meant that nobody knew exactly or could understand the composition of their investments, not even those who sold the instruments.

Developed countries with multiple financial circuits, such as the US and the UK, clearly show that compared to other types of loans, mortgages are a relatively small share of all loans, even if most households have mortgages. It is important to note that the same low level of mortgage loans to total loans in economies marked by a small elite of super rich individuals has a different meaning in the US and UK: hence, Russia's extremely low incidence of residential to total loans in the economy is an indication of a narrow mortgage market (mostly for the rich and very rich) and the fact that there are vast financial circuits centred on other resources.

It is important to emphasise that the viral infection of sub-prime mortgages originated in the US but spread to other countries via the globalisation of financial markets. This spread was helped by the fact that non-national investors are, as a group, the single largest buyers of some of the weakest types of mortgage instruments. Together with banks, non-national mortgage buyers are over a third of all sub-prime mortgage holders. Foreign ownership strengthens the potential for spill over effects well beyond the US.

An important question raised by these developments is the extent to which developed and developing countries will follow this troublesome "development" path (see Sassen, 2008b). It has become another way of extracting value from individuals. In this case, through home mortgages that even very poor households are invited to buy, partly because the sellers are merely after the contract that represents an asset, in order to bundle them up and sell the package to an investor, thereby passing on the risk and removing an incentive to care whether the home owner manages to pay the mortgage.

8. Conclusion: Land is in. People are out.

The potential for global replication of the financial innovation that destroyed many million households in the US, therewith devastating whole neighbourhoods is the systemic equivalent, albeit on a much smaller scale, of the global South countries devastated by an imposed debt and debt servicing regime which took priority over all other state expenditures. These are two manifestations of a systemic deepening of advanced capitalism, one marked by its potential to spread globally and the other marked by its full enactment in the global South.

Both cases can be seen as part of a much larger process of financial deepening, one of today's major dynamics characterising advanced capitalist economies. Financial deepening requires specific mechanisms, which can be extremely complex, as in the case of the type of sub- prime mortgage examined in this chapter, or they can be quite elementary, as in the debt servicing regime that took off in the 1990's. I examined these two cases through a specific lens: the transformative processes that expand the operational space of current advanced capitalism. Particular attention went to the assemblages of specific processes, institutions, and logics that get mobilised in this systemic transformation/expansion/consolidation.

The result is an expulsion of people from their land and livelihood both in the global South and in the North even as it incorporates rural and urban land into new organising logics. The devastated economies of the global South subjected to a full decade or two of debt servicing, are now being incorporated into the circuits of advanced capitalism through the accelerated acquisition of millions of hectares of land by foreign investors—to grow crops and extract water and minerals, all for the capital investing countries.

This also holds for such a radically different instance as the sub-prime mortgage crisis, a largely global North dynamic. I see the sub-prime mortgage as extending the domain for high finance but in a way that delinks the financial circuit from the actual material entity that is the house, and hence from the neighbourhood, and from the people who got the mortgage.

Thus the land and the devastated neighbourhoods I examined here are expelled from what are, strictly speaking, traditional circuits of capital. It is akin to wanting only the horns of the rhino, and throwing away the rest of the animal, devaluing it, no matter its multiple utilities. Or using the human body to harvest some organs, and seeing no value in all the other organs, let alone the full human being – it can all be discarded.

References

Anseeuw, Ward; Alden Wily, Liz; Cotula, Lorenzo; Taylor, Michael. 2012a. Land Rights and the Rush for Land: Findings of the Global Commercial Pressures on Land Research Project. Rome: International Land Coalition.

Anseeuw, Ward; Boche, Mathieu; Breu, Thomas; Giger, Markus; Lay, Jahn; Messerli, Peter; Nolte, Kerstin. 2012b. Transnational Land Deals for Agriculture in the Global South: Analytic Report based on the Land Matrix Database International Land Coalition. Bern/Montpellier/Hamburg: CDE/CIRAD/GIGA. URL: http://www.landcoalition.org/publications/transnational-land-deals-agriculture-global-south (accessed 28 July 2012).

Arrighi, Giovanni. 1994. The Long Twentieth Century. London: Verso.

Beneria, Lourdes; Feldman, Shelley (eds). 1992. Unequal Burden: Economic Crises, Persistent Poverty, and Women's Work. Boulder, CO: Westview.

Bello, Walden. 2004. Deglobalization: Ideas for a New World Economy. London: Zed Books.

Borras, Saturnino M. Jr.; Hall, Ruth; Scoones, Ian; White, Ben; Wolford, Wendy. 2011. Towards a better understanding of global land grabbing: an editorial introduction. Journal of Peasant Studies, 38:2, 209–216.

Bose, Christine E.; Acosta-Belen, Edna (eds). 1995. Women in the Latin American Development Process. Philadelphia: Temple University Press.

Bradshaw, York; Noonan, Rita; Gash, Laura; Buchmann, Claudia. 1993. Borrowing against the future: children and third world indebtedness, Social Forces, 71(3), pp. 629–656.

Brautigam, Deborah; Xiaoyang, Tang. 2011. African Shenzhen: China's special economic zones in Africa.Cambridge: Cambridge University Press.

Buechler, Simone. 2007. Deciphering the local in a global neoliberal age: three favelas in Sao Paulo, Brazil, in Sassen, Saskia (ed.), Deciphering the Global: Its Scales, Spaces, and Subjects (New York: Routledge), pp. 95–112.

Carrington, Damian. 2011. UK Firm's Failed Biofuel Dream Wrecks Lives of Tanzania Villagers. The Guardian. Available: (http://www.guardian.co.uk/environment/2011/oct/30/africa-poor-west-biofuel-betrayal).

Colchester, Marcus. 2011. Palm oil and indigenous peoples in South East Asia. FPP contribution to ILC Collaborative Research Project on Commercial Pressures on Land. Rome: ILC.

Cotula, Lorenzo. 2011. The outlook on farmland acquisitions. IIED contribution to ILC Collaborative Research Project on Commercial Pressures on Land. Rome: ILC.

Deininger, Klaus; Byerlee, Derek; Lindsay, Jonathan; Norton, Andrew; Selod, Harris; Mercedes Stickler. 2011. Rising global interest in farmland: Can it yield sustainable and equitable benefits? Washington, D.C.: World Bank.

De Schutter, Olivier. 2011. How Not to Think of Land Grabbing: Three Critiques of Large-Scale Investments in Farmland. Journal of Peasant Studies 38:2, pp. 249–279. Available: (http://dx.doi.org/10.1080/03066150.2011.559008).

Dossou, Paulin Jesutin. 2011. Evolution and impacts of coastal land use in Benin: The case of the Sèmè-Podji Commune. VADID contribution to ILC Collaborative Research Project on Commercial Pressures on Land. Rome: ILC.

The Economist. 2009. "Outsourcing's Third Wave." The Economist. Available: (http://www.economist.com/node/13692889).

The Economist. 2009. Economic and financial indicators: Food, 23 May.

FAO [Food and Agriculture Organization]. 2011. "Land Grabbing: Case studies in 17 countries of Latin American and the Caribbean." New York, NY. United Nations. Available: (http://www.tni.org/sites/www.tni.org/files/download/borras_franco_kay__spoor_land_grabs_in_latam__caribbean_nov_2011.pdf).

Frank, Andre Gunder. 1998. Re-orient: Global Economy in the Asian Age. Berekely: University of California Press.

Friis, Cecilie; Reenberg, Anette. 2010. Land grab in Africa: Emerging land system drivers in a teleconnected world. GLP Report No. 1. Copenhagen: GLP-IPO. URL: http://farmlandgrab.org/wp-content/uploads/2010/08/GLP_report_01.pdf (accessed 29 July 2012).

Furman Center for Real Estate & Urban Policy. 2007. New Housing Data Continue to Show Signs of Danger for New York City's Homeowners, Furman Center Analysis Concludes, 15 October. New York: New York University (http://furmancenter.org/files/FurmanCenterHMDAAnalysis_000.pdf).

Galeano, Eduardo H. 1997. Open Veins of Latin America: Five Centuries of the Pillage of a Continent. New York: Monthly Review Press.

Globalizations. 2010. Special Issue: Globalization and Crisis. Globalizations 7: 1–2. Available: (http://www.tandfonline.com/toc/rglo20/7/1-2).

Hall, Ruth. 2011. Land Grabbing in Africa and the New Politics of Food. Future Agricultures, Policy Brief 041.

Harvey, David. 2003. The New Imperialism. Oxford: Oxford University Press.

International Monetary Fund (IMF). 2005. Coordinated Compilation Exercise (CCE) for Financial Soundness Indicators. FSIs. 31 December. Washington, DC: International Monetary Fund.

International Monetary Fund. 2006. Household credit growth in emerging market countries, in Global Financial Stability Report: Market Developments and Issues, September. Washington, DC: International Monetary Fund. (http://www.imf.org/External/Pubs/FT/GFSR/2006/02/pdf/chap2.pdf).

International Monetary Fund. 2007. Coordinated Compilation Exercise for Financial Soundness Indicators. Washington, DC: IMF Legal Division.

International Monetary Fund. 2008. Global Financial Stability Report: Containing Risks and Restoring Financial Soundness. Washington, DC: International Monetary Fund. (http://www.imf.org/external/pubs/ft/gfsr/2008/ 01/pdf/text.pdf).

International Monetary Fund. 2009a. Factsheet: Poverty Reduction Strategy Papers (PRSP), 14 August, (https://www.imf.org/external/np/exr/facts/prsp.htm).

International Monetary Fund. 2009b. Factsheet: Debt Relief Under the Heavily Indebted Poor Country (HIPC) Initiative, 22 September. (http://www.imf.org/external/np/exr/facts/hipc.htm).

International Monetary Fund. 2015a. Factsheet: Poverty Reduction Strategy in IMF-supported Programs, September 17, 2015. (https://www.imf.org/external/np/exr/facts/prsp.htm).

International Monetary Fund. 2015b. Factsheet: Debt Relief Under the Heavily Indebted Poor Country (HIPC) Initiative, September 17, 2015. (http://www.imf.org/external/np/exr/facts/hipc.htm).

International Monetary Fund (IMF) Financial Soundness Indicators (FSIs). November 5, 2015c. (Washington, DC: International Monetary Fund). (http://data.imf.org/?sk=9F855EAE-C765-405E-9C9A-A9DC2C1FEE47).

International Monetary Fund. 2015d. Vulnerabilities, Legacies, and Policy: Risks Rotating to Emerging Market. Global Financial Stability Report, October 2015. Washington, DC: International Monetary Fund. (https://www.imf.org/External/Pubs/FT/GFSR/2015/02/index.htm).

International Monetary Fund. 2015e. Factsheet: Debt Relief Under the Heavily Indebted Poor Country (HIPC) Initiative, September 17, 2015. (http://www.imf.org/external/np/exr/facts/hipc.htm).

Jubilee Debt Campaign UK. 2007. Debt and Women. (http://www.jubileedebtcampaign.org.uk/Debt%20and% 20Womenþ3072.twl).

Jubilee Debt Campaign UK. 2012. Angola, country information. (http://jubileedebt.org.uk/countries/angola).

Jubilee Debt Campaign UK. 2013. How Big is the Debt of Poor Countries?, (http://jubileedebt.org.uk/faqs-2/how-big-is-the-debt-of-poor-countries).

Jubilee Debt Campaign UK. 2013. Hasn't All the Debt been Cancelled?, (http://jubileedebt.org.uk/faqs-2/hasnt-all-the-debt-been-cancelled).

Kyle, David; Koslowski, Ray. 2001. Global Human Smuggling. Baltimore, MD: Johns Hopkins University Press.

Lucas, Linda (ed). 2005. Unpacking Globalisation: Markets, Gender and Work. Kampala, Uganda: Makerere University Press.

Krueger, Anne O. 1993. Economic Policy at the Cross-Purposes: The United States and the Developing Countries. Washington DC: Brookings Institute.

Krueger, Anne (ed). 2002. Economic Policy Reforms and the Indian Economy. Chicago: University of Chicago Press.

Land Matrix. 2012. The Land Matrix, Beta version: The online public database on land deals. ILC/CIRAD/CDE/GIGA/GIZ. (http://landportal.info/landmatrix, accessed 29 July 2012).

Land Matrix. 2014. (http://www.landmatrix.org/en/get-the-idea/dynamics-overview/).

Lucas, Linda (ed.). 2005. Unpacking Globalisation: Markets, Gender and Work. Kampala, Uganda: Makerere University Press.

Maldonado-Torres, Nelson. 2007. On the Coloniality of Being. Cultural Studies 21(2): 240–270.

Marx, Karl. 1992. Capital, vol. 1, Part VIII, Ch. 26–31. London: Penguin Classics, pp. 873–931.

McKinsey & Company. 2008. Mapping Global Capital Markets Fourth Annual Report, McKinsey Global Institute, January, (http://www.mckinsey.com/mgi/reports/pdfs/Mapping_Global/MGI_Mapping_Global_full_Report.pdf).

Mignolo, Walter. 2007. Delinking: the rhetoric of modernity, the logic of coloniality, and the grammar of de-coloniality. Cultural Studies. 21(2): 449–514.

Migrant Remittances. 2008. Worldwide Trends in International Remittances, May, 5(2), Electronic newsletter jointly sponsored by DFID and USAID, (http://www.thedialogue.org/PublicationFiles/Migrant%20Remittances—May%202008-FINAL.pdf).

Miles, David; Pillonca, Vladimir. 2007. European economics: financial innovation and European housing and mortgage markets, Morgan Stanley Research Europe, 18 July. New York: Morgan Stanley. (http://www.germany-re.com/files/00034800/MS%20Housing%20Report%202007.pdf).

Mishel, Lawrence. 2007. Who's grabbing all the new pie? Economic Snapshots, 1 August. Washington, DC: Economic Policy Institute. (http://www.epi.org/content.cfm/webfeatures_snapshots_20070801).

Molnar, Augusta; Barney, Keith; DeVito, Michael; Karsenty, Alain; Elson, Dominique; Benavides, Margarita; Tipula, Pedro; Soria, Carlos; Shearman, Phil; France, Marina. 2011. Large acquisition of rights on forest lands for tropical timber concessions and commercial wood plantations. Rights and Resources Initiative (RRI) contribution to ILC Collaborative Research Project on Commercial Pressures on Land. Rome: ILC.

Orozco, Manuel et al. 2005. Transnational Engagement, Remittances and their Relationship to Development in Latin America and the Caribbean. Washington, DC: Georgetown University, Institute for the Study of International Migration.

Oxfam International. 1999. Oxfam International Submission to the Heavily Indebted Poor Country (HIPC) Debt Review. (http://www.oxfam.org.uk/resources/policy/debt_aid/index.html).

Putzel, Louis; Assembe-Mvondo, Samuel; Bilogo Bi Ndong, Laurentine; Banioguila, Reine Patrick; Cerutti, Paolo; Chupezi Tieguhong, Julius; Djeukam, Robinson; Kabuyaya, Noël; Lescuyer, Guillaume; Mala, William. 2011. Chinese trade and investment and the forests of the Congo Basin. Synthesis of scoping studies in Cameroon, Democratic Republic of Congo and Gabon. Working Paper 67. Bogor, Indonesia: CIFOR.

Quijano, Anibal. 2000. Coloniality of Power, Eurocentrism and Latin America. Nepantla: Views from the South, 1(3): 533–580.

Ratha, Dilip, et al. 2009. Migration and Development Brief 11: Migration and Remittance Trends 2009: A Better-than-expected Outcome for Migration and Remittance Flows in 2009, but Significant Risks Ahead, 3 November, (Washington, DC: World Bank, Migration and Remittances Team, Development Prospects Group), http://siteresources.worldbank.org/INTPROSPECTS/Resources/334934-1110315015165/ MigrationAndDevelopmentBrief11.pdf

Ratha, Dilip, et al. 2015. Migration and Development Brief 24: Migration and Remittances: Recent Developments and Outlook. Special Topic: Financing for Development. April 13, 2015. http://siteresources.worldbank.org/INTPROSPECTS/Resources/334934-1288990760745/MigrationandDevelopmentBrief24.pdf.

Ravanera, Roel and Gorra, Vanessa. 2011. Commercial pressures on land in Asia: An overview. IFAD contribution to ILC Collaborative Research Project on Commercial Pressures on Land. Rome: ILC.

Rawat, Vidya Bhushan; Bhushan, Mamidi Bharath and Surepally, Sujatha. 2011. The impact of special economic zones in India: A case study of Polepally SEZ. SDF contribution to ILC Collaborative Research Project on Commercial Pressures on Land. Rome: ILC.

Safa, Helen. 1995. The Myth of the Male Breadwinner: Women and Industrialization in the Caribbean. Boulder, CO: Westview.

Sassen, Saskia. 1982. Recomposition and peripheralization at the core. In: The New Nomads: Immigration and Change in the International Division of Labor, M. Dixon and S. Jonas (eds.) San Francisco, CA: Synthesis, pp. 88–100.

Sassen, Saskia. 1988. The Mobility of Labor and Capital. Cambridge: Cambridge University Press.

Sassen, Saskia. 1991. The Global City: New York, London, Tokyo. Princeton: Princeton University Press.

Sassen, Saskia. 2008a. Territory, Authority, Rights: From Medieval to Global Assemblages, revised 2nd ed. Princeton: Princeton University Press.

Sassen, Saskia. 2008b. Mortgage capital and its particularities: a new frontier for global finance. Journal of International Affairs, 62(1), pp. 187–212.

Sassen, Saskia. 2008c. Two stops in today's new global geographies: shaping novel labor supplies and employment regimes, American Behavioral Scientist, 52(3), pp. 457–496.

Sassen, Saskia. 2013. When Territory Deborders Territoriality. Territory, Politics, Governance, Vol 1, Issue 1, 2013: pp. 21–45

Sassen, Saskia. 2014. Expulsions: Brutality and Complexity in the Global Economy. Cambridge, Mass: Harvard University Press/Belknap Book.

Tinker, Irene. (ed.) (1990) Persistent Inequalities: Women and World Development. New York: Oxford University Press.

UNCTAD [United Nations Conference on Trade and Development]. 2008. World Investment Directory Volume X: Africa. New York: United Nations.

UNCTAD [United Nations Conference on Trade and Development]. 2009. Investment Report: Transnational Corporations, Agricultural Production and Development. New York, NY. United Nations. Available: (http://unctad.org/en/docs/wir2009_en.pdf).

UNCTAD [United Nations Conference on Trade and Development]. 2015. World Investment Reports. New York: United Nations. http://unctad.org/en/pages/DIAE/World%20Investment%20Report/WIR-Series.aspx.

UNDP [United Nations Development Programme]. 2005. A Time for Bold Ambition: Together we can Cut Poverty in Half: UNDP Annual Report. New York: UNDP.

UNDP [United Nations Development Programme]. 2008. Human Development Report 2007–2008, UNDP Annual Report. New York: UNDP.

United Nations Conference on Trade and Development (UNCTAD). 2008. World Investment Directory Volume X: Africa. New York: United Nations.

United Nations Development Programme (UNDP). 2005. A Time for Bold Ambition: Together we can Cut Poverty in Half, UNDP Annual Report. New York: UNDP.

United Nations Development Programme (UNDP). 2008. Human Development Report 2007–2008, UNDP Annual Report. New York: UNDP.

UNDP [United Nations Development Programme]. 2014. Human Development Report 2–015, UNDP Annual Report New York: UNDP. http://hdr.undp.org/sites/default/files/hdr14-report-en-1.pdf.

United Nations Statistics Division (IAEG), Inter-Agency and Expert Group on MDG Indicators. 2009a. Millennium Development Goals Indicators: Debt Service as a Percentage of Exports of Goods and Services and Net Income, last updated 14 July, http://mdgs.un.org/unsd/mdg/SeriesDetail.aspx?srid1⁄4655.

United Nations Statistics Division, Millennium Development Goals Indicators. Debt Service as a Percentage of Exports of Goods and Services and Net Income Updated July 6, 2015. http://mdgs.un.org/unsd/mdg/SeriesDetail.aspx?srid=655&crid=

US Department of State. 2004. Trafficking in Persons Report. Washington, DC: Office to Monitor and Combat Trafficking in Persons.

US Department of State. 2015. Trafficking in Persons Report. Washington, DC: Office to Monitor and Combat Trafficking in Persons. http://www.state.gov/documents/organization/245365.pdf.

Varchaver, Nicholas and Benner, Katie. 2008. The $55 trillion question: special report issue 1: America's money crisis, CNNMoney.com. http://money.cnn.com/2008/09/30/magazines/fortune/varchaver_derivatives_short.fortune/index.htm.

Von Braun, Joachim and Meinzen-Dick, Ruth Suseela. 2009. Land grabbing by foreign investors in developing countries: risks and opportunities, IFPRI Policy Brief 13 (Washington, DC: International Food Policy Research Institute). http:// www.ifpri.org/publication/land-grabbing-foreign-investors-develop ing-countries.

Warnock, Veronica and Warnock, Francis. 2008. Markets and housing finance, Social Science Research Network Working Paper Series, February. http://ssrn.com/abstract1⁄4981641.

Wiener Bravo, Elisa. 2011. The concentration of land ownership in Latin America: An approach to current problems. CISEPA contribution to ILC Collaborative Research Project on Commercial Pressures on Land. Rome: ILC.

World Bank. 2005. Increasing aid and its effectiveness, in Global Monitoring Report: Millennium Development Goals: From Consensus to Momentum (Washington, DC: World Bank), pp. 151–187, http://siteresources.worldbank.org/INTGLOBALMONITORING/Resources/ch5_GMR2005.pdf.

World Bank. 2006. Global Economic Prospects: Economic Implications of Remittances and Migration. Washington, DC: World Bank.

World Bank. 2008. Migration and Remittances: Top Ten, March, http://econ.worldbank.org/WBSITE/EXTERNAL/EXTDEC/EXTDECPROSPECTS/0,,contentMDK:21352016□pagePK:64165401□piPK:64165026□theSitePK: 476883,00.html.

World Bank. 2015a. Global Monitoring Report: Development Goals in an Era of Demographic Change. ttp://pubdocs.worldbank.org/pubdocs/publicdoc/2015/10/503001444058224597/Global-Monitoring-Report-2015.pdf.

World Bank. 2015b. Global Economic Prospects: The Global Economy in Transition. Washington DC: World Bank. http://www.worldbank.org/en/publication/global-economic-prospects.

World Bank. 2015c. Migration and Remittances: Prospects. http://econ.worldbank.org/WBSITE/EXTERNAL/EXTDEC/EXTDECPROSPECTS/0,,contentMDK:21121930~menuPK:3145470~pagePK:64165401~piPK:64165026~theSitePK:476883,00.html.

Part II. Globalisation, Crisis of Territoriality, and Reshaping of Communities

Martin Belov

Globalisation, Crisis of Territoriality, and their Effects on the Constitutional Principles

Abstract

This paper explores the effects of the globalisation and the crisis of territoriality on the main constitutional principles. The constitution is supposed to be a traditionally territorial phenomenon. The information revolution, the global fluidisation and dispersion of the demos and the territorial irresponsibility of the global financial capital as phenomena related to the territoriality crisis affect directly the constitutional axiology. They produce not just functional but also structural changes in the value core of the constitution and in the constitutional infrastructure of the territorial state and public power. The paper tries to problematise the influence of the globalisation on the constitutional infrastructure of the power and to explore whether the territoriality is still solid element of the statehood. If not, we should start looking at new concepts, paradigms, and "supportive ideologies" in order to reaffirm the capability of the constitution to serve as reliable frame for democracy, rule of law, solidarity, welfare, and identity. Such conceptual change may be fostered by the global governance paradigm.

1. Introduction

Globalisation is a system of social, political, economic, and cultural processes which jointly change the socio-political conditions for policy making and governance as well as the power infrastructure on local, national, and supranational levels (see Sassen, 2007). Thus it also affects central political concepts developed during the last centuries and enshrined in the code of the constitutional territorial nation state. Consequently these issues need a deliberate, rational, and explicit response from a constitutionalist point of view.

The constitution is traditionally a territorial phenomenon. It presupposes territory based socio-political community – usually a nation and in some cases multicultural society, as an addressee of its provisions. Moreover the constitution is designed to frame and limit the functioning of the public power within clear territorial and personal jurisdictions, which ideally have to have a more or less perfect match. The constitution has to provide solutions for the political issues of a territory bound community governed by territory based institutions of public power. In addition the public sphere and civil society players also have to be referential to a specific state territory.

Basic constitutional principles are experiencing massive and important influences by globalisation. The changes in the territoriality (see Teivainen, 2000; 715, Ruggie, 1993, pp. 139–174; and Parrish, 2011, 1100) affect not only the axiology of the constitution consisting in the constitutional institutionalisation of principles and values based on initially meta-legal normativity but also its functionality. The way constitutional law and constitutional theory reflect the globalisation and the crisis of territoriality (see Cuttitta, 2006, pp. 27–39) determine the effectiveness, legitimacy, and functionality of the constitution in the age of global governance. Hence the conceptualisation of the territoriality of constitution and the effects of the globalisation on it deserves special attention.

Three main phenomena associated with globalisation directly affect the territoriality as political and constitutional conceptualisation of the territory. These are the rise of the political prominence of territory unrestrained financial capital, the global fluidisation and dispersion of the demos and the information and communication revolution. They lead to the disintegration of the "territorial container" (see Brenner, 1999, 55), reconfiguration of territoriality, diminution of the role of territory as the only basis for political socialisation, political participation and political community building, relativising of the absolute and necessary bond between the people and the territory as state building components (see Jellinek, 2010) as well as to necessity for the public power and the constitution to adapt to this new context.

Both the new phase of capitalistic development consisting in the emergence of territory detached and territory irresponsible financial capitalism and the global fluidity of the demos are products of the crisis of territoriality. At the same time they contribute to its further deepening. The information and communication revolution is also related to the increased territorial detachment of the social and political relations and fosters the deterritorialization of public governance and community building. The rise of the political prominence of financial capital, the global fluidisation of the demos, and the information and communication revolution produce important structural and functional changes in the constitutional principles. Both the key constitutional principles and the adequate context for their consistent application are directly affected by the current phase of globalisation with its crisis of territoriality, predominance of financial capitalism, and reconfiguration of space.

This paper aims to explore exactly the challenges that the increased mobility and migration, the new information and communication technologies, the emancipation of the financial capital, and the emergence of new actors of global governance such as supranational regimes, multinational and transnational companies, sovereign funds and global non-governmental organisations (NGOs) pose to constitutional law with regard to its fundamental principles – sovereignty, democracy, welfare state, and rule of law. The influences of the above mentioned phenomena on the constitutional principle of separation of powers will be left aside due to space constraints. An attempt will be made to draw up also some conclusions and to map out the possible directions in which the constitutional principles will and should evolve in the course of their response and adaptation to the social context as redesigned by the globalisation and the crisis of territoriality.

2. Sovereignty

The indivisible sovereignty and the monolithic common good are among the main "supportive ideologies" of classical constitutionalism and modern statehood. Sovereignty as the essence and the source of public power is supposed to be thematically indivisible and a holistic category (see Rousseau, 1968) which penetrates all spheres of government where public interest is at stake. Sovereignty resides in a single power centre usually personified by a political player (monarch, dictator, or political party) or by a composite entity with presumed common will (state, nation, or people). It qualifies that player or entity as the supreme holder of public power that can take fundamental decisions with existential character (see Schmitt, 1970, pp. 75–87). The "common good" – a brand serving for denomination of the set of aims, values, principles, and policies that have to be jointly pursued by the community, is also typically conceptualised as a holistic category that is not sector specific.

However the current phase of globalisation which has started at the end of the 1970's and has gained momentum since the 1990's has led to the fragmentation of sovereignty, substantial proliferation of constitutionalism, and strategic redefinition of the demarcation lines between the private and the public.

The fragmentation of sovereignty consists in the fact that the taking of the key decisions and the determination of the policy guidelines in the different socio-political spheres is accomplished not by a single but more and more frequently by different and even competing players. The traditional understanding is that the sovereignty belongs to the state as a holistic entity and is put into practice and driven by either the monarch, or the nation, or the people through the state institutions.

Currently we are witnessing an increasing divergence and mismatch between the holders of supreme decision making power in the different fields of socio-political relations. The state formally retains its legal sovereignty (see Agnew, 2005, 437). Internally it is still quite visible in many spheres – police matters, taxation, education, etc. However in other aspects – foreign policy, public finance different from taxation, human rights protection, etc. – the state sovereignty is more and more becoming a politically and socially nominal category.

This is due to losses and transfers of sovereignty on the vertical scale of territorial distribution of power – upwards to the EU and downwards to federal, quasi-federal, and regional units as well as to autonomies. The more challenging process is the transfer of sovereign power in favour of sector specific supranational regimes such as the World Trade Organisation (WTO) and North Atlantic Treaty Organisation (NATO) and even to non-governmental players. Very frequently such a transfer is done gradually but persistently and in a manner that does not coincide with the idea of people's and national sovereignty and constituent power. In most of the countries such a transfer has not been legitimised through the special procedures of constituent power. Typically no referenda on transfer of sovereign powers have been accomplished with the exception of the transfer of sovereignty to the EU. Usually there are also no explicit constitutional provisions in most of the state constitutions providing for the conditions for accession and withdrawal from such supranational organisations as well as for procedural and substantial limits to the transfer of sovereignty. The only exceptions again are the EU's integration clauses as well as other constitutional provisions concerning the EU's membership of the states.

In the cases where sovereign power is tacitly "outsourced" to non-governmental players of the global governance such democratically legitimate procedures for transfer of sovereignty are even harder to imagine. This is due to the lack of constitutional conceptualisation of the influence of the non-state players of global governance on the constitutional principles in general and on the sovereignty in particular. The idea that sovereign powers may be accomplished by formally private actors contravenes the very logic of the establishment of the modern constitutional state which was directed towards diminishing the power fragmentation and power privatisation, the enhancement of the concentration of public power in the state, and the legitimation of a publicly controlled common platform and frame for the realisation of government.

There is an increasing mismatch between legal and political sovereignty (see Tanchev, 2003, pp. 258–282) as well as between territorial, personal, and substantial (especially financial) sovereignty (for the territorial sovereignty see Cuttitta; 2006, 32; Agnew 2013, 2; Benhabib, 2005, 674). John Agnew opposes the "effective sovereignty" of the state due to its traditional but declining "legal territorial sovereignty" (see Agnew, 2005, 437).

Some of the reasons for the decline of the monolithic state sovereignty and the emergence of the mismatch between its different aspects are the global mobility of capital, the "territorial entrenchment" of the politicians and the citizenry, the increase of the foreign investment flow, the radical privatisation of the economy and the service sector which leads to the emergence of political power gained by the transnational and multinational corporations, and the role of offshore zones, sovereign funds, and global cities (for the concept of global city see Sassen, 1991, pp. 193–321). Other reasons are the intensification of the global flow of people – refugees, migrants, job seekers, etc. According to S. Benhabib (2005, 675)

> "'vis-à-vis peoples' cross-border movements, the state remains sovereign, albeit in much reduced fashion. Vis-a-vis the movement of capital and commodities, information and technology across borders, by contrast, the state today is more hostage than sovereign."

Hence there is an asymmetry between the cross-border mobility of people and the transborder movement of capital. The movement of people is much more territory related because people move from one territory into another. That is why it can be classified as "cross-border movement." The movement of capital is much more territory-detached. We are witnessing a capital flow that is both supraterritorial and transterritorial. The capital flow is supraterritorial because it is almost territorially unrestrained and virtual in the sense of being spaceless. It is transterritorial due to the fact that it may penetrate simultaneously several territories without the need for a territorial linkage between them. The last phenomenon is facilitated by the "space-time compression" (see Brenner, 1999, 39).

To sum up, currently state sovereignty is a package category that has been cut in some aspects, enhanced in others, or has been leaking in favour of actors that are different from the state. The increase of the importance of "emergent jurisdictions and orderings that override the state's territoriality," such as "the World Trade Organisation (WTO), the International Criminal Court (ICC) and the UN humanitarian system" has been already recognised in the scientific literature (see Sassen, 2013, 23). Thus the military sovereignty of the state is becoming limited by its participation in NATO or other military organisations. The financial sovereignty of the state is partially restrained by the European Central Bank (ECB), the IMF, the World Bank and other financial institutions which determine huge parts of the financial policy of the state. The same is true with regard to the economic sovereignty that is framed by the WTO. The information sovereignty in the sense of control over the direction, intensity and content of data currents via different communication means gets step-by-step taken on by social networks such as Facebook, Twitter, Google+ as well as by other information networks and agents of globalisation. Last but not least the different human rights regimes and institutions vastly influence different parts of the state sovereignty via human rights understood as practical, moral, and legal restraints of the public power and as new ideology of the Western world that has achieved almost the status of a new religion.

It has to be taken into account that although these supranational or non-state actors limit the state sovereignty in some aspects they also enhance it in others. This is due to the fact that they provide the state, its society, and its citizens with additional military, financial, economic, information, or moral resources that otherwise could hardly be gained or put in practice by it as a sole player. Thus globalisation, supranationalisation, and global governance do not unilaterally diminish the role of the state. They contribute to the limitation of some of the aspects of the state's sovereignty but also provide new governance instruments, new policy making platforms, and new opportunities. Moreover the state is both an important player and key playground in the mosaic power and institutional infrastructure of global governance because its capabilities are still of crucial importance to the governability of the world (see Sassen, 2006, pp. 21, 148–204). That is why the current round of globalisation is defined in the theory as a "rescaling of nationally organised forms of territoriality" (see Brenner, 1999, 62) leading to the reshaping and not to the demise of the role of the state.

We are currently living in the most interconnected world that has ever existed in human history. This interconnectedness leads to increased interdependence not only of the states and the international organisations but also of the people and their profit and non-profit organisations. New spheres of social relations, i.e. in the domains of technology, ecology, culture, finance, and economy have gained political importance producing their constitutional prominence. The increase of the substantial diversity of the social relations with constitutional character leads to the emergence of new types of constitutionalism – financial, economic, ecological, information, and technological, etc. This process can be defined as substantial proliferation of constitutionalism.

The non-recognition of the distinct meaning of financial and economic sovereignty and constitutionalism leads to the weakening of the regulative function of the constitution. If constitutional law leaves politically important issues aside without any attempt at rational, deliberate, and democratic framing and regulation then the players and processes in these non-constitutionalised constitutionally sensitive spheres will probably produce democratically uncontrollable outputs. This is the reason why the substantial proliferation of constitutionalism is intrinsically intertwined with the fragmentation of sovereignty.

The strategic redefinition of the demarcation lines between the private and the public consists in two processes. The first one is the gaining of public and political importance of issues that were conceived as private and non-political or not directly political in previous times. Such issues are i.e. corporate finance, foreign investment, and new technologies. The second one is the increase of the public importance of players that formally have private character such as sovereign funds, international and transnational corporations, global charity funds, and NGOs. These processes produce a structural reshaping of the social and political playground that constitutional law is supposed to regulate. They will either get constitutional reflection or will lead to the "twilight of constitutionalism" (see Dobner et al., 2010, 4) or "waning constitutionalism" (see Rasmussen, 2006, pp. 149–156).

Now let's turn to the territorial mutations of sovereignty. Contemporary constitutional law and constitutional science must at least raise questions if not give answers concerning the structural changes and remodelling of the concept and the principle of state sovereignty. Most of these changes are inflicted by the crisis of territoriality in conjunction with the fragmentation of sovereignty, the substantial proliferation of constitutionalism, and the strategic redefinition of the demarcation lines between the private and the public.

The absolute monarchy and its successor – the nation state, have developed tools for protecting and imposing the state's sovereignty over "territory based enemies or competitors" – other states, separatists, local landlords, and even international organisations. However the modern state – doesn't matter whether it is a nation state or multicultural society, is unprepared to reassert its sovereignty against non-territorial competitors for sectoral sovereignties.

International and multinational companies, sovereign funds, and NGOs penetrate deep into the state's sovereignty producing "transversally bordered spaces" (see Sassen, 2013, 23). They start to claim implicitly and even explicitly participatory rights for the determination and execution of sector policies leading in fact to the partial privatisation of sector sovereignties. This tendency is especially visible with regard to the financial and economic sovereignty but is beginning to spread also to the humanitarian, information, and cultural sovereignty of the state. Consequently there is an increase of instances of jurisdictional conflicts and an emergence of "informal jurisdictions" (ibid., 23).

We are witnessing the emergence of non-territorial and aterritorial sovereignties (see Cuttitta, 2006, pp. 32–33) that parallel the dismantling of the sovereignty as a monolithic concept. The power of supranational and transnational actors to impose their will on the states in important domains of public interest such as corporate finance, public finance, economy, management of natural resources, and even identity politics are key examples of their role as competitors for sovereign power with the states and the territory based politicians.

At the same time these non-territorial and aterritorial quasi-sovereign power centres allocated in the global governance grid continue to use the state infrastructure due to its retained military, educational, healthcare, and policing advantages. Hence the non-territorial and aterritorial sovereignties are not only competing with and destroying the state. They need the state as a still sovereign entity and the network of sovereign states as a necessary logistical infrastructure that has proven its advantages in providing education and health care to the population and military aid when needed. Hence the state sovereignty is going to be fragmented and weakened but not destroyed by the new non-territorial and aterritorial players of global governance.

It has to be clarified why international and transnational corporations, global NGOs, and sovereign funds can be defined as atteritorial and non-territorial actors bearing a sovereignty-like potential. Sovereignty has traditionally been defined as a concept that belongs exclusively to the state in general and its leading power centre in particular. The state has always been a fixed territory based concept with the partial exception of nomadic states. Hence historically the sovereignty is a territorial concept monopolised by the state.

If we deconstruct the concept of sovereignty and interpret it functionally, we can come to the conclusion that the supreme decision making power in some spheres of social relations currently and factually may also belong to non-state entities. It is obvious that international and transnational corporations indeed set guidelines for the economic, financial, labour, ecology and other policies of many states due to their overwhelming financial, lobby, organisation, and information power. This is especially true for the so called "growth triangles" (see Ong, 1999, pp. 221–222) and to the poorer parts of the world but is also occurring in the leading economic powers.

Foreign investments, more precisely those which are done via international and transnational corporations, may actually function as forms of aterritorial financial sovereignty. When the investments are accomplished by sovereign funds one can speak of transplantation of foreign sovereignty that is politically and ontologically territorial but functions as aterritorial through the activity of the fund. Hence the state to which the sovereign fund belongs invests its sovereignty into an aterritorial functional financial quasi-sovereignty of the fund which then transplants it into the domain of the recipient state thus limiting its sovereignty. This is especially true when sovereign funds invest in state debt instruments of foreign states. In fact this is a case when one state via its sovereign fund buys out particles of the financial and thus indirectly of other parts of the sovereignty of another state. Here one can speak of atteritorial sovereignty because the sovereign fund functions on many locations of the globe although initially based in its sovereign state holder territory.

Private actors of global governance such as international and transnational corporations, sovereign funds, and NGOs with exorbitantly high public influence paralleling, competing, and even driving the state power may formally have a seat and some form of territorial coverage of their management, offices, branches, and investments. However the territoriality as an aggregate form and dimension of territory produced through political engineering, imposition of state power, and the collective imagination of a territory based community is not a necessary precondition either for their functioning or for the accumulation and use of their power (for the difference between territory and territoriality and their relationship see Sassen, 2013, pp. 21–45). In that sense they are transterritorial, non-territorial, and even aterritorial.

The aterritoriality, transterritoriality, and non-territoriality here consists in the simultaneous and global functioning of the power of these actors enabled by the new information, communication, and transportation technologies as well as by the virtual, non-territorial, and global nature of the financial capital. Hence the emergent quasi-sovereignty of financial capital actors of global governance is intrinsically virtual, global, and territory detached. That is why while the state sovereignty remains territory dependent even in case of superpowers the quasi-sovereignty of transnational corporations and other private actors of global governance is aterritorial. Its aterritoriality is enabled and enhanced by mutually interdependent processes and phenomena such as the "time-space compression," (see Eriksen, 2014), globalisation, and the information revolution.

An important characteristic of the holders of aterritorial sovereignty is that they can easily escape democratic oversight and accountability than traditional territory-based sovereignty. They can function simultaneously in different territorial jurisdictions avoiding the territorial constraints experienced by traditional sovereignty holders such as monarch, people, nation, and their agents – the "territorial politicians" (EU, national, or subnational). Last but not least the atteritorial sovereignty is usually not a holistic category. It is a sector specific and policy oriented power to impose key decisions. Typically the atteritorial sovereignty concerns the financial, the economical, and the humanitarian sphere.

One of the key elements in the construction of the nation state has been the establishment of the state as a "territorial container" (see Brenner, 1999, 55). This means that the state was conceived as a self-sufficient territory based entity capable of maintaining compact nations with cultural and social homogeneity controlled by the sovereign power.

The territorial closure of the nation is no longer available. The presumed self-sufficiency and solipsistic introversion of the nation is fractured by the tremendously increased information, capital, and migration flow as well as by the "time-space compression" (see Eriksen, 2014). With the advance of information technologies, the increase of the international and transnational job, education and leisure opportunities and the "democratisation of the transport" in terms of cheaper and accessible transportation means the nation becomes more and more fragmented. Hence the nation as origin, history, culture, and territory based community is currently competing with multiple interest and value based communities, subcultures, and sub-societies. Some of them have global character and are territory detached due to the universality of their shared interests, goals and values spread, shared, discussed, and developed through the new information technologies.

The emergence of multiple attachments and affiliations crosscutting each other and functioning without the need of the state and its composing elements – the compatriots, the public power, and the territory (see Jellinek, 2010) – creates multilayered and globalised open societies (for open society see Popper, 2013). Their members are more and more interconnected with people from different parts of the world and their group affiliations do not always coincide with the traditional forms of territory based group solidarities. Hence the sovereignty cannot be further conceptualised in terms of territorial closure due to the fact that the "territorial container" (see Brenner, 1999, 55) is increasingly dysfunctional and is competing with the global network as an explanatory concept and as a power, authority, and community paradigm.

Currently we are witnessing the rise of the epoch of *global fluidity of demos*. The demos and the nation as coherent territory based social groups are being partially transformed into a network. This network escapes the restraints imposed by territoriality and is semi-detached from its territorial origin – the nation state. The territorial state with its national imaginaries and social and cultural infrastructure will remain the most important base for the demos. However the demos is now able to spread to many places and locations of the globe. Thus many nations will gain space reflection on a world scale resembling a network with the nation state of origin as a central node of it. These world diasporic networks will remain interconnected. Their territoriality mode will not be limited to one place but will change and follow the move of the demos and its spread throughout the global and globalised space. Hence the "territorial container" (see Brenner, 1999, 55) will be transformed into a territorial centre paralleled by globalised "space of flows" (see Castels, 2010, pp. 407–460).

Great shifts and movements of populations have been witnessed throughout different periods of human history. However none of them has challenged so profoundly the very basis and existence of the territorial state. The great migration of people occurred in the middle ages before the emergence of the nation state. The migration of people from the former colonies to the metropolis in the post-colonial age has not formally challenged the substance, the constitutional principles, and constitutional infrastructure of the territorial state. It was not a challenge to the territoriality of the state. In some cases it has introduced changes in its national character thus producing multicultural societies framed by territorial states.

The current wave of migration, on the contrary, has the potential to challenge the very essence of key political and constitutional concepts such as border, territorial sovereignty, national identity, nation, liberal democracy, and territory based social solidarity. It transplants subcultures, challenges the idea of dominant culture and of national homogeneity and diminishes both the personal and territorial sovereignty of the state.

According to P. Cuttitta

> "today sovereignty does not consist anymore – or at least not only – in the mere control of territorial areas. But it more and more depends on the control over the different flows running inside and through territories. If we consider that states are no longer the only – and often not even the main – actors which can take decisions regarding such flows, we can say that sovereignty reveals itself in the very modalities through which such decisions are taken and implemented" (Cuttitta, 2006, 37).

Hence the emphasis of the territorial sovereignty of the state has shifted from the preservation and increase of the territory to control over the migration flows and thus to channelling the fluidity of the personal element of statehood. In that aspect the personal sovereignty as the power to take fundamental decisions for the community has gained momentum and has superseded in importance its territorial sovereignty understood as the power to reassert the territorial scope of the state.

In other words one of the key tasks of the states of emigration is to preserve some form of durable political linkage with the former citizens and the citizens living abroad. At the same time the crucial challenge to the states of immigration is to control the incoming flow of people and to provide identity policies and accomplish identity politics that are in compliance with two simultaneous conditions. First, they have to be non-discriminatory and preserve human rights.

Second, they should safeguard a sufficient level of social homogeneity and social integration that would allow the maintenance of a viable democracy based on solidarity that stems out of group identity. The structural problem here is that in some instances these two conditions might contradict each other so a political choice that is pro-human rights or pro-community integrity has to be made.

There are different types of migrations – emigrations and immigrations, migration of refugees, economic migrants, students, workers, and highly paid professional elites. Many of the migrating people move from state to state for different reasons – education, work, social benefits, holidays, preservation of their life and dignity, etc. They develop multiple affiliations that in many cases are not attached to a certain territory and cannot be grasped and conceptualised sufficiently by the nation state's citizenship. Thus the nation state's citizenship is paralleled by other forms of territorial (i.e. city or regional patriotism) and non-territorial (i.e. corporate, professional or religious) social group affiliations.

Citizenship becomes not only multiplied in the territorial aspect in the form of dual citizenship, EU citizenship, or sub-state unit citizenship. It is made to some extent obsolete due to two parallel processes. The first one is the granting of quasi-citizens' political and social rights to non-citizens such as voting rights in local elections and in referenda, rights to establish and join a political party, health care and social insurance rights, etc. The second one is the growth of the importance of territory detached forms of socialisation, i.e. transborder, non-territorial, and virtual social networks.

Emigration is challenging predominantly the personal sovereignty of the state and the immigration – mostly its territorial sovereignty. This is due to the fact that the emigration turns the state into a "leaking container" increasing the depopulation and the establishment of global diaspora whereas immigration is reshaping the national identity of the territory carefully modelled in the last centuries. There is also a reversed relation between migration and sovereignty although in a much weaker version. It has already been mentioned that immigration is an issue that concerns also the personal sovereignty and the identity policies of the state. On the other hand, emigration can be tackled also as a burden to the territorial sovereignty of the receiving state because it challenges its capacity to manage the transborder flow of people and to reaffirm its territoriality.

Emigration produces the depopulation of states, diminishes their productive economic capacity (in the rich Western countries) or on the contrary serves as a demographic valve (in the less developed countries). The key constitutional dilemma posed by emigration concerns the question of how can the states keep the link with their citizens living abroad or with their diaspora of former compatriots thus reasserting the remnants of their personal jurisdiction and personal sovereignty. Immigration, on the other hand, challenges the identity policy of the state, its value and infrastructure character as republican-liberal and national or as a multicultural society. In that case the state is doomed to exercise its jurisdiction over the "newcomers" due to its inherent territoriality.

In some cases the huge migration streams directed from one state to another may function as an instrument for "investment" or transplantation of "personal sovereignty." This is because such streams may lead to the emergence of important subcultures and sub societies in the core of the dominant culture and society that is supposed to serve as a basis for the statehood of the territorial nation state. Moreover they can be nodes in the global diasporic networks spreading from other territorial nation states as their source and centre. The "investment of foreign personal sovereignty" via migration flows beyond certain degree erodes the conditions for the existence not only of liberal-republican democracy but also the usually fragile equilibrium of established multicultural democracies. The reason is that it biases that equilibrium in favour of some of the co-existing sub societies or subcultures or creates new non-integrated communities. Thus the ethical, religious, interest and value toleration will have to be redefined in order to enable the maintenance of social, political, and constitutional consensus.

3. Democracy

Several territorial challenges to democracy caused by migration (emigration or immigration) can be outlined. Excessive immigration may lead to the diminution of the critical degree of social homogeneity and thus of the chances and prerequisites for democracy. In a pluralist democratic society both the socio-political and constitutional conflict and the socio-political and constitutional consensus are needed (see Nuscheler et al., 1982). The non-conflict homogeneous society is a dangerous authoritarian utopia. The same is true for the society without a need for a common core of political, social, and cultural values recognised by the constitution and shared by the majority of citizens. However in the latter case the utopia is a libertarian one. Hence the existence of a pluralist society is dependent upon the toleration of diversity and the recognition of the official and system building values of the pre-existent territorial community.

The current huge wave of immigration to the EU's member states produces a conceptual clash between liberalism and democracy taken in their pure and radical forms. In fact this is not the first instantiation of the antagonism and contravention between these two leading Western ideologies enshrined by all EU member states' constitutions in the form of constitutional principles. However in the post-World War II period, they have coexisted in the context of a modus vivendi that has been wisely elaborated by the constitutional and political theorists as well as by the politicians.

The absolute version of liberalism presupposes that human liberty of all people in the world should be safeguarded at any price and should enjoy primacy over other values and principles such as democratic self-determination of the community, social solidarity, and protection of the national interest. The absolute version of democracy presumes that the collective will of the citizens should prevail over liberty and rights if the decision is a product of free and active participation of the demos and has been taken via just and inclusive democratic procedures. As S. Benhabib puts it:

> "democratic sovereignty is based on three regulative ideals: public autonomy, that is, that the people are the author as well as the subject of the laws; the ideal of unified demos, and a self-enclosed and autonomous territory over which the demos governs" (see Benhabib, 2005, 675).

The extraordinary and excessive immigration flow we are currently witnessing in Europe is undermining the conditions for democracy. The emergence of substantial non-integrated subcultures in European societies which are not sharing their basic values, the sharp contrast between the personal and group values of the "newcomers" with the already established constitutional and political consensus may lead to the "implosion" of European democracy, which is undermined by other factors. Another systemic peculiarity of Europe is that the nation state tradition is deeply rooted in its constitutional code. The constitutional patriotism and political nation options (see Habermas, 1998, pp. 632–660) potentially capable of sustaining multicultural democracy are traditionally weak on national, subnational, and supranational levels. Thus the eventual replacement of republican liberalism with multiculturalism on the level of EU member states would in fact undermine democracy not only in their domestic constitutional politics and constitutional infrastructure but also on the level of the EU.

Multiculturalism depends on two main prerequisites. First, there should be a set of shared public aims, values, and principles that could make possible the coherent functioning of the society and the achievement of common political goals. Second, the subcultures have to recognise each other's mutual right of peaceful parallel coexistence. Toleration and "differentiating recognition" (I am grateful to Prof. Mark Arenhövel for that term) should be the operational values of a multicultural democratic community. Unfortunately it remains unclear whether such demanding conditions can be achieved in the EU, in Europe, or in many other parts of the world.

Another problem of uncontrolled migration is that the states cannot open their borders for all possible types of migrants because this will lead to the inability of the public power to manage such an exploding diversity. It is obvious that democracy needs more or less integrated demos capable of collective action whereas the uncritical recognition of the primacy of the libertarian variant of a human rights based world community is irreconcilable with the idea of an activist and coherent democratic community.

Uncontrolled immigration may also produce a structural exclusion of immigrants. According to S. Benhabib "the entitlement to rights is no longer dependent upon the status of citizenship" (see Benhabib, 2005, 675). Moreover N. Brenner believes that we are experiencing a "global crisis of territorialized definitions of citizenship" (see Brenner, 1999, 60). In spite of that, we are witnessing that in the short-term or even in the midterm that immigrants do not achieve full integration and full equality in the society. This leads inevitably to the immigrant's frustration and dissatisfaction with the receiving state and society and their basic rules and values. The formal recognition of certain amount of rights does not automatically produce inclusion and the feeling of horizontal togetherness and vertical belongingness (see Belov, 2011, 406) that are structural prerequisites for the permanent reaffirmation of an integrated community.

With the diminishing of the importance of belongingness to the "traditional nation" and with the "decline of the unitary model of citizenship" (see Benhabib, 2005, 675), we are experiencing a crisis of the criterions through which the public power can serve as a distributor of rights and can demand obedience and observation of duties by the people. Who is the demos – the former citizens who have emigrated and live abroad, the people from the diaspora spread though the world, the immigrants that have recently received citizenship, or all of them? The delimitation of the demos as one of the pillars of the statehood (see Jellinek, 2010) is of crucial importance to the legitimacy and efficacy of the state power and the policies that it should provide. The lack of clarity regarding the scope of the demos and the criteria for inclusion and exclusion in the democratic community is an important aspect of the crisis of territoriality produced by globalisation.

Emigration and the increasing density and velocity of transnational diasporic population movements (see Brenner, 1999, 60) may lead to the erosion of territory based democratic community. This erosion occurs in two different and opposite aspects.

First, the exclusion of the "former citizens" through deprivation of political and other rights stemming out of the citizenship limits the demographic power of the community and tears to pieces the bond between the initial demos and the world diaspora. Hence the territorial dispersion may produce irreversible disintegration of the national community. This is especially problematic for countries that have experienced huge emigration waves.

Second, in cases that former citizens are allowed to preserve all or some of their political rights the demos commences to function as a fluid global community partially detached from the territoriality of the state and drifting with its periphery in the globalised space. Such a hypothesis is based on the principle of constitutional equalisation of the political status of the citizens living inside the "territorial container" and the members of the world diaspora allocated outside of it. However this principle does not recognise the fact that the results of such partially territory detached decision making will have consequences predominantly for that part of the "fluid demos" that lives in the framework of the initial territorial jurisdiction. Thus there will be a mismatch between decision making subject and addressees of the political decisions. It is well known that this is an important structural prerequisite for democracy. "Democratic laws require closure precisely because democratic representation must be accountable to a specific people" (see Benhabib, 2005, 675).

It is widely recognised in the theory that the remoteness of the decision making subject from the addressees of the decisions taken by him diminishes the chances for democratic government and governance. The broader the scale and the scope and the remote the power the more elitist, non-controllable, and non-accountable is the government. The peculiarity here is that the global fluidity of the demos and the political empowerment of the diasporic network create a democratic deficit of the decision making, which is not due to elitist rule.

Here we are confronted with another "problem of scale" namely whether it is democratically justifiable to allow parts of the demos that have escaped the restraints of the territoriality of power to influence the lives of the territorially entrenched part of the demos without immediately experiencing the results of their decisions. In other words could we define democracy as a system of territory semi-detached network governance if the policy making of a national community that comprises both the demos of the state of origin and the demos spread out as diaspora becomes virtual and even global but many of its effects are by nature territorial? Moreover how can we render the diaspora territorially responsible if this is a precondition for the preservation of the democratic nature of the civic participation of the people that belong to it?

Here we touch upon two conceptual issues. The first one is could tfluid demos and especially those parts of it that have escaped the borders of the "territorial container" be non-democratic due to the irresponsibility to the initial territorial community. Is it possible to assume that the extraterritoriality and the physical distance produce territorial irresponsibility and "democratic fracture" of the globalised demos? These questions are related to the fundamental problem under which circumstances and on the basis of which criteria can the exclusion or inclusion in the demos be legitimate. Could the territorial detachment or vice versa the territorial entrenchment be among these criteria and conditions?

The second conceptual issue concerns the following two interrelated questions. Could we have not only territorial but also aterritorial and non-territorial democracies? Is the democracy necessarily territory restrained phenomenon based on permanent territorial attachment or can it be achieved also virtually, i.e. through Internet based social networks? The difference between aterritorial and non-territorial democracy is that the former is virtual, Internet based and fully independent of the territory whereas the latter may have territorial forms and manifestations but they are subordinate to its non-territorial aspects. Moreover they are not limited to a single state territory but may occur on different territories.

Both issues are stemming out of the crisis of territoriality in conjunction with the global fluidisation of the demos in the context of the information and technology revolution. The information and technology revolution has made possible the enhanced virtual participation of the citizens living abroad, the emigrants, and even the diaspora in the social and political life of the state of origin. Currently a partially non-territorial democracy is thinkable if we do not consider it as a fully-fledged holistic concept but as a discourse that supports and upgrades the territory-based democracy. Presumably the non-territorial democracy may be conceptualised as an Internet-based network of citizens upgrading other territory based forms of civic activism that facilitates the deliberation and participation of the territory detached parts of the fluid demos in the decision making processes of the state of origin. The forms of such non-territorial, diasporic and globalised democracy are the e-voting, the e-petitioning, the deliberative pools, the Internet based pressure groups, the platforms for idea sharing, and decision making, etc.

Hence the territory detachment of such a democracy is not absolute. It presumes the territoriality of some of its elements – state institutions, technical infrastructure, etc. The non-territorial democracy of a globalised diasporic national network is combining territorial and non-territorial, network, and hierarchy elements.

The more challenging issue is whether the Internet can serve as a space for global aterritorial or non-territorial and non-national democracy in the form of a discursive networked global civil society which is based on "space-time compression" (see Brenner, 1999, 39). The normative idea behind such a proposal is that new technologies allow for the emergence of virtual communities of "idea compatriots" that can perform critical, deliberative, and controlling functions and thus serve as a functional equivalent of a territory detached and non-national political community.

Indeed such global networks can be very important in channelling the political participation of different world communities, in fostering the political inclusion independently of states, governments, territories, and nations and in enabling the emergence of critical public opinion on a global scale. The hope is that this emergent discursive, virtual, and network civil society could eventually produce limits to the otherwise democratically irresponsible actors of global governance and that the development of global public opinion is potentially capable to foster democratic accountability.

However doubts remain whether such discursive non-territorial democratic networks and non-territorial forms of community and authority that should produce global democratic accountability are viable without a coherent, national and territory based demos. Questionable is also if they will be really authentic forms of civic participation and engagement that are independent from the actors they are supposed to criticise, control, and render accountable. Moreover is the "virtual global demos" based simultaneously on the territory, the professional and personal relations and on Internet communities a possible functional equivalent to the nation as demos grounded on territory, history, and ethno-cultural proximity?

I will leave these questions to remain rhetorical due to space constraints. There should be a systematic effort for the encouragement of the emergence of such global virtual network communities. The irreversibility of the information revolution is a fact that has to be recognised. The advantages of the new information and communication technologies have to be deliberately used for limitation of their disadvantages. In fact the fostering of such virtual and global participatory and deliberative networks can reduce the information advantage of the financial capital in terms of uncontrollability and unaccountability stemming out of the "space-time compression" (see Brenner, 1999, 39). Thus the unaccountability produced by the virtual and global character of the financial capitalism may at least to some extent be limited by the virtual character of the emergent global civil society. This may lead to an increase of the democratic control of the new category of global active citizenry. Although it will probably not render the financial capital territorially responsible.

4. Rule of law

It might seem at first glance that the global fluidity of demos undermines the conditions for maintenance of the constitutional principle of rule of law. Immigrants are usually not accustomed with the legal provisions and especially with the legal culture of the receiving state. The knowledge of the legal culture is an important condition for the achievement and maintenance of the substantial rule of law especially with regard to the horizontal effect of human rights. In many cases, immigrants are also not willing to adapt to the new legal context and institutional infrastructure of the state in which they are supposed to live.

There might also be an opposite problem namely that the receiving state does not provide for sufficient civic education which will enhance the inclusion of immigrants in the new legal culture and that will allow them to make use of the institutional channels for integration in the socio-political, economic, and cultural life of the receiving community. The mismatch between the legal culture of the migrating people and that of the states and societies through which they migrate or in which they reside for the short term or permanently may produce anomia, a clash of legal cultures or a conflict of jurisdictions.

One of the historical reasons why the rule of law has emerged in the Western legal tradition (for the concept of legal tradition see Glenn, 2000, pp. 1–30) is the need for integration and sufficient legal harmonisation of initially fragmented societies with differing ethical, religious, and other types of metalegal normative systems of the composite subcultures and sub societies. The pre-modern European states were loose frames of fragmented, mosaic, and diverse societies. The establishment of the broad scale territorial nation states required a legal unification based on recognition of a legal system that is common for all subcultures and sub societies. It should have to consist of rational, abstract, and as much as possible morally, religiously, and culturally neutral rules that have to be equally valid for all parts of the society. Such neutrality was much more presumed and ideal than real but it was part of the "supportive ideologies" of the modern constitutional statehood institutionalised as legal equality, equal treatment, due process of law, etc.

Even if the state is a Rechtsstaat or a state which is ruled by law and provides for advanced institutional infrastructure safeguarding human rights, liberty and freedom with the huge immigration and the emergence of vast subcultures it might become inadequate to the legal culture of the migrants. Hence it has to be either reconciled with the culture of the new inhabitants or they have to change and accept it. Both options may become obsolete under certain conditions. It is not clear from a democratic and sovereignty point of view why the dominant or traditional culture should start to adapt to the culture of the immigrants. On the other hand, the immigrants may also not want to accept the dominant culture. Moreover they may belong to different traditions that are also irreconcilable with each other.

In such case the formal variant of rule of law that is value detached and neutral might seem like a solution (for the formal rule of law see Tanchev, 2003, pp. 314–315). However this option is problematic in many aspects. First, it is open to authoritarianism and might be taken over by radical political, social, or religious factions using its formality. Second, it does not provide for real remedies of substantial problems exactly because it is "blind to the context." Anyway the larger the scale of the society and the greater its diversity the more formal the rule of law can be. The EU with its accent and focus on formal legal integration and with substantial unification lagging way behind is an example of that principle.

It is clear that the current round of globalisation produces social and political outcomes that are opposite in many aspects to the processes which have led to the establishment of the nation state. Globalisation diminishes the social homogeneity and in many cases produces pluralistic, multicultural, and even fragmented societies. It undermines the conditions for preservation of the territorial sovereignty of the nation states and for the maintenance of liberal-republican neutrality of the state because it fosters the emergence and development of religious and culture based sub societies.

The current emerging proliferation of legal subcultures combined with vertical pluralisation of the normative orders creates a social and political situation which can be best described as a "Kandinski painting" – a metaphor used by Martti Koskenniemi in his keynote speech to the XXII IACL World Congress. The constitutional pluralism (see MacCormick, 2002, 104; Maduro, 2012), the religious, ethical and legal multiculturalism, the normative inflation, the emergence of cross-cutting jurisdictions (see Sassen, 2013, pp. 21–45) and the territorial proliferation of the normative and institutional systems reinforce each other producing the feeling of an increasing normative chaos and thus of non-governability of the processes on local, national, regional, supranational, and global levels. The increasing number and complexity of subnational, national, supranational and international legal provisions not only does not reduce the legal anomy of the fragmented societies but actually they widen the gap between the "official" legal culture of the state and the "real" legal cultures of the social fragments.

Hence we are in deep need for a common denominator and a common core of legal provisions that can serve as an inclusive grid and regulative framework both for the increasingly pluralist territorial states and societies and on supranational and in some sense supraterritorial level – also for the global society. Thus one can suppose that the same reasons that have produced the need for rule of law in the period of establishment and consolidation of the territorial nation states are once again important and pressing in the context of constitutional pluralism, globalisation, and global governance.

It is obvious that we are going to live in pluralist societies that will never again get as presumably homogenous as in the epoch of the rise of the nation state. This is due to reasons "from inside" – the diminishing of social solidarity and social cohesion within the nations, dysfunctionality of the national imaginary and mythology and "from outside" – the migratory waves of different kinds of migrants, booming information flow, and the influence of supranational and international normative orders.

It is also clear that people cannot be the only agent that can rearrange and adapt the normative system and achieve the necessary degree of normative coherence and socio-legal and cultural homogeneity. Such coherence and homogeneity are needed not only for the maintenance of democracy and people's sovereignty but also for the normal functioning of the legal system. Legal certainty has to be secured and the legal expectations of the people should be safeguarded. Moreover not only the predictability and legality but also the legitimacy of the acts and behaviour of the institutions of public power, the other legal subjects, and especially the global governance actors have to be secured and provided. This can be done through the reassertion of the rule of law in the framework of the state but also on supranational and even global levels.

Hence we are confronted with several possible future developments of the global rule of law. The need for conceptualisation of the constitutional principle of rule of law as supranational and even global legal and political principle is provoked by several postmodern challenges. The most important among them are the fluidity and global dispersion of the demos, the non-accountability of financial capital to territory entrenched public power, and the information revolution that produces territorial detachment of the human relations in parallel with the emergence of new virtual borders, communities, and restraints.

The first option is the maintenance of several levels and spheres of rule of law that are coordinated with each other. The limited number of basic principles further developed via sector specific political and legal acts and loose institutional system adapted much more for debating and popularising them than for their systematic implementation and safeguarding could be conceived as a universal system of rule of law. Then this fragile and underdeveloped universal system should be paralleled by regional, supranational, and national systems of rule of law generally coordinated with each other.

This model has many issues. Some of them are the formality of the global level of the system that does not provide for a substantial rule of law and the lack of sufficient coordination thus producing normative gaps and jurisdiction collisions. Another problem is the entrenchment of most of the actors – especially the public and democratically controllable, in one of the systems that enables other actors that have the knowledge and institutional capacity to function across the different systems and levels to get profit of that situation. Moreover such a system is not genuinely universal due to the lack of developed mechanisms for the implementation and safeguarding of the rule of law as well as of value consensus underlying the formal rules.

The normative collisions and antinomies in the spheres of human rights, migration, military action, finance, ecology, and new technologies are especially problematic. They demonstrate the limited ability of the "coordination model" to manage the diversity of contexts, beliefs, interests, and actors and to provide viable solutions to problems that are stemming out of the incongruence between the subsystems, the formality of rule of law, the "cross-cutting jurisdictions," the "jump-scaling," and the "nested games" (see Tsebelis, 1990).

The second option is the emergence and the development of a global rule of law which should not only be institutionally and procedurally harmonised but also adjusted to the material scope and content of the rule of law in the framework of the territorial states and the international and supranational organisations and regimes. The most logical and feasible option would be that such rule of law should be formal and neutral. Otherwise it can be based on the imposition or voluntary acceptance of one or more key metalegal systems defined as an official variant of the substantial rule of law. Another possibility is the negotiation of a substantial rule of law based on a negotiated and mixed metalegal normativity.

The establishment of a genuine global rule of law has many advantages. It allows for the application of common rules for a presumably world community which enhances the business and facilitates the rule recognition by the people. At the same time it imposes limits to currently almost unrestrained factors such as the financial capital and migration flow as well as diminishes the normative gaps of the information societies. Such a concept is actually not absolutely novel because its seeds and general theoretical prerequisites have been launched in the intellectual debate by Kant in his book "Perpetual Peace" (see Kant, 2008).

However this option does not take into account the natural diversity of normative beliefs shared by different societies. Thus it may turn to be just formally observed while at the same time it may lack real acceptance, recognition, and obedience. Moreover it is questionable whether such a global normative network can be paralleled by the necessary and coordinated institutional network with sufficient democratic legitimacy. In other words the problem is could such a global rule of law be also democratically enacted, maintained, and safeguarded by sanctions.

The renationalisation of the rule of law is impossible. The states are highly interconnected, the demos become more and more fluid and even globally dispersed, the information and capital flow is worldwide. These are just some of the most important reasons why the territorial states cannot achieve legal equilibrium framed by purely national law. The full globalisation of the rule of law is also utopia for the moment. It is illegitimate and practically dysfunctional due to the non-recognition of the plurality of contexts that are still very much territory restrained by the states as institutional frames for the societies.

The information revolution and the subsequent emergence of a globalised and even to some extent global information society introduce the issue of the necessary adjustment of the principle of rule of law to this new information context and a set of new problems. Can we apply the constitutional and international rule of law provisions developed in the age before the information revolution to the new technological and communication infrastructure or we have to adapt it to the emergent global territory detached social and political relations and communities which are virtual, simultaneous, and based on a "space-time compression?" Should and could we have a global set of unified rules regarding Internet based issues? Will the adoption of such rules, i.e. in the framework of the United Nations (UN), lead to the increased legality and legitimate pluralism of the world information flow or vice versa – to informational authoritarianism? These are just some of the questions imposed by the application of the rule of law in the new information context. They will have to be left to remain rhetorical due to space constraints.

5. Welfare State

Initially the welfare state was created as a result of the consensus between the labour and the (predominantly industrial) capital politically represented by the social democrats and the Christian democrats. The social contract on the establishment of a welfare state in Europe has horizontal and vertical dimensions. Horizontally it is a pact between compatriots for mutual support and solidarity and for recognition of a minimal degree of dignity based on reflexive and reciprocal responsiveness. Vertically the welfare state is a contract between the people, the capital, and the politicians established for the peaceful coexistence of all social strata in the context of market based economy. The welfare state is a cornerstone of the post World War II consumerist society and social market economy in Western Europe. It is based on the social, economic, and cultural rights providing for fair working conditions, social security, a sufficient degree of education and healthcare, and access to culture.

The information and technology revolution creates new challenges to the principle of a welfare state. The information and technological dimension of the welfare state consists of the right to access sufficient information and fundamental technological developments by all parts of the society. The quantity and quality of information as well as the possession of adequate technical skills and technologies are important for the development of a society based on information and technology inclusion. The current degree of technological advance produces new types of labour markets, and economic, cultural and political exclusion for the citizens that do not have the sufficient education and access to technological resources. The information and technology equality is nowadays not less important than the other forms of social equality.

The information and technology revolution changes profoundly the way business is done. It facilitates the global forms of capitalism and creates new types of deals and businesses that are based on the "space-time compression." They are territory detached, could be virtual, and may function simultaneously on many places on Earth. The advance of the new technologies empowers the capital to get global and thus independent from concrete community and territory attachments and affiliations. The deterritorialisation of the capital is not paralleled by the development of sufficient compensatory mechanisms for the maintenance of social justice and solidarity on supranational, national, or subnational levels.

This new production and business infrastructure based on the new information and technological context does not allow the protection of fair working and social conditions to be accomplished only in the framework of the territorial state. The labour competition in many branches of the economy and in the non-production sector is increasingly international and even global. Hence the protection against social dumping and social exclusion and the provision of a minimal standard of welfare cannot be safeguarded anymore in the narrow frames of the "territorial container."

Moreover all "territorial political elites" – national, subnational and even the EU, have to simultaneously produce two competitive advantages which are mutually exclusive. On the one hand, they have to provide for a developed welfare state in order to preserve the demographic and productive potential of their nations or other types of communities (subnational or supranational) by preventing depopulation, social degradation, emigration and collapse of the adequate degree of education and health of the human capital. On the other hand, they have to engage in a "race to the bottom"[1] in order to minimise the labour and production costs of the business, attract foreign capital and prevent the fleeing of the national capital. The creation of a capital friendly environment is supposed to be based on minimising taxation, ecology and social protection costs that produces a constant erosion of the welfare state.

The current phase of capitalism is characterised by the enhanced importance of financial capital. The specificity of financial capital is that it is intrinsically global, territory detached, and in many cases virtual. Hence financial capital is hard to restrain by the welfare state infrastructure and the instruments available to the territorial state. The territorial irresponsibility of the financial capital infringes the principles of democracy and welfare state and undermines the social consensus achieved in the decades after World War II between the industrial capital, the agrarian capital, and the rest of the society – politicians, workers, and the citizens engaged in the non-productive sphere financed by redistribution (education, culture, healthcare, etc.).

The welfare state is a territoriality based concept. It is preconditioned upon the territorial responsibility of capital and the solidarity of a territory framed community. The welfare state is dependent on the territoriality of power and production resources. It needs territorial closure due to the fact that it is dependent on solidarity and redistribution which are possible only in a territorially framed community and economy. It has to be kept financially balanced and directed towards people who are determined in advance with regard to their needs and contributions. The welfare state depends on the financial balance between revenues and spending which is conditional upon the stability and predictability of the public finance. Moreover the redistribution presupposes social solidarity that in the long term can be systematically achieved only in the framework of territory based demos bound by feelings of togetherness and belongingness to a political community.

The information and technology revolution proliferates the non-territorial forms of engagement and prosperity and stimulates the search of aterritorial welfare. Social prosperity is frequently searched for not only beyond the borders of the state of origin but also beyond any type of space via the Internet or through virtual global communities which do not have a special territorial allocation. In addition financial capital can hardly be rendered socially responsible and accountable to a territory based community neither with democratic nor with authoritarian means. Traditional capital restraints and forms for the production of welfare output

1 The notion "race to the bottom" has been used in the 1933 US Supreme Court decision Ligget Co v. Lee.

such as taxation, social security systems and labour and ecology legislation remain obsolete. This is due to the fact that they are functional and operational upon concrete state territory and thus remain territory entrenched whereas the information, capital, and investment flow and to a much limited extent the flow of workers are increasingly territory detached.

Global fluidity of the demos challenges all constitutional principles of the modern state. Intense global and regional migration undermines the conditions for maintenance of the welfare state. It has been mentioned that the welfare state is a redistributive state that is based on a necessary equilibrium between financial input and financial output. Hence exorbitant emigration deprives the national economy of working force and creates impediments for its social systems whereas extreme immigration makes the maintenance of high social standard practically impossible.

The global or regional mobility of the working force may be useful in some cases for the achievement of a match between the distribution of people, resources, and capital. However the structural problem caused by migration is that there is no global or regional state or other form of public power that can provide the migrants with a protective legal and administrative framework and can serve as a democratic forum that may grant them not only fair working conditions but also instruments for political participation and civic inclusion. The only exception is the EU with its free movement of people as a fundamental principle and the social policy and social and labour EU law.

Hence the welfare society is by definition territorially referential and cannot be global or open to everyone on the principle of universal humanity. The inclusion of people that do not belong to the citizenry in the social benefit schemes can be justified, i.e. through the Kantian principle of ethical personalism or via obligations for maintenance of world peace and equilibrium. However such recognition has its limits in the priority of the interest of the territorial community.

A world welfare system is thinkable only in the form of the UN system of humanitarian aid. However this system is also territorially entrenched due to the fact that it is financed by territorial states and serves for support of citizens of territorial states. In addition it is based on the value of universal humanism and not on the principle of social solidarity. This is due to the fact that there are universal and inviolable core elements of the human identity and human dignity but no universal community or universal society and thus no imperatives for universal social solidarity.

6. Conclusions

The fluidity of demos, the territorial irresponsibility of financial capital and the increased influence of the new information, communication, and transportation technologies are symptoms of the great systemic change and transition we are currently experiencing. These processes are not only functional. They are changing profoundly the structure of the constitutional, political, and social relations and the context in which the constitution is supposed to function.

The constitutional principles are elaborated in order to function in a territory based and territory framed context. The sovereignty and the welfare state are essentially territorially entrenched. Although state sovereignty is challenged by the emergence of aterritorial and sector specific quasi-sovereign global governance players, it remains a territory based concept due to several reasons. A worldwide or global sovereignty is impossible at this current stage of historical development. The transfer of sovereignty towards the EU is again territory referential. Even the actions of the above mentioned aterritorial factors with quasi-sovereign power are directed towards one or more state territories.

Moreover the welfare state is very much predetermined by territoriality with regard to both its input and output side. On the input side the revenue gathering in general and the taxation in particular remain key competence of the territorial states. On the output side the criterions for welfare distribution are directed towards a territory based community – the EU's citizens or the citizens of its member states.

The only constitutional principles that may retain their logic and functionality also in the territory detached and increasingly globalised context are the rule of law and to a limited extent –democracy. The determinants and the possible ways for the emergence of a global rule of law have already been explained above. The eventual deterritorialization of democracy may be conceptualised with regard to two phenomena. The first one is the networked diasporic extraterritorial democracy encompassing both the "internal" and "external compatriots." It may be produced as a result of the global fluidity of the demos. The second one is the global Internet based forms of democratic deliberation, participation, and community building. They may eventually lead to the emergence of an Internet democracy. Most probably such virtual democracy will not be a holistic category but sector specific and a discursive form of democratic entanglement.

Even in the current age of crisis of territoriality, some form of territorial closure has to be achieved in order to reassert the conditions for maintenance of sovereignty, rule of law, democracy, and the welfare state. It is not necessary for the territoriality to persist in the form of nation state territoriality. It may be achieved in the framework of regional or supranational unions. However global democracy as a holistic category which is fully detached from definite demos and some form of territoriality as well as the welfare state without a referential community with a degree of cohesion and solidarity cannot be realistic options. This is to some extent true also for the rule of law if it has to be substantial, value oriented, and context adequate and thus to be really accepted by a certain community of people.

References

Agnew, John. 2013. Editorial. *Territory, Politics, Governance*, Vol. 1, Issue 1: 1–4.

Agnew, John. 2005. Sovereignty Regimes: Territoriality and State Authority in Contemporary World Politics. Annals of the Association of American Geographers. Vol. 95, Issue 2: 437–461.

Belov, Martin. 2011. EU Citizen – Market Agent, Political Player or a New Dimension of the Personal Identity. Is There Any Chance for a 'Supranational Nation' on EU Level? In *Europe – A Continent of Immigration? Legal Challenges in the Construction of European Migration Policy*, 2011, edited by Daniel Thym and Francis Snyder, 405–431. Brussels: Bruylant.

Benhabib, Seyla. 2005. Borders, Boundaries and Citizenship. *Political Science and Politics*. Vol. 38, № 4: 673–677.

Brenner, Neil. 1999. Beyond state-centrism? Space, Territoriality and Geographical Scale in Globalization Studies. *Theory and Society* 28: 39–78.

Castels, Manuel. 2010. The Rise of the Network Society. Oxford: Blackwell.

Cuttitta, Paolo. 2006. Points and Lines: A Topography of Borders in the Global Space. *Ephemera* Vol. 6, № 1: 27–40.

Dobner, Petra, Loughlin Martin (eds.) 2010. The Twilight of Constitutionalism? Oxford: Oxford University Press.

Eriksen, Thomas, H. 2014. Globalization. Key Concepts. London: Bloomsbury.

Glenn, Patrick, H. 2000. Legal Traditions of the World. Oxford: Oxford University Press.

Habermas, Jürgen. 1998. Faktizität und Geltung. Frankfurt/Main: Suhrkamp.

Jellinek, Georg. 2010. Allgemeine Staatslehre. Charleston: Nabu Press.

Kant, Immanuel. 2008. Perpetual Peace. San Diego: The Book Tree.

MacCormick, Neil. 2002. Questioning Sovereignty: Law, State and Nation in the European Commonwealth. Oxford: Oxford University Press Nuscheler, Franz, Steffanie Winfried. 1982. Pluralismus. Konzeptionen und Kontroversen. München: Piper Verlag.

Maduro, Miguel Poiares. 2012. Three Claims of Constitutional Pluralism, in Constitutional Pluralism in the European Union and Beyond, edited by Matej Avbelj and Jan Kom6rek, Oxford:Hart Publishing.

Ong, Aihwa. 1999. Flexible Citizenship. The Cultural Logiscs of Transnationality. Durham: Duke University Press.

Parrish, Austen, L. 2011. Rehabilitating Territoriality in Human Rights. *Faculty Publications*. Paper 881: 1099–1141.

Popper, Karl. 2013. The Open Society and its Enemies. Princeton: Princeton University Press.

Rasmussen, H. 2006. Denmark's Waning Constitutionalism and Article 20 of the Constitution on Transfer of Sovereignty. In: The European Constitution and National Constitutions: Ratification and Beyond, edited by Albi, Anneli and Ziller, Jacques. 149–156, Deventer: Kluwer.

Rousseau, Jean-Jacques. 1968. The Social Contract. London: Penguin Books.

Ruggie, John G. 1993. Territoriality and Beyond: Problematizing Modernity in International Relations. *International Organization* Vol. 47, № 1: 139–174.

Sassen, Saskia. 1991. The Global City. Princeton: Princeton University Press.

Sassen, Saskia. 2007. A Sociology of Globalization. New York: W. W. Norton & company.

Sassen, Saskia. 2013. When Territory Deborders Territoriality. *Territory, Politics, Governance*. Vol. 1, Issue 1: 21–45.

Sassen, Saskia. 2006. Territory, Autority, Rights. From Medieval to Global Assemblages. Princeton: Princeton University Press.

Schmitt, Carl. 1997. Verfassungslehre. Berlin: Duncker&Humblot.

Tanchev, Evgeni. 2003. Introduction in the Constitutional Law. Sofia: Sibi (in Bulgarian).

Teivainen, Teivo. 2000. Towards a Democratic Theory of the World-System: Democracy, Territoriality and Transnationalization. *Journal of World-Systems Research*. Vol. VI, № 3: 706–725.

Tsebelis, George. 1990. *Nested Games. Rational Choice in Comparative Politics*. Berkley: University of California Press.

Mate Paksy

Justice, Territory, and National Minorities: Critical Assessments

Abstract

The rights of national minorities as territorially homogenous sizeable groups can be protected by means of two seemingly contradictory sets of techniques. One of these techniques uses the principle of the territoriality and the other is based on the personality principle. Both techniques can be traced back to the political-legal discourse of the declining Austro-Hungarian Empire and the rising Germany. Notably the idea of the territorially based nation-state as a normative methodological construction was clearly expressed by the famous three-elements definition of Georg Jellinek. Simultaneously the idea of the non-territorial cultural autonomy was born thanks to Otto Bauer and Karl Renner. These techniques of protection had extremely important impacts on the nation-building strategies in the Central European countries and these theories have their own renaissance today. This is especially true for Will Kymlicka, the Canadian scholar, who, on the basis of a slightly modified theory of John Rawls rejected the personality principle as a unique solution for the difficulties in the Central European countries and suggested instead a theory of the multicultural citizenship. In the present study I am paying particular attention to the apparent contradiction between the bases of the different means of the protection, namely, the territory as a fact and the justice as a normative claim. I will try to show not only that this contradiction is not an essential one because "territory of the state" is rather a social construction and part of the national identity than a physical-geographical (material) datum but also that the above mentioned techniques, having the same intellectual origin, are much closer to each other than we usually think.

1. Introduction

It is in the nature of things that justice can only be universal and eternal. By the same token, territory can only be local and concrete. In Kantian terms, justice is something "that ought to be" while territory belongs to the world of facts.[1] This distinction still may prove helpful even in the age of the globalisation when:

1 Local justice is usually called "equity" and I do not need to mention that universal territory is not a contradiction in terms either; it is called "space." This dialectic has been refrained in Kasier's study where he speaks about the procedure of "nationalizing space / territorialisation of the nation." The goal of this procedure is a "homeland-creation,"

> "we can expect global law to have characteristics that are significantly different from our experience of the law of the nation state: …The boundaries of global law are formed not by maintaining a core »territory« and expanding on a federal basis as Kant perceived in terms of nation-states, but rather, by »invisible colleges«, »invisible markets and branches«, »invisible professional communities«, »invisible social networks« that transcend territorial boundaries but nevertheless press for the emergence of genuinely legal forms" (see Teubner, 1997, pp. 7–8).

Despite this unrestrainable globalisation, which destroys our well-established categories, justice as norm, and territory as fact still remain parts of our world's different spheres. Nevertheless they share at least one common feature in their side-effects, namely, both are susceptible to bring about conflict which means that the current *status quo* based peace would not last much longer.

Hence political theorists spare no pains to find techniques to justify the maintenance of the actual status quo. They think that even a "just" secession implies necessarily the disintegration of the state and keeps the ethnic nationalism alive. It sounds familiar to say that in Central and Eastern Europe the territorial claims mobilised against the given political status quo are usually based on the argument from the historical injustice. Thus, many of these theorists are trying to put forward practical or political arguments against plans to territorially organise national minorities self-government. According to them national minorities should not even think about further federalisation of the state since it would be a sign of impending doom of their broader multi-ethnic political community. Therefore they go along with the suggestion of the de-territorialised protection of national minorities, such as the extended use of the principle of anti-discrimination or the cultural autonomy. The realistic-amoral approach disregards the question of the allegedly universal principles of justice in favour of collective security and efficient risk management.

Far be it from me to say that I agree with this "realistic" approach but unfortunately for the time being I do not have any fully fledged normative-federalist theory of the minority protection in my pocket either. On account of this manqué, I am going to limit myself to mapping some relevant theories and criticise them in the hope that this can be helpful for those who have more straightforward answers.

---

since it is "not ready-made, but rather the outcome of the national construction of social space" (see Kaiser, 2002, 231).

2. Jellinek and his Hidden Legacy: Theory of the Modern State and its Impacts on the Theories of Minority Rights

I venture to say that that almost all geographically concentrated, sizeable national minorities claim to be empowered morally to practise their rights of national self-determination. Nonetheless the meaning, the use and scope of the use of the "national self-determination" is still extremely uncertain, these national minorities do not consider the chance to think about themselves as "ministates" as ill-acquired gain.

Let me begin my reflections with a short overview of Georg Jellinek's theory of state. My personal choice of him is because he was a great Neo-Kantian philosopher, who took the "to be /ought to be" distinction fairly seriously and he is also a positivist lawyer and probably the most influential German founding father of the general theory of state. He was the scholar who conceptualised in a most influential way the territorially based state. If a national minority claims to have a right to achieve independence, the first of the fulfilment of the criteria should be proved which is determined by Jellinek regarding the statehood.

Jellinek nails down in his *Allgemeine Staatslehre* that territoriality of the state is a modern phenomenon. Using the term *a quo*, he famously defined it with its three conceptual elements: territory, population, and authority.[2] In addition to that his theory of right is fairly well-known. He advocated against French republican scholars like Boutmy on a theory of individual right as a "Teutonic concept," traceable to the emergence of the Protestant vindications for religious tolerance and not to Rousseau's political theory (see Kelly, 2004). It seems to me that there is no necessary link between his theory of right, his proposal for the protection of (any) minority, and his influential draft on the judicial review of the constitution.

Let me come back to his *opus magnum* (see Jellinek, 1922), in which one might discover that territory is under scrutiny in both parts of the book. At the very beginning, the author gives an interpretation of the territory as a sociological fact

2 He refers to a certain Klüber article from 1817, which defined the state *mit einem bestimmten Landbezirk* (with a determined territory). Before that even a "state-emigration from one territory to another" was conceptually feasible. (see Jellinek, 1922, 395s) This claim is quite arguable. It is a cliché in political philosophy that the territoriality was an essential feature of the statehood as early as in Saint Augustine's thinking. Everybody knows the quotation form the City of God: "Justice being taken away, then, what are kingdoms but great robberies? For what are robberies themselves, but little kingdoms? The band itself is made up of men; it is ruled by the authority of a prince, it is knit together by the pact of the confederacy; the booty is divided by the law agreed on."

whereas in Chapter 13, he interprets it as a part of the juridical definition of the state. Indeed, he is definitely reluctant to decide whether the factual-sociological or the normative-juridical side of the territory should prevail. The same goes for the two other elements of the state: the questioned unity of the population by the minority and the divisibility of the authority are analysed without any references to a conceivable challenge raised by the national minorities.

As to the territory, Jellinek's reluctance can be generalised. Usually, the definition of national minority follows the definition of the state and both refer to the territory and have indeed an explicit or implicit reference to the territory. Compare for instance the definition offered by Francesco Capotorti, Special Rapporteur of the United Nations Sub-Commission on Prevention of Discrimination and Protection of Minorities with reference to the culture[3] with Article 1 of the Montevideo Convention[4] providing a definition of the state as a spatially demarcated entity.

Debating the best practise of the accommodation of national minorities claims, it appears that the cultural-political context of Jellinek's theory is probable more thought-provoking than his oeuvre itself. Hence the renewed interest in the Austro-Hungarian Empire is justified for multiplied reasons.

On the one hand, this was a historical context for theories of state that shape our understanding of political communities. This dual Empire had hegemony over national minorities, which used the principle of national self-determination coupled with ethnic-cultural nationalist ideology when the Empire finally split up. It is worth mentioning however that the link between liberalism and the question of the best practise in the field of minority rights is contingent. While many republican theories are malignant towards group rights and the examples of the illiberal uses of these rights are well-known (see e.g. the analyse of the Turkish millet system in Tas, 2014), not only Jellinek, but many contemporary liberal thinkers can assume without making a conceptual mistake that Western liberalism can accommodate minority rights of national sub-state groups. Well, this is not

3 E/CN.4/Sub.2/384/Rev.1, para. 568.: A group numerically inferior to the rest of the population of a State, in a non-dominant position, whose members—being nationals of the State—possess ethnic, religious or linguistic characteristics differing from those of the rest of the population and show, if only implicitly, a sense of solidarity, directed towards preserving their culture, traditions, religion or language.

4 *Montevideo Convention on the Rights and Duties of States*, Signed in Montevideo on December 26, 1931. Art. 1. The state as a person of international law should possess the following qualifications: a) a permanent population; b) a defined territory; c) government; and d) capacity to enter into relations with the other states.

so obvious. Many theorists prefer the "easier" way of the theory-construction and exclude normative-moral considerations from the argumentation. Among these theories there are some that can be traced back to the first "antifederalist" authors of the late Austro-Hungarian Empire.

3. Renner, Bauer, and the Challenge of Non-Territorial or Cultural Autonomy

Various contemporary political theorists – who work driven by the desire to promote stability and eternal peace in international relations – suggest that the "de-territorialised" theory based on the cultural autonomy should be considered as a panacea for the whole Eastern and Central European *misère*.[5] This is because, while the real impact of national boundaries is gradually weakening under the political pressure of the increasing European Union, the issue of self-determination by means of secession in Europe is still not overcome. In many cases the tension between the "be" and the "ought to be" is very high.[6]

Among others Nimni, Maloy and Smith take priority of the de-territorialised protection of the minority rights. They seem to think that the federalisation of a multi-ethnic state is the penultimate step before the secession and as a result its disintegration. In order to keep unchanged the geopolitical balance of power, they prefer and promote "non-territorial" or cultural autonomy (see Nimni, 2007; Maloy 2009; Smith 2013). A fine example for speaking of de-territorialisation in a seemingly critical, but in fact, rather glowing terms is Maloy:

> "The aim of the NTA provisions of the Lund Recommendations was to lead governments away from fearing territorial autonomy claims towards contemplating NTA as alternatives. In other words, if national security and unity could be achieved through NTA, there would be no need for governments to accept demands for territorial autonomy. This is a noble aim…"

The first theories of cultural autonomy were elaborated by great scholars such as Karl Renner and Otto Bauer. Let me survey these theories.

5 See Malloy, 2009 providing an overview on the influence of the non-territorial autonomy (or arrangements) in the OSCE states. Further to the non-territorial (or personal or cultural) autonomy see Quer, 2013 and Smith, 2013.

6 While the introduction of cultural autonomy in the Baltic states cannot prevent these political communities from all possible conflicts, in many European countries the ethnically justified federal autonomy functions fairly well (see South Tyrol or the Aaland Islands).

Renner's "State and Nation" was not only a political pamphlet promoting cultural autonomy but it also contained the intellectual and political seeds of a modern theory of state as cultivated in the German and Austrian universities. It was published in 1899, only one year before Jellinek's grand synthesis in which he elaborated the three-component definition of the state.

Renner's theory was not a political one. He tried to distance himself from politics as his friend Kelsen did and as it was required by positivistic ideology. I quote Renner:

> "The jurist is as such not a politician. It is his task to clothe given political postulates in a juridical form, to strip the slogans appealing to the emotions of their mystificatory quality and to translate them into bare relations of will' and 'We believe that we have now honestly attempted to solve the task of the theoretician with reference to jurisprudence. And the theoretician cannot aim for or achieve anything more than the delineation of the constitutional legal principles according to which a solution is conceivable" (see Renner, 2005, pp. 36, 45).

Not surprisingly Renner echoes Jellinek's definition of the state, saying, the state is "a legal territorial domination" (see Renner, 2005, 27). After contrasting it with the nation, he defines national minority as a "factual personal association" which at the same time has a "rights holder legal personality" (see Renner, 2005, 27) He uses a legal analogy to compare the declaration of the membership in a nationality with declaration of paternity and imagined the organisation of this community like a Christian church.

Even if we take no notice of the scientific-technologic development in the field of the human reproduction (e.g. artificial insemination, test-tube babies) and the related bioethical and legal issues (e.g. surrogate mothers, same-sex marriage, etc.), I firmly believe that none of these analogies work. Let us suppose for an instant indeed that Renner had in his mind a "paradigmatic" family living under "ordinary" conditions to produce descendants. Even in this case we can argue that (1) the declaration of paternity is only a subsidiary possibility when establishing the status of the child: if fatherhood began in marriage (or before during certain period of time), his paternity is assumed. (2) This declaration cannot be done without the mother's consent. (3) Such a declaration is not only a source of the rights, but a set of obligations (e.g. feeding the children) and these obligations exist independently from rights. It is not the case in the rights and duties derived of the membership of a non-core, ethnic group.

It appears to me that instead of paternal recognition, the declaration of a religious affiliation is a more subservient normative analogy, which, by the way, sustains Jellinek's claim according to which religious liberty is the origin of all rights.

Therefore it would be better to establish an analogy between the declaration on the membership in a given minority group and the declaration on the membership in a religious group. Unfortunately this Protestant analogy is unserviceable in cases of those churches that have remained intact from the spirit of the Reformation (e.g. Roman Catholic Church or Russian Orthodox Church). In these – usually sizeable and "historical" religious groups, the membership should be established usually immediately after birth using religious rituals such as baptism, dipping or circumcision. These rituals cannot be interpreted as free and personal declarations of adult and independent men or women. Though if it is not this kind of personal choice, its analogical use might lead back to the "ethnicist" concept of the minority. Using this concept one would be compelled to concede that the membership is clearly factual, or in the worst case "supposed" (and not contractual like in a club). This is precisely what Renner seeks to avoid.

Renner emphasises that courts do not have the competence to decide in cases in which the nation's rights have been involved. There is a conflict between majority and minority if the latter is organised by the law territorially:

> "the territorial principle can never produce compromise and equal rights; it can only produce struggle and oppression because its essence is domination" (see Renner, 2005, 28).

If we juxtapose Renner's definition of the state and this remark, we can shed light on the fact that finally he considered the territorially organised national minority as a "ministate" and the origin of the conflictual situation is the fact that this "ministate" claims to have dominion over own territory.

Compared to Renner, Bauer's squarely political theory gives priority to economic considerations over the legal and constitutional aspect in his *opus magnum* (see Bauer, 2000). In the meantime, at one important point at the very beginning of his book, the German political scientist enters into the general argument. Carl Friedrich Savigny's "national spiritualism" (see Bauer, 2000, 23) uses the reference to the "spirit of the people" as a motor of national action. Bauer claims on the basis of Kant's transcendental philosophy that a substantialist vision of the nation that tries to make us believe that the nation thinks and acts according to its "spirit" cannot be accepted on materialistic-individualist premises. Bauer criticised Savigny on the same line with von Jhering in his Kampf ums Recht (1872), as the young Marx's anti-Hegelian papers did.

Savigny's historical school promoted the organic development of a society that seeks to sterilise the political community from fight and conflict. He assessed that the socio-legal development of the political community should be compared to the silent evolution of the language. Bauer, on the contrary, conceptualised the problem of national sovereignty and minority issue in terms of fight and conflict:

among so many critics of the territorial principle, Bauer fears that "national self-determination on the basis of the territorial principle would simply provoke renewed struggles" (see Bauer, 2000, 271).

This conflictual situation is not specifically German or Austro-Hungarian. According to Bauer, it is indeed generalised, extended to "all nations" (see Bauer, 2000, 266). This generalisation ambiguously implies what Kymlicka claimed in the current scholarly debate on nationalities. He is of the opinion that there is a problematic Western choice between promoting the theory of justice and saving security. That strategy, he argues, over-emphasises the question of security at the expense of justice if the question is Central Europe. According to him, the Western strategy is neither legal, nor does moral reason support the realisation of the theory of non-territorial cultural autonomy in this region of Europe instead of further federalisation of the states:

> "Experience to date suggests that most viable democratic settlement for such sizeable potentially secessionist national groups involves territorial self-government. I believe that this is a clear lesson from the accommodation of sub-state nationalism in the Western democracies, and I see no reason to think that the lesson does not apply to Central and Eastern Europe, or elsewhere around the world. … It is almost certain that several of the Western countries that have adopted territorial autonomy would have faced much greater threats of violence if they had not accommodated the desire for the territorial autonomy" (see Kymlicka, 2005, pp. 138–139).

Kymlicka finds fault with Renner's plan which probably unintentionally took for granted the dual (Magyars vs. Austrians) territorial division of the Austro-Hungarian Empire:

> "the main point is that the model of the national-cultural autonomy presupposes that we have already determined the territorial units. … The 'personality principle' operates within the pre-existing territorial boundaries and administrative structures" (see Kymlicka, 2005, pp. 141–142).

4. Schmitt, Smend, and Others: Between Political and Normative Theories of Territory

It is arguable that the "or" in the option of the "territory or justice" should be an exclusive one: a normative theory of the ethno-cultural justice based on deliberation instead of conflict can antedate the security issue which contingently follows it. In most cases, the risk of (armed) conflict in the EU is very low, almost zero. On the other hand, the mere fact of the appearance of violence does not let us coercively believe that opposing nationalities have already lost their sense and need of justice.

Several theories frame the nationality question in terms of geopolitics and conflicts and because of this influence the territory was slowly but surely becoming "essentialised." Carl Schmitt is probably the best-known antipluralist republican guilty of the direct or indirect "essentialisation" of the territory. But he is not the only one. When the French Constitutional Court declared that under the French Constitution of the 5th Republic "Corsican people do not exist," the judges intended to say that the territory of France is the essence of France and that its monadic unity cannot be divided by nationalities, such as the people of Corsica.[7]

At first glance, Schmitt seems to eliminate the whole question of territoriality by treating the question of the "political" before the above-mentioned three-component definition of the state. The "political" is a sovereign's pre-state decision on the enemy. There is no such approach that one would call the "general theory of the decision" or "of the enemy" or "of the state," since a decision on the enemy is always concrete and existential. According to this well-known situationalist – decisionist theory given political community either exists factually in a historically given context and in a historically shaped territory or it does not exist at all. The question of territory follows the factual-internal power of the dominant group and the amoral balance of international centres of interest-oriented power (see Schmitt, 1927).

Obviously I am not saying that one should find the most important use of the territory in the *Concept of Political*[8], but it is probably worth to mention that – although less polemically – Kymlicka used the idea of the "societal culture as a context of choice" when he assessed critically and "completed" Rawls's theory of justice. If the territory is a substantive-cultural phenomenon then it should bear an importance in a multiethnic theory of justice (see Kymlicka, 1995, Ch. 5).

What about other republican theorists? Let us take a discursive look at Rudolf Smend's theory of integration. He distinguished between three forms: personal, symbolic and functional integration. Instead of opposing nation and state, as

7 The Decision 91–290 DC OF 9 May 1991 "Act on the statute of the territorial unit of Corsica" of the French Constitutional Council rejected the use of the concept of the "Corsican people" (Art. 1.) claiming that it is not in conformity neither with the preamble to the Constitution of 1958, which postulates the "unity of the French people," nor with Article 2, which enshrines the indivisibility of the Republic, nor with Article 3, which designates the people as the sole possessor of national sovereignty; moreover, Article 53 of the Constitution refers to the "the population concerned" in a territory and not to the concept of the people.

8 See rather Schmitt, 1950, 155s.

Renner did, Smend tried to reconcile them. Among the three above mentioned factors territory is as substantive as element as in Schmitt.

Smend's peaceful "essentialisation" of the territory has at least one positive outcome. In the field of social science in which we understand that "nation," "state," and similar concepts are imaginations (see Andersen, 1991), hence, in this sense the "territory" cannot be conceived as a mere geographical *datum* either. Smend uses the term "space" (*Raum*) instead of territory, in which the personified state lives. The state as an organism can be founded by individual will or by some irrational factor such as ethnic relation, history, or religion. What is important for our purpose is the fact that the personified state lives in a determined place. Let this person-state be a *Gemeinschaft*- or *Gesellschaft*-type it has the right to live somewhere: indeed every state has the right to have a territory that is a part of the national self-determination. Smend emphasised that neither causal nor metaphysical reasons can determine alone the particularity of the state (see Smend, 1968, pp. 136–180, Section 7).

The anti-metaphysical stance upon which Bauer introduces the term of the "national character" puts him closer to Schmitt and Smend than to Kelsen's normativism. Nevertheless liberal nationalism[9] or a normative theory of ethno-cultural justice can indeed accommodate the territory without referring to any primordialist or groupist criterion. In the field of social science, the expert should try to understand that a given territory is not simply a neutral geographical unity, but a particular space in which the political community lives and should live irrespective of its ethnical composition.

Meanwhile, Hans Kelsen, on behalf of legal science, made a robust effort to deterritorialise the concept of the state. He famously argued that the law and the state are only two sides of the same coin, as opposed to the three-element definition of the state developed by Jellinek. Therefore the territory of the state is no more and no less than one form of the scope of the valid legal system:

> "The state territory is a certain delimited space. … The so-called state-territory can only be defined as the spatial sphere of validity of a national legal order" (see Kelsen, 1967, 288).

The personal and the temporal validity of the legal system are the other two forms. His pure theory indeed marginalised the question of territory: if the borderline has changed then it is nothing but a change of the territorial scope of the legal system.

---

9 As to the perspectives of the liberal nationalism in Eastern and Central Europe, see Auer, 2004.

The territorial autonomy seems to promote a better practise than federal autonomy if the minority lives homogenously, there is a kin state in the neighbourhood, and it is generally claimed that territory of the state was shaped by unjust historical circumstance. Kymlicka thinks that the homogenous geographical situation alone is a sufficient reason in itself to reject non-territorial cultural autonomy (see above Kymlicka.). Furthermore Buchanan's and Brilmayer's studies can be mobilised in order to justify that any minority can legitimately claim for the secession, *a majori ad minus*, for federal territorial autonomy.

Meanwhile the normative approach survived Kelsen. Currently scholars analyse the problem of national minorities in terms of legal pluralism. European legislation uses territorial legal techniques as the most expedient means to solve present day legal problems and to settle legal disputes. For instance, the connection factor of the "domicile" (a place where a citizen of the EU intends to settle down) is extensively used as a means of determining the law to be applied in family law cases instead of the principle of citizenship in the European Union. In a recent overview, Giovanni M. Quer analysed the de-territorialisation of minority rights in terms of legal pluralism, where one of his examples was the recognition of the decisions of the shari'a court in the UK (see Quer, 2014).

5. Final remarks

Let us make a short conclusion. In the age of globalisation the mainstream legal, political, and constitutional theory is post-national, but it does not offer different plans for different regions of the world. A constitutionally controlled legal pluralism and an interpretative theory of the territory may lead to a better understanding of minorities claims for autonomy. It may also lead to accommodating these claims.

The territory of the state is essentially not physical, but a social construction. When a community is created, this social construction takes part of this narrative as the language does in case of national identity (see Schöpflin, 2001). If there is a problem with the secessionist minority nationalism, it is not linked to the territory itself, but to the idea of the territorially based nation state. Its counterpart, possessive individualism is still a dominant ideology and it still legitimises minority groups' claims based on the understanding that the territories are exclusively "their territories." They claim to possess territory not because of the legacy of the "dark medieval times," but because of our own worldview. Hence the geographical location of the citizen can entitle him or her to have specific rights as well.[10]

Consequently the principle of territoriality will always preserve its priority over the principle of personality in general and, for the time being, there is no specific reason why the principle of territoriality should be limited geographically to Western multi-ethnic states.

References

Auer, Stefan. 2004. *Liberal Nationalism in Central Europe*, London, New York: Routledge.

Andersen, Benedict. 1991. *Reflection on the Origin and the Spread of Nationalism*. Rev. ed. London: Verso – New York [1983] 1991.

Bauer, Otto. 2000. *The Question of Nationalities and Social Democracy* [1907] ed. Ephraim J. Nimni, trans. Joseph O' Donnell. London: University of Minnesota Press.

Jellinek, Georg. 1922. *Allgemeine Staatslehre* [1900]. Berlin: Springer 3rd ed.

Kaiser, Robert K. 2002. Homeland Making and the Territorialization of National Identity, in Daniele Conversi (ed) *Ethnonationalism in the Contemporary World*, London, New York: Routledge. 229–47.

Kelsen, Hans. 1967. *Pure Theory of Law*, Berkley, Los Angeles: University of California. Transl. Max Knight.

Kelly, Duncan. 2004. Revisiting the Rights of Man: Georg Jellinek on Rights and the State, *Law and History Review*, 22:3 Fall (2004) 493–529.

Kymlicka, Will. 1995. *Multicultural Citizenship: A Liberal Theory of Minority Rights*. Oxford: OUP.

Kymlicka, Will. 2001. *Politics in the Vernacular: Nationalism, Multiculturalism and Citizenship*. Oxfor: OUP.

Kymlicka, Will 2005. Renner and the Accommodation of Sub-state Nationalisms, in ed. Ephraim Nimni *National Cultural Autonomy and its Contemporary Critics*. London: Routledge. 137–49.

Maloy, Tove H. 2009. The Lund Recommendations and Non-Territorial Arrangements: Progressive De-territorialization of Minority Politics" in *International Journal on Minority and Group Rights*, Vol. 16, No. 4. 665–79.

10 It is a telling fact that Scotland's 2014 referendum on independence was territorially organised. It excluded people who lived elsewhere in the UK who identify themselves as (ethnic) Scots.

Nimni, Ephraim. 2007. National-Cultural Autonomy as an Alternative to Minority Territorial Nationalism, 6:3 *Ethnopolitics*. 345–64

Quer, Giovanni M. 2013. De-Terrorializing Minority Rights in Europe: A Look Eastward. *Journal on Ethnopolitics and Minority Issues in Europe* 12.1: 76–98.

Renner, Karl. 2005. State and Nation [1899]. Ed. Ephraim Nimni. *National Cultural Autonomy and its Contemporary Critics*. London: Routledge. 27–32.

Schöpflin, George. 2002. Liberal Pluralism and Post-Communism. Eds. Will Kymlicka, Magda Opalski. *Can Liberal Pluralism Exported? Western Political Theory and Ethnic Relations in Eastern Europe*. Oxford: OUP. 109–25.

Rudolf, Smend. 1968. Verfassung und Verfassungsrecht [1928], in *Staatsrechtliche Abhandlungen und andere Aufsätze*, Berlin: Duncker und Humblot, 2nd ed.

Schmitt, Carl. 1950. *Der Nomos der Erde im Völkerrecht des* Jus Publicum Europaeum, Köln: Greven Verlag.

Smith, David J. 2013. Non-Territorial Autonomy and Political Community in Contemporary Central and Eastern Europe. *Journal on Ethnopolitics and Minority Issues in Europe* 12.1: 27–55.

Tas, Latif. 2014. Myth of the Ottoman Millet System: Its Treatment of Kurds and a Discussion of Territorial and Non-Territorial Autonomy. *International Journal on Minority and Group Rights* 21.4: 497–526.

Teubner, Günther. 1997. "Global Bukowina": Legal Pluralism in the World Society, in Teubner, Günther: *Global Law Without State*, Aldershot, etc.: Dartmouth. 3–28.

Michele Saporiti

The Concept of Sovereignty and the Transnational Challenge of Global Religions. A Theoretical Framework

Abstract

This paper aims at analysing the concept of sovereignty from a peculiar perspective. Instead of the typical global powers considered by scholars (economic and financial powers), it will pay specific attention to global religions. After an initial clarification of what "religions" are intended to be from this viewpoint, the paper will discuss the idea, proposed by an eminent academic, to consider global religions as "new transnational nations." Does this idea represent only a useful metaphor or a realistic perspective not to be underrated? May we make a persuasive comparison between the classic elements of a state and the contemporary structure of global religions?

1. Introduction: Sovereignty, again

As Norberto Bobbio (1999, 183) notably stated "the most important idea shared by juridical as well as political studies is power."[1] These words perfectly summarise the core concept in sovereignty studies: power. From a theoretical viewpoint, there are some preliminary questions: is this concept still useful? Or does it represent a useless, anti-democratic, and imperialistic idea? Whereas Kelsen's (1920) theoretical concerns on sovereignty are consistent, contemporary global relations are still ruled by the appeal to sovereignty. Therefore, we could argue that, as Ferrajoli (2012, 492) convincingly wrote, "the history of sovereignty is far from being over." Consequently, legal and political theoreticians need to investigate its metamorphoses.

This paper will seek to show why sovereignty does not exclusively concern states. The main reason is the emergence of new international actors in the last few decades. Some of them are intertwined with the capitalist economy: they are the financial and economic global players. There are many academic publications on their influence and strategies. The contribution of this paper to the current literature may be summed up in one main concern: the description of a parallel

1 The passages excerpted from Ferrajoli's, Ferrari's, and Graziano's works have been translated by the author of this paper.

and underrated trend. I refer to the "return" of different global actors: religions. After a long exile from the public arena, religions have increasingly become a pressing issue in global politics. Terrorism, new forms of nationalism, military campaigns: these are few examples of contemporary urgencies associated with religions. Firstly, this paper will address the power issue from the viewpoint of the international relations theory. Secondly, it will take into account different levels of political and legal institutions. It will also pretend to apply these levels to global religions. Finally, the idea of religions as "new transnational nations" will be under close scrutiny.

2. Soft Power, Strong Power: What About Religions?

I will not focus on the legal meaning of power, which is generally involved in normative elaboration and implementation. I will refer to power as "the production of intended effects" (see Russell, 1960, 25) instead. These effects will be connected with certain capacities, and these capacities will be described within the globalisation process. As overlapping of different dimensions (economic, legal and social ones) and confusion (*cum fundere*) of traditional categories (such as public-private/ local-global / economic-politic), globalisation has transformed the power phenomenology. In order to explain how this phenomenology has changed over time, I will suggest some keywords or expressions:

1) dissemination and fragmentation, Foucault's (1975) *microphysique du pouvoir*; contextually, big concentrations and self-expansion, a sort of *macrophysique du pouvoir*;
2) a progressive diversification in the way power is exercised;
3) new power holders or possessors, along with public subjects (see Ferrara, 2014, 36).

As referred to the second point mentioned above, I will focus on Nye's notorious distinction between soft and strong powers. First of all, with "soft power" he means:

> "the ability to get what you want through attraction rather than through coercion or payments. It arises from the attractiveness of a country's culture, political ideals, and foreign and domestic policies. When our policies are seen as legitimate in the eyes of others, our soft power is enhanced" (2004, 12).

Secondly, Nye uses "hard power" to refer to the capacity of using or threatening to use military, financial, or diplomatic force. At a later stage, Haynes (2012, 11) elaborated Nye's idea of soft power, which:

> "refers to the capacity of an entity, usually but not necessarily a state, to influence what people do through persuasion, not force or threats. […] Soft power convers certain attributes – including, culture, values, ideas – collectively representing different, but not necessarily lesser, form of influence compared to 'hard' power."

Therefore, soft power uses persuasion (that is, the ability to convince using argumentations) and attraction (that is, the ability to be thought-provoking). Indeed, it tries to reach common shared views on specific values in order to achieve specific goals. Strong power uses or threatens the use of force, instead: it is *contra nolentes*, beyond spontaneous acceptance.

Despite the need for an in depth analysis of these two categories, which is however an area beyond the charge of my discussion, it may be observed that Nye's distinction between strong and soft power is not of a rigid kind in power phenomenology. For example, he added a third category in his theory of international relations, termed smart power (see Nye & Armitage, 2006.). This latter is a combination between soft and strong power in order to plan a winning strategy for action.

Thus, we can argue that strong and soft powers only represent two extremities of a power *continuum*. Within this power *continuum,* I will pay close attention to specific entities, historically possessing soft powers (see Nye 2004, 98; Hynes, 2012): religions, or, on a worldwide scale, global religions. In the first place, I will keep both the above mentioned distinction and the idea of religions as barely soft power holders. I will argue against this distinction in my conclusions.

In spite of that, my current interest is to understand the political and legal impacts of this analysis on the concept of sovereignty. To this purpose, I will take into account three different levels (national, international, and supranational) of political and legal institutions. In addition to them, I will propound a fourth level of analysis: the transnational. Within these levels I will try to point out three models of sovereignty. Eventually I will try out these categories on global religions.

3. National, International and Supranational Level: Different Models of Sovereignty

First of all, let us start with the *national* level, which is grounded in the Westphalian concept of a nation state. The three main elements of this model are: a territory, a population, and an authority with legitimate and exclusive use of force. Furthermore, the 1648's peace created a first model of sovereignty: the nation state sovereignty. As external sovereignty[2], this model led to the age of nationalisms from the second half of 19th century to the first half of the 20th century: a Hobbesian *bellum omnium contra omnes* between sovereign states on a world scale (see Ferrajoli, 2004). Moreover, it must be noticed that relevant geographic differences marked the development of the nation state model. For instance, in the Mediterranean region, as Alessandro Ferrari (2014, pp. 16–17) wrote, nation state has undergone a different development on the north and south shores. On the north one, it has been gradually absorbed by broader international or supranational political entities, as the UN and the EU. Instead, on the south one it has slowly emerged, as neo-Westphalian legal system, intertwined with the religious element (see also Ferrari, 2016).

Secondly, let us turn our attention to the *international* level that deeply changed after the failure of the League of Nations and the tragic events of the Second World War. The 1945 Charter of the UN marked a political and legal revolution. International law, as Ferrajoli argued (2012, 490), passed "from a system of force-based relations between sovereign states, easily degenerating into world war, into a legal system […] based on two principles: war ban and protection of the fundamental rights of all human beings." Under the auspices of the UN a new model of sovereignty started. On the one hand, this new model denies the original idea of a *summa potestas superiorem non recognoscens.* On the other hand, it formally (maybe just formally) establishes the equality principle regarding states sovereignty, along with the aforementioned binding limitations.

Finally, let us briefly analyse the *supranational* level (e.g. the federal or confederal forms or states unions). It provides a system of progressive and specific limitations of internal or external state sovereignty. Within supranational systems, third institutions exercise delegated sovereign powers over a group of states. We could argue that the international and the supranational levels are conceptually different. Nevertheless, the former is increasingly similar to the latter nowadays. As Dan Sarooshi wrote (2005), exercise of sovereign powers by international organisations throughout conferrals of states is a contemporary trend. The more powers are delegated to international organisations (let us think of the WTO), the more states' autonomy in the decision making process is limited.

2 'External sovereignty' is the relationship between each nation state and other subjects possessing international legal personality. It states the autonomy and political independence of any state towards other international subjects, as original institution. 'Internal sovereignty' is the relationship between the state, its territory and citizens living within it. It states the absolute supremacy of state power towards any other subject, power or institution acting within the same territorial borders (see Zolo, 2000).

The current state-centred world relies on these three political and legal levels. As a matter of fact, this framework embodies the traditional articulation of possessed, delegated, and shared sovereign powers. Nevertheless, a further level marks the age of globalisation: the *transnational* level, where global powers address their influence towards states. In fact, a-territorial powers act within a single state, among a group of states and beyond the states on a planetary scale. In this scenario a fundamental switch took place. The focus is no longer on sovereign subjects (that is on the question: who *is* the sovereign?) but on sovereign powers (that is on questions concerning who *has* the sovereign powers (see Aalberts, 2012) and where these sovereign prerogatives do move). In other words, we have a complex system of concurrent sovereignties involving state actors as well as non-state or private actors in global politics.

To sum up, after *the nation state sovereignty model* (boundless and conflicting) and *the UN Charter sovereignty model* (formally egalitarian and legally bounding), a third model emerged: *the global powers sovereignty model*. This latter is based on a conception of shared sovereignty (no more exclusive holders) that coincides with the idea of governance, engaging both public and private powers. It also represents a potential clashing mechanism between sovereignty and counter-sovereignty, as I will try to instantiate in the following paragraphs.

4. From States to Religions

Can we apply this multi-level analysis to religions? In order to positively answer this question several premises are needed. First of all, I will use only three levels: national, supranational, and transnational. In the current legal-political scenario, the international level is also present in religious field. As a matter of fact, a remarkable number of different international religious organisations have emerged on a global level. Nevertheless, this level does not provide a sound framework for the religious phenomenon in my political perspective. Secondly, the analysis might significantly vary according to religions we are considering. Thirdly, these conceptual frames are not rigid or mutually excluding. In fact, some religions might have simultaneously a national and a transnational organisation, without any supranational structure. In general terms, these three levels represent a framework suitable for being applied to religions from a political viewpoint. Considering these premises, we will now address national, supranational, and transnational religions.

First of all, *national religions* are an organic part of the nation state. The Orthodox Church[3] is a paradigmatic case. As Silvio Ferrari (2007, 6) wrote "the territory on which the state exercises its own sovereignty coincides with the territory on which the church claims exclusivity in face of other religions." Moreover, as Olivier Roy (2013, 91) has pointed out, Christian orthodoxy presents "the most explicit forms of religious nationalism, [...] where the identification between Church and people relies on a close link with the state."[4]

Secondly, there are *supranational religions* as the Roman Catholic Church or the Anglican Church. In history, these religions have often created an identity opposition: on the one hand a national identity (depending on the secular power); on the other hand, one clashing religious identity[5]. In addition, in supranational religions there is a unitary centre of power control (as in the Holy See) along with a national and local power network.

Finally, *transnational religions* are marked by the absence of a unitary centre of power. Consequently, they typically use an effective group of concepts, which transcend territorial boundaries[6]. The idea of *Umma* in Islam presupposes the above mentioned logic. Indeed, the Islamic community goes far beyond states' borders and local ethnicities and affirms an identity based on common faith and shared religious rituals (see Cook, 2014). Haynes (2012, 43) argues that Islam is, "a religious, social and cultural system grew to become a global religion via the growth of a transnational religious community." Furthermore, this transnational frame is suitable for being applied even to the Jewish community, or, to some extent, to the evangelic "born again" movement or the Buddhist concept of Sangha, as spiritual community.

Clearly, these categories may overlap and do overlap. For instance, the national level of Islam, with its local organisations, is closely connected with its predominant transnationality. Instead the Catholic church has a ruling supranational level, governing and safeguarding the unity of each national entity. In the light of these

3 The Orthodox Church has a polycentric system of power: each Orthodox centre rules the surrounding national territory. This is the reason why the Orthodox Church is a national religion.

4 By "religious nationalism" Roy means "a religious institution identifies itself with a state and people" (see ibid., 90).

5 The papist accusations, which crossed our history for centuries, is a notable example of this clash.

6 The transnational level might put into question the traditional Islamic cosmogony. As a matter of fact, there we find the dichotomy between "dar al Islam" (territory of Islam) and "dar al Harb" (territory of war).

examples it is clear that religious transnationality represents a pressing issue in international relations studies. *Religious transnational actors* will increasingly have a considerable influence on global politics in the coming years. In spite of their relevant differences, the Catholic church, the Anglican church, the Shiromani Gurdwara Parbandhak Committee, the United Sikhs, the Organisation of the Islamic Conference, Tablighi Jamaat, and al-Qaeda are all significant examples of these actors (see Shani, 2009)[7].

5. Religions as "New Transnational Nations?"

By assuming that religious global powers and actors possess different peculiarities, we can generally assert that they hold sway in two main and opposite directions.

A) On the one side, religious global players are able to *help the democratic order.* Consequently, they are committed to promoting a peaceful, international, and state-centred world (e.g., the considerable influence of Roman Catholic Church and of John Paul II on the democratic transition in Central and Eastern European regimes). Within the exercise of internal sovereign powers, religious actors often play a central role in the legislative decision making process on sensitive issues in consolidated democracies (e.g., bioethical issues, education, family issues or, in general, the "politics of intimacy" issues (see Dobbelaere & Pérez-Agote, 2015)). As for the exercise of external sovereign powers, they can influence international strategies instead, by encouraging policymakers to incorporate certain values into foreign politics (e.g., the references to the Evangelical values in G.W. Bush's public speeches during the U.S. military campaigns (see Lincoln, 2006)).
B) On the other side, religious global players represent an alternative *counter-model* for the sovereignty-based international order. In fact, this counter model might be expressly against preservation of any public and democratic order. I refer to the terrorist and armed activities of transnational religious actors such

7 Undoubtedly they differ significantly and broadly. In particular, the case of Islam is notably complex. Indeed, religious powers and state organisations often overlap in the Islamic world. In such cases, pinpointing the influence of religious powers on state sovereignty might be difficult. In fact, completely different cultural backgrounds create difficulties in transposing certain political concepts. The Organisation of the Islamic Conference is paradigmatic in this sense. Its members are all state-nations. Nevertheless, even within this transnational organisation, profound differences persist in conceiving the Islamic State and constitutionalism. For a detailed analysis on transnational religious actors see Haynes, 2012.

> as al-Qaeda or Boko Haram. Conversely and without referring to violence or terror, this counter model might also reshape religions as a persuasive alter ego of the nation-state. In this perspective, religions act as the "new transnational nations" (see Ferrari, 2007, 10). In order to analyse this hypothesis, I will compare the nation state model and global religions from the political and legal theory's viewpoint.

We can point out at least three traditional elements which constitute states: 1) a territory, as a well identified space limited by boundaries; 2) a permanent population, intertwined with the idea of nation;[8] 3) a government, as legitimate authority with the exclusive use of force.[9] The legal expression of the nation state is, as Irti (2006) wrote, "geo-law." The existence of this kind of law is strictly linked with the power of country boundaries. As a matter of fact, it limits and circumscribes; it includes and excludes; it separates who is in and who is out. The ones who are in have their own identity, as part of the *civitas*. All the others are excluded from national societies.

I would like to investigate what occurs if we apply these categories to religions. It must be noticed that much depends on the global religion we are considering. In fact, this is a highly general approach, and concepts might significantly change in specific cases. Notwithstanding differences, I argue that common features can be pointed out. First of all, the notion of national territory limited by frontiers corresponds to a non–territory. This non-territory radically lacks boundaries: in this sense it is transnational. Secondly, the notion of permanent population, intertwined with the very concept of nation (in this perspective, populations become people) corresponds to the idea of a worldwide community of believers or members of given ethnical group (as is the case of Jewish). Thirdly, legitimate and exclusive authorities using force or coercion correspond to different authorities or *auctoritates*. These *auctoritates* are able to influence what people do only by persuasion[10]. Finally, the "geo-law" of the nation state corresponds to the "theo-law" of global religions. The latter crosses the frontiers, "without losing its attraction power, coming from historically and geographically entrenched identity" (see

8 For historical and conceptual overview of the concept of nation see Habermas, 1992.

9 There is a further element: the capacity to enter into relation with other states (see Article 1, Montevideo Convention). Although this element is negligible in my analysis, it deserves a general comment: these constitutive elements with their fixed traditional configuration are rather anachronistic. Consequently, each one of them should be put into question and scrutinised, in order to have a realistic political portrait (e.g., for the territory element see Sassen, 2008).

10 In this case I obviously do not consider terroristic actors or the Islamic State (see below).

Ferrari, 2007, 9). Furthermore, the nation state idea of a local territorial identity is replaced with the idea of identity as belonging, acceptance or adhesion. Consequently, this "theo-law" fulfils important functions. It gives a worldwide status and sense of belonging to believers.

From a theoretical viewpoint, the concept of "transnational nation" does not provide a fully convincing framework. Indeed, coupling the idea of nation with trans-nationality denies the very concept of a Westphalian nation. On the one hand, this latter exists within and is limited by country boundaries. On the other hand, trans-nationality is a border crossing mechanism. Conversely, when a group of states passes under the control of a unique authority or of a third institution, we have a supranational (not a transnational) form along with sovereign powers conferral. A transnational nation means a *cosmopolitan* nation: that is, any form of nation even in the post-Westphalian world.

Despite this theoretical remark, the core idea of *identity* is undoubtedly compelling in Ferrari's analysis. It should be noticed that the conceptualisation of sovereignty as identity is present in international relations theories (e.g., Alexander Wendt's version (see Wendt, 1999)). As a result, we could easily grasp the impacts of an identity approach both to sovereignty and to religions on a global scale.

In fact, overruling the idea of identity as bare territorial origins, global religions were able to build up a thick sense of belonging out of sovereign states. In this perspective, the globalisation process represents the ideal context. In addition, the epoch-making change of mass migration towards Western countries has created new and impelling claims of identity.

In general terms, as cultural anthropology often argues religion is one of the most powerful means for personal identity building, if not the "identity paradigm" (see Remotti, 1996, pp. 42–43). But there is a second political element: religions have never completely relinquished their role of *political identity makers* even in the secularised world.

On the one side, we could argue that the more globalisation forces states, the more states lose their identity peculiarities. Consequently, the less states give convincing political identity to new and old generations, the more religions emerge. In such a conundrum, global religions have shown their ability to capture a dissatisfied wish of identity inside contemporary societies. On the other side, religions are able to reinforce national identities, even outside the Muslim world. The revival of nationalist religious political movements or parties are remarkable example of this trend. For example, the triumphal electoral result of the hindu nationalist Bharatiya Janata Party in India in 2014 proves this revival best. In other words, contemporary global religions are showing their ancient and ambivalent role:

identity-catalyst for nationhood, or a credible substitute for any nationhood. It might sound contentious or rather simplistic: are religions claiming back their pre-Westphalian role?

6. A Brief but Necessary *Excursus*

My previous analysis did not take into account a relevant issue in contemporary geo-politics. I refer to the Islamic State (IS). This topic would deserve the attention of a dedicated paper[11]. Nevertheless I will try to briefly address this issue. Although the IS does not represent a necessary political outcome of Islam, some aspects in its geo-political evolution need to be taken into account. In contemporary times the IS tries to rebuild a typical institution of political Islam: the Caliphate. As a matter of fact, quoting Michael Cook, Sharīʿa conveys "the idea of a divine monopoly in the domain of law" as "core component dell'Islam" (see Cook, 2014, 270). As an expression of an all-embracing political and legal conception, already present in the early stages of Islam, the Caliphate:

> "provides an emotionally powerful antidote to the sense of geopolitical deprivation arising from the current distribution of global power; it furthers a sense of Muslim unity across the globe; and it invokes a component of the religious tradition that is associated with a glorious past" (see ibid., 326).

Hence the appeal to the Caliphate is meant to give an "antidote" to the geopolitical deprivation of global powers (mostly the economic and financial ones). In addition this appeal is strengthened by an ideological claim to the Islamic tradition. In fact the IS's allusion to the Caliphate seems to be a "brand reference" rather than a cultural, historical, or religious reference. Beyond their fundamentalist doctrinal positions, their view on the Caliphate lacks sound theological contents or historical arguments. As Graziano (2014, pp. 215–216) wrote on Islamic fundamentalism, they "would like to create a never existed Islam." In general terms, the IS and the powerful reference to the Caliphate should be considered as a highly structured and dangerous expression of the Jihadi-Salafism, or jihadism.[12]

Besides the reference to the Muslim world community and to the Koran transnational message, the use of force and coercion are typical nation state elements in the IS. Indeed the IS's strategy is ambivalent. On the one side, it uses a global and effective ideological and social media strategy. In this way, it attracts new adherents

---

11 For an updated in-depth analysis see Lister, 2015; Cockburn, 2015; Filiu, 2015; Isakhan, 2015. For an historical reconstruction of the Caliphate see Kersteen, 2015.

12 For an analysis of contemporary jihad see Kendall and Stein, 2015; Turner, 2014.

or participants to the jihad cause. On the other side, the IS began a campaign of territorial expansion, using military forces and coercion against opponents (or "the infidels"). Thus, the terrorist attacks are just a part of its offensive actions. Consequently, we can argue that it is aggressively acting as state strong powers are able to do. Within this framework, the IS also raises challenging questions for additional theoretical research developments, like for instance: which is the political and legal idea of sovereignty asserted by contemporary global religions? How could religious conceptions on sovereignty influence on the fragile equilibrium of globalisation? Shall we identify soft and hard models of counter-sovereignty in religious global powers?[13] Will states be able to react to this clash of sovereignties?

7. Some Conclusions

In this paper I have tried to give a theoretical framework of sovereignty and the transnational phenomenon of global religions. My analysis was focused on a plausible transposition of several political and legal categories to contemporary religions, that is, an attempt to apply conceptual structures to different fields. In addition, global religions, as the new transnational nations, have been scrutinised with reference to the core idea of identity. In these conclusions I wish to point out two additional remarks.

The first remark addresses an epistemological issue. I refer to the distinction between soft and strong powers. In the first part of this paper, I kept this distinction, without questioning it. As we all know, dealing with power is always problematic. Nye's theory aims to examine the phenomenology of power in international relations. His analysis focuses on the distinction between several typologies of power, with reference to their means. Based on Nye's analysis, Haynes applied the category of soft power to global religions in international policy making. As far as this transposition is concerned, it may be observed that the above mentioned power distinction (soft/strong) is suitable for being applied to religions with the following remarks.

First of all, the huge variety of contemporary religious subjects may use their ability to convince (e.g., to influence foreign policies with their values or persuade people to join an ideological struggle). Nevertheless, they may also couple this ability with force or violence (e.g., religious terrorism or the abovementioned IS). Therefore, if power is the "ability to get what you want," quoting Nye (2004, 12), then contemporary religions exercise both soft and strong powers in their action.

13 For example, all-embracing religions may possess a hard model of counter-sovereignty. In this sense, Islam best represents what Cook calls "divine jealousy."

Secondly, we cannot definitively define global religions as soft or strong powers. In other words, in order to maintain Nye's distinction an instrumental conceptualisation of power is needed (that is how religions act) rather than an ontological one (what religions are). As a matter of fact, we use "power" with two different meanings. When we say that religions are global powers, "power" refers to non-state *institutions* with a global influence. In the expression "religious soft or strong power," "power" refers to peculiar means of political influence.

Consequently, global religions are neither strong nor soft power. If this is the conclusion of this paper, it may be observed that it leaves scope for inquiry into whether a more specific classification of global powers has to be elaborated[14] for global religions. Nevertheless, these theoretical remarks might prevent misleading interpretations by showing the direction of a further and deeper analysis of this issue.

The second remark concerns the relationship between the mutation of religions due to globalisation and the nation state crisis. Olivier Roy (2013, pp. 6–7) has clearly highlighted this relationship, when he focused on two crucial aspects of religions' transformation: *deterritorialisation* and *deculturation*.

> "Deterritorialisation is not only associated with the movement of people (which only affects a small percentage of the population), but also with the circulation of ideas, cultural objects, information and modes of consumption generally in a non-territorial space. But in order to circulate, the religious object must appear universal, disconnected from a specific culture that has to be understood in order for the message to be grasped. Religion therefore circulates outside knowledge. [...] Deterritorialisation is also a consequence of the crisis of the territorialized nation-state, to which political secularism still clings."

Deterritorialisation and deculturation are two key words defining a relevant religious phenomenon. I refer to fundamentalism, defined as the "most suited to globalisation, because it accepts its own deculturation and makes it the instrument of its claim to universality" (see ibid., 5). Not surprisingly, nation states express similar claims to universality. As a matter of fact, they claim to be both the universal political archetype and the global model for democracy export strategies. This is the reason why I have often used the expression "clash of sovereignties" in this paper. But a relevant difference still exists among these actors. Global religions differ from states in terms of the strategy's effectiveness. Unlike global religions,

14 In this sense, the idea of "power of statelessness" elaborated by Grygiel (2009) is a helpful category within religions and politics. The Catholic Church might represent a perfect example of those powers "capable of achieving their objectives and maintaining their social cohesion without a state apparatus."

which have taken the opportunity offered by globalisation in order to expand beyond boundaries, states are still too concentrated on their local business. In other words, they do appeal to universality, but they use ineffective local references.

A geopolitical turmoil is taking place in recent years: the global shifts of power are increasingly compelling states to reconsider their political role and their legal monopoly. Within this historic change, religions are key actors for present and future political challenges. In fact, they gave proof of their remarkable ability and versatility in managing power. Consequently, the bare appeal to state sovereignty is no longer effective when facing non-state actors, especially religions. Beyond economics and finance, contemporary nation states should be able to reshape their identity. In this process, they can learn from global religions the best way to build up a successful and inclusive strategy. We should always consider that religions are much older than the Westphalian actors. They were probably the first actors who used the logics of globalisation in history.

Acknowledgments

I want to express my deepest appreciation to Prof. Alessandro Ferrari for his wise suggestions and precious corrections. I also want to express my gratitude to my colleagues Post Docs at the *Groupe Sociétés, Religions, Laïcités* (EPHE Sorbonne – CNRS) for the constructive remarks that emerged during our seminars in Paris. Last but not least, I would like to thank Dr. Silvia Salardi for her precious linguistic overview.

References

Aalberts, Tanja E. 2012. Constructing Sovereignty Between Politics and Law. London and New York: Routledge.

Armitage, Richard L.; Nye, Joseph S. Jr. 2006. A Smarter, More Secure America. CSIS Commission on Smart Power, Washington [http://csis.org/files/media/csis/pubs/071106_csissmartpowerreport.pdf].

Bobbio, Norberto. 1999. Teoria generale della politica, edited by Michelangelo Bovero. Torino: Einaudi.

Cockburn, Patrick. 2015. The rise of Islamic State: ISIS and the new Sunni revolution. London: Verso.

Cook, Michael. 2014. Ancient Religions, Modern Politics: The Islamic Case in Comparative Perspective. Princeton: Princeton University Press.

Dobbelaere, Karel; Pérez-Agote, Alfonso (eds). 2015. The intimate. Polity and the Catholic Church. Leuven: Leuven University Press.

Ferrajoli, Luigi. 2012. Principia iuris. 2. Teoria e della democrazia. Roma-Bari: Laterza.

Ferrara, Pasquale. 2014. Global Religions and International Relations. A Diplomatic Perspective. New York: Palgrave Macmillan.

Ferrari, Alessandro. 2014. Dove va la libertà religiosa: percorsi comuni tra le due sponde del mediterraneo. Stato, Chiese e pluralismo confessionale 5 [http://www.statoechiese.it/images/stories/2014.2/ferraria.m_dove_va.pdf].

Ferrari, Alessandro. 2016. The "Right to Religious Freedom" on the Two Mediterranean Shores: an Interconnected History. In: Religions and Constitutional Transitions in the Muslim mediterranean: the Pluralistic Moment, edited by Ferrari, Alessandro and Toronto, James. Furnham: Ashgate.

Ferrari, Silvio. 2007. Tra geo-diritti e teo-diritti. Riflessioni sulle religioni come centri transnazionali di identità. Quderni di diritto e politica ecclesiastica 1: 3–14.

Filiu, Jean-Pierre. 2015. From deep state to Islamic State: the Arab counter-revolution and its Jihadi legacy. London: Hurst & Company.

Foucault, Michel. 1975. Surveiller et punir. Naissance de la prison. Paris: Gallimard.

Graziano, Manlio. 2014. Guerra santa e santa alleanza. Roma-Bari: Laterza.

Grygiel, Jakub. 2009. The Power of Statelessness. Policy Review 154: 39–50.

Habermas, Jürgen. 1992. Staatsbürgershaft und nationale Identität. In Id., Faktizität und Geltung – Beiträge zur Diskurstheorie des Rechts und des demokratischen Rechtsstaats, Frankfurt am Main: Suhrkamp.

Haynes, Jeffrey. 2012. Religious Transnational Actors and Soft Power. Furnham: Ashgate.

Irti, Natalino. 2006. Norma e luoghi: problemi di geodiritto. Roma-Bari: Laterza.

Isakhan, Benjamin (ed.). 2015. The legacy of Iraq : from the 2003 War to the 'Islamic State.' Edinburgh: Edinburgh University Press.

Kelsen, Hans. 1920. Das Problem der Souveränität und die Theorie des Völkerrechts.Tübingen: Mohr.

Kendall, Elisabeth; Stein, Ewan. 2015. Twenty-first century Jihad: law, society and military action. London: I.B.Tauris.

Kersten, Carool. 2015. The Caliphate and Islamic statehood: formation, fragmentation and modern interpretations. Berlin: Gerlach Press.

Linconl, Bruce. 2006. Bush's God Talk. In Political Theologies. Public religions in a post-secular world, edited by de Vries, Hent and Sullivan, Lawrence E., 269–277. New York: Fordham University Press.

Lister, Charles R. 2015. The Islamic State: a brief introduction. Washington, D.C.: Brookings Institution Press.

Nye, Josef. 2004. Soft Power: The Means to Success in World Politics. Washington DC: Public Affairs.

Remotti, Francesco. 1996. Contro l'identità. Roma-Bari: Laterza.

Roy, Olivier. 2013. Holy ignorance: when religion and culture part ways. Oxford: oxford University Press.

Russell, Bertrand. 1960. Power: a New Social Analysis. London: Unwin Books.

Shani, Giorgio. 2009. Transnational Religious Actors and International Relations. In Routledge Handbook of Religion and Politics, edited by Jeffrey Haynes. London: Routledge.

Sarooshi, Dan. 2005. International Organizations and Their Exercise of Sovereign Powers. Oxford: Oxford University Press.

Sassen, Saskia. 2008. Territory, Authority, Rights: From Medieval to Global Assemblages. Princeton: Princeton University Press.

Turner, John A. 2014. Religious ideology and the roots of the global Jihad: Salafi Jihadism and international order. Basingstoke: Palgrave Macmillan.

Wendt, Alexander. 1999. A Social Theory of International politics. Cambridge: Cambridge University Press.

Zolo, Danilo. 2000. Sovranità. In Enciclopedia Italiana – VI Appendice [http://www.treccani.it/enciclopedia/sovranita_%28Enciclopedia_Italiana%29/].

Part III. Constitutional Geometry and Constitutional Identity in an Increasingly Pluralist Global Legal Setting

Anna Kalisz, Monika Zalewska

Hans Kelsen in a Multicentric (Legal) World

Abstract
Multicentrism is perceived nowadays as one of the leading paradigms describing legal reality. Multi-level legal systems and legal orders are linked to each other on both legislative and decisional dimension. Since multicentrism means "many centres" – it admits and even emphasises that there are several bodies empowered to pass legal provisions or take decisions, which makes the entire process more complex and exposed to risk of conflicts. It does reshape the classic concepts and paradigms of law and challenges the legal theory and practice. On the other hand, European legal culture has been and still is dominated by Kelsen's well-established *Pure Theory of Law* that equalises law and state (so-called "identity thesis").

The main goal of this paper is to pursue a question: are these two theories (approaches) really incompatible and whether it is possible to combine them successfully? The authors have been tempted to suggest the possible "Kelsenian replies" to the multicentric legal reality. They are linked to the dynamic structure of law and – maybe even more – to the modern concept of state.

1. Introduction

Phenomena of globalisation and global governance (as well as the "European governance") are the most widely discussed issues in social sciences. Transnational actors bear more and more power and it affects traditional concepts of state, law, and sovereignty. Such a situation results with the questions about a new role of national legal orders in a complex legal reality. One of the theories trying to cope with the problem is multicentrism.

In recent decades, it seems two opposing concepts compete with one another: Hans Kelsen's XX century vision of law described in his *Pure Theory of Law*, and more recently developed *Multicentrism* theory. This article asks, whether these two theories are actually as disparate as believed. In answering this question, the relationships amongst classic notions of "(legal) system," "legal order," "law," and "state," will be explored in brief.

First a slight, but significant difference between the notions of legal system and legal order exists. Nevertheless, these concepts are often inaccurately used as synonyms. Legal order may be described as a set of all norms, rules, principles, and standards of different origins (derived from "soft" legal sources with no binding force) that may serve as the ground for valid legal decisions. Legal system is understood in a more structured, "positivist" way and may be defined as a totality of legal norms and principles arising mainly from binding legal provisions given by the state. The crucial difference is, not the origin of the norms, but the term "binding." Legal order is larger and contains – apart from aforementioned legal norms – elements with the potential of influencing a decisional process. Considering this – Hans Kelsen's theory regards rather legal system, while legal order matches the multicentric vision of the (legal) world.

Secondly – the relation between law and state shall be examined and challenged in the light of a multicentric concept. At the present time, *Multicentrism* is perceived as one of the leading paradigms describing legal reality (see further Golecki, Wojciechowski, & Zirk-Sadowski, 2009, *passim*). Multi-level legal systems and legal orders are linked to each other on a legislative and a decisional level. *Multicentrism* emphasises that there are several bodies empowered to pass legal provisions and make legal decisions making the entire process more complex and exposing it to the risk of conflict.

The current European situation may illustrate such a case. Within the territory of a state, the law of the given state (national/domestic legal system), the EU law, and the law created in the framework of the Council of Europe apply simultaneously as a legal order. Thus, a possibility exists to have the law without the state – the stateless law (see further: Dedek, van Praagh, & Donlan, 2015, *passim*). This in turn reshapes the classic concepts and paradigms of law and challenges the legal theory and practice.

The notion of "stateless law" may be viewed as a set of pluralistic concepts of law that co-exist simultaneously (see Golecki, Wojciechowski, & Zirk-Sadowski, 2009, 9). The common ground of these co-existing laws is that they share a transitional space. Such a legal structure might result in losing the ability of unifying all legal orders by a traditionally understood state. Thus the state may no longer be a *sine qua non* condition to account for the validity of legal acts.

On the other hand, European legal culture continues to be dominated by Kelsen's well-established *Pure Theory of Law*. This theory stems from classical continental legal positivism and is based on its critique. In European legal culture, *Kelsenism* is viewed as a continuation of the classical positivistic tradition. This includes the idea of duality of law and state, and, national and international legal orders thesis. Such an approach is described by Marek Zirk-Sadowski's *Soft-Kelsenism* (see Zirk-Sadowski, 2009).

In fact, Kelsen's *Pure Theory of Law* can be perceived as an antithesis to a positivistic vision of law. Not only has Kelsen added to his theory's philosophical background and strict criteria of methodological correctness embodied in duality of *Is* and *Ought* thesis, but also recognised law as a set of legal norms. The implications of these clarifications are significant. If law is a set of legal norms then the role of a state is severely weakened. Moreover, in such case, the ability to distinguish national and international legal orders is not readily present. They are intertwined. Basic norm (*Grundnorm*) is an original component defined by Kelsen as a hypothetical assumption made by each lawyer. In the hierarchy, a basic norm resides at the top of the pyramid of norms, above the first constitution. This paper argues that these elements can be a solid basis for multicentric theories.

The authors of this paper suggest a possibility of utilising "Kelsenian answers" to the multicentric legal reality in an attempt to thoroughly examine the potential relationship between the two theories. Such answers are linked to the dynamic structure of law and to Kelsen's concept of state. In light of this, the article examines the *Multicentrism* concept in relation to Kelsen's concept. Furthermore an explanation of possible reconciliation between the two approaches will be provided. In doing so, the concepts of the state, hierarchical structure of law and relations between international and national (domestic) law will be analysed. Finally, a discussion of several issues that the *Pure Theory of Law* fails effectively to address will be presented.

2. Multicentrism vs. Kelsen

As mentioned above, law understood as a system of norms (and meta-norms, as legal principles) is traditionally associated with the state ("identity thesis"). The positivist tradition is not the only one emphasising such a notion. In the history of European legal philosophy, law is viewed as a social phenomenon within the state and the state is seen as a *sine qua non* condition to account for the validity of legal acts (see further Somek, 2006, *passim*). Nevertheless, contemporary legal systems fit into this idea with ever greater difficulty. Such traditional categories as 'state,' 'sovereignty,' or citizenship in a multicentric world lose their meaning (see Golecki, Wojciechowski, & Zirk-Sadowski, 2009, 9).

In times of globalisation, regionalisation, and European (Union) integration, (and – what follows – the global or at least European governance) the paradigm of a legal system shall no longer be described as a Kelsenian "pyramid" with the sovereign state at the top (see Zirk-Sadowski, 2009, 61). Such a situation results in a multitude of alternative concepts offered to explain the notion and the nature of the law. One of the most popular among them is the *Multicentrism* theory, particularly in its external aspect.

The first challenge of the law and the state relation seems to be the increased role of the international law (see further: Jovanović M.A., 2013, pp. 4–13). Such law has always differed from the state law, mainly through the lack of a superior sovereignty, a graduated system, and a hierarchy of norms, as well as in different ways of creating the norms. International law has been a result of negotiations rather than a command, and is not binding in the same way as a state law. As a result, positivists were sceptical in the treatment of international law as "real" law. Additionally, a belief exists that the normativism treated as traditional monist theory of law (see Golecki, Wojciechowski, & Zirk-Sadowski, 2009, 7) is not far from legal positivism. On the other hand, the nature of both – state and international law have changed and nowadays seems to be more converged. On the international level, few bodies and institutions dedicated to the creation and application of the legal norms have been established, and the state law is not a command any longer, but rather the result of social dialogue and discourse. Thus, initial differences are often not visible.

The second challenge arises from international law's continuing close relation to *statu nascendi* – supranational law, understood mainly as the EU's law. It is a network configuration of legal norms, principles, and standards arising from binding legal acts, non-binding legal acts as well as, subsidiary, but significant case law. Such legal *order* is separate from international law, but forms an integral part of the legal *systems* of the EU member states.

Both challenges are a consequence of the globalisation process and a European reply to it. Both result in modifications in the concept of sovereignty and in the liaisons between law and state.

In a generalised vision of contemporary law and relations between the concepts of *the Pure Theory* and *Multicentrism*, Kelsen's thought and qualification can be easily rejected as out-dated. However, it does not seem proper. The multiple thesis presented above, named by Zirk-Sadowski *Soft-Kelsenism* (see Zirk-Sadowski, 2009, pp. 59–61) ascribed certain concepts to Kelsen, such as: traditional meaning of a state (law within state) or duality of international and domestic legal order. In fact, Kelsen, never expressed these. Furthermore, *Soft-Kelsenism* ignores the methodological and philosophical dimensions of the *Pure Theory of Law*.

In fact *Soft-Kelsenism* is a compilation of several classical positivistic theses with most being a subject of Kelsen's explicit critique. Kelsen believed that jurisprudence not only operates on an unified subject of study, but that it is itself an unified discipline, equipped with a methodological tool-kit equally applicable to various branches and levels of law, including international. The crucial aspect was the presence of sanctions (such as restrictions, reprisals, and even so called "just war"). Kelsen was not against the international (present legal reality also European) law dealing with challenges differently in comparison to the state law.

Kelsen's actual views on state, international law, and the hierarchical structure of law will be elaborated below.

3. Kelsen and Multicentrism. Can There be Reconciliation?

Nowadays, Kelsen's well-established ideas are often improperly analysed and misunderstood. Curiously, some positivist concepts he opposed have been ascribed to him.

A notion placing *Pure Theory* opposite of *Multicentrism* is a typical case of misunderstanding. In the following paragraph it will be argued that Kelsen's theory is supportive of *Multicentrism* or at least does not create an antagonism between the two theories. In order to support such a thesis, the concept of state will be presented along with a hierarchical structure of law. Then the relation between domestic (national) and international *legal order*[1] will be analysed.

3.1 The Concept of State in *Pure Theory of Law*

As mentioned above, it is common to ascribe to Kelsen the "law within state" concept, which obviously cannot be compatible with the idea of multicentric legal order. In fact, such an approach characterised legal positivists prior to Kelsen and it is incorrectly associated with Kelsen's thought. Kelsen found this concept metaphysical and deprived of scientific character (see Kelsen, 1967, pp. 284–286). In order to comprehend Kelsen's arguments we have to examine Kelsen's understanding of state.

Kelsen distinguished two meanings of a state. The first one defines the state as a *legal order*, which is identified with the law (aforementioned "identity thesis"). The second meaning describes a state as a *legal person* (see Kelsen, 1967, pp. 286–292), and is a metaphor for the concept of the state's institutions in relation to other actors of the legislative scene. In this case, state is defined as a legal person entering into legal relations with other subjects. From the multicentric point of view, only the first meaning (state as a *legal order*) is significant.

Kelsen also differentiated law *sensu stricto* and law *sensu largo*. Law *sensu stricto* equals state providing *legal order* as centralised and organised. For Kelsen, such a definition of state is only possible in legal science. On the other hand, duality of law and state involves metaphysical assumptions, transcendence of state in relation

1 It is worth noting that it is not determined yet whether Kelsen's understanding of legal order is the same as a contemporary one. Thus when referring to Kelsen's legal order, it will be marked with the cursive.

to the law. Resulting in the concept of state as a meta-legal being, which consequently leads to ideologising the legal science (see Kelsen, 1967, pp. 284–286). For Kelsen both: a metaphysical assumptions and ideology cannot be accepted for a theory aspiring to be "scientific." Additionally, a concept of law *sensu largo* includes international law and supranational law, as well as domestic legal order.

The unity of law and state can be a theoretical support for *Multicentrism*. Law *sensu stricto* equalised with the state means not only the rejection of "law within state" doctrine, but also brings a new quality into a discourse. For Kelsen, the category of state seems to be of minor significance since the central category is the law. This conclusion creates new possibilities in defining relations between domestic and international *legal order*. When the state category is eliminated no clear boundaries of particular *legal orders* exist. Hence, Kelsen's idea of state will be examined in the context of relation between international and national law.

Another implication of such an idea of the state is bound with state *sensu largo*. If law can be understood not only in national, but also in international terms then the appropriate relation between law and the state is not "law within the state," but rather "state within law." This notion implicates that domestic legal system would be part of a bigger *legal order* and its complexity.

To summarise, Kelsen's idea focusing on the "law-and-law" rather than "state-and-law" relation, where state plays a minor role, allows this concept to be more comprehensible. Basic and simultaneously sophisticated solution provides a firm foundation for the multicentric theories. At the same time Kelsen's concept of state appears to support the "stateless law" doctrine as well.

3.2 Hierarchical Structure of Law

Although the Kelsenian concept of state provides an explanation of the relations between law and state it cannot explain how the domestic, the international, and the EU's legal systems work together. In order to comprehend it an introduction of hierarchical structure of law is necessary.

Kelsen's first steps towards a *Pure Theory of Law* were taken in Vienna, where he had created with Merkl and Verdross "wiener rechtstheoretishe Schule." During this period of time he enjoyed a unique opportunity to develop his theory and one of the most important results was the concept of the hierarchical structure of law (Stufenbau) with its dynamic aspect. Adolf Merkl differentiated between dynamic and static normative systems. Static systems, distinctive for morality (also for the variant linked to religion), are based on the substantive content of norms. The content of the norm highest in the hierarchy (superior) allows deriving a content of the lower (inferior) norm. For example, the norm: "you shall love your neighbour as you love yourself" allows deriving lower norms – "you shall not steal" or "you shall not kill."

By contrast, dynamic systems, such as law, put a special emphasis on formal connections between the norms, where the key role is played by the competence.

The schema of the dynamic structure is as follows: The institution A issues the competence to the institution B to create the norm with a specific content. This norm can also contain a competence for the institution C to issue another norm and such a process may continue (see Kelsen, 1967, pp. 195–198). Hence in Kelsen's vision of law the norms are bound in chains where the highest and the first one is a basic norm and the last one – an individual decision.

This concept explains how international or supranational law can be incorporated into a domestic legal system and becomes legally binding in Kelsenian's terms. Basically, at some point the competence for the EU or other international institution is delegated, hence, such institution holds certain influence on the national *legal order*.

The concept of a hierarchical structure of law is particularly visible in the area of "divided sovereignty" (see more Pavel, 2014, *passim*) – the competences of the EU shared with member states. According to "divided sovereignty" theory the state through its own institutions (bodies) can delegate specific competence to another institution or organisation.[2] In such case the external authority would be empowered to make provisions and decisions in a binding way unless the state decides to withdraw this empowerment. It provides the basis for European governance. When an interaction between the state and the external authority occurs, law contains a broader meaning than state and "the roots" of European or international law are placed within the state(s), national law, national legal systems and orders. Even if particular state acknowledges supremacy of some European Union bodies and institutions (see more Schütze, 2012, 350), it is accomplished according to its own will to join and remain in the EU's structures. Thus divided sovereignty enables distinguishing diffusion of supranational and national law.

The dynamic nature of law based on the delegation of the competence can explain to some extent the process of the decision making in a multicentric legal world. Unfortunately the hierarchical structure of law contains one more assumption treating the law as a pyramid of norms. In a pyramid-of-norms theory, the

2 E.g. art. 90.1 of the Polish Constitution which states, that: "*The Republic of Poland may, by virtue of international agreements, delegate to an international organisation or international institution the competence of organs of State authority in relation to certain matters.*"

relation between superior and inferior is a basic issue. However nowadays in a multicentric legal reality such schema might not always work.

Zirk-Sadowski has argued that in the case of a soft law (typical occurrence for the EU law and – even more – for the Council of Europe law) the idea that law has a purely hierarchical structure is inadequate. The example is norms that set specific goals to be pursued by the EU as well as the member states. The hierarchy in this case is questionable because the main role in such situations is played jointly by legal interpretation and the strong position of the Court of Justice of the European Union (CJEU) (see Zirk-Sadowski, 2009, 63).

In this part, Kelsen's theory was not flexible enough. Nevertheless, Kelsen's claim on such matters is not fundamental to his work. Therefore this element of *Pure Theory of Law* can be regarded as out-dated without any harm to the body of work.

On the other hand, the multicentric reality does not mitigate the fact that legal systems are usually hierarchically structured. Even if the multicentric European legal order leans toward the network configuration its subsystems (national legal systems) retain their hierarchical structures.

Moreover the metaphor of a pyramid presents a dilemma concerning two elements- institutions (or bodies) and legal norms. While Kelsen's view of a legal norm of a lower level being a result of a higher norm was quite right (even considering a multicentric reality), it would not make sense to picture a legal system in terms of a strict hierarchy of institutions and/or bodies. More so, such an idea would not make any sense in domestic and traditionally understood *legal order*.

The point where Kelsen's dynamic structure of law might not fit appears to be the issue of binding legal interpretation. However this can also be explained. The legal interpretation of the court is a result of one chain of norms that in the future chains become a binding norm itself. It is worth mentioning that Kelsen also used the metaphor of a chain with respect to the dynamic structure of law (see Kelsen, 1967, 25).

Although the concept of a pyramid seems to contradict the complexity of multicentric structures a reconciliation of both ideas is possible with an appropriate interpretation of Kelsen's dynamic structure.

3.3 Relations Between Domestic and International Legal System

As it has been demonstrated already Kelsen's view on the relationship between state and law supports a multicentric paradigm rather than creates antagonism. However the key relation between international (including European) and national (domestic) law demands further elaboration.

The traditional positivist concepts recognised international law as a distinct *legal order* separated and independent from the national law. Hence these two *legal orders* need to be both valid at the same time or one of them must be invalid. As a result international law could not be regarded as law but rather as an international morality. Since traditional positivist theories hold that both *legal orders* are valid such theories are untenable (see Kelsen, 1967, 330).

Instead Kelsen proposes another solution – the unity of national and international *legal orders*. In order to argue this thesis Kelsen demonstrates that international law may fit the definition of law in its traditional meaning. According to him international law can be understood as *legal order* if two conditions are fulfilled. First, international law should concern human behaviour – and it does indirectly (see Kelsen, 1967, 320). Second, it should react to a violation of legal norms with sanction and coercion. Kelsen argues that special sanctions of international law are reprisals, restrictions of various kinds and, as a last resort, war. The difference between national sanctions and international sanctions is that the latter are aimed (at least directly) against a state rather than individuals (see Kelsen, 1967, 320).

Kelsen also points out that no actual conflicts between national and international legal norms exist. For Kelsen international and national law orders are unified which in the future could even lead to one *legal order* and world state (see Kelsen, 1967, 329). Hence norms of international and national law are perceived as a whole.

Kelsen explained such vision of law by identifying that the denial of the unity of *legal orders* exists only if two systems of norms have unsolvable conflicts. This idea was common for traditional legal positivists and was used as an argument against unity of international and national law. An example of the most popular case of such conflict occurs between a domestic act and an international agreement. On the contrary Kelsen holds that there is no such conflict. The domestic act can be valid and at the same time can be in conflict with an international agreement. Validity of this international agreement arises from the right to impose the sanction by other member states or an international court (see Kelsen, 1967, 331).

Kelsen finds international *legal order* to be analogous to a national one. The difference between them is the subject. In national *legal order* the role of subjects is played by individuals. In international *legal order*, the subject, a state has a collective nature.

In the relation between two unified *legal orders* of such a kind (national and international), the one is superior to the other. Thus there are two concepts to consider. (1) The basic norm of the superior *legal order* is also a basic norm for the inferior one. (2) Alternatively unity can be guaranteed by the third superior *legal order.* The inferior *legal orders* (domestic legal systems of the states) are unified in a manner where territory and time constrain their validity. In such case the superior *legal order*, which is international law, sets rules for the inferior ones. Additionally, it also provides ways for the rules to be created as well as determines their boundaries and limits. In other words – coordinates them.

Kelsen perceives national *legal orders* as delegated from international one. At the top of such a legal system, the basic norm belongs to the international *legal order*. International order is not acknowledged as valid by a state but rather is transformed into national legal system (see Kelsen, 1967, pp. 332–337).

Thereby the first concept views one *legal order* as being incorporated into another. In such case the supreme *legal order* is the domestic (national) one. As a consequence, the international *legal order* is delegated by national norms and at the top of the hierarchy of norms lays a national basic norm. Such a construction seems to be a reminder of a traditional, dualist understanding of the relationship between international and national law and is strictly bound within the concept of sovereignty (see Triepel, 1899, pp. 21, 121–122 and, with regard to Kelsen, & Brunkhorst , 2014, pp. 329, 353–354).

The question of the origin of the basic norm might be answered with a help of monistic and dualistic concepts forming a traditional theory of international law. According to the first one the obligations that stem from a ratified treaty are incorporated directly into domestic legal order and become automatically binding. The latter concept demands a previous incorporation of rights and obligations deriving from international treaties into national legal order.

The way the treaty becomes effective in national legal order might be a good clue which basic norm – international or national one – stands at the top of an entire system. However there are terminological differences in the traditional theory of international law and Kelsen's thought. According to Kelsen a system with a national basic norm on the top is not impossible. It means that his monistic theory accepts potential situations when the international treaty must be incorporated into the national legal system by virtue of domestic acts. Such a mechanism is typical for the traditional dualistic theory and it is worth to point out that Kelsen rejected the duality of national and international law. Hence one can raise the question if Kelsen is right accepting national basic norm in a monistic legal system. Kelsen explains it by the rule of delegation characteristic of dynamic system of law. Either international law is delegated by national *legal order,* or *vice versa*. In the context of *Stufenbau* theory both options are possible (see Kelsen, 1967, 333).

Such a concept seems to resemble the EU's legal order. Nevertheless in issues such as: coordination, partial influence on national legal order (in the area of norm creation), and delegating competences for national legal orders based on the rule of divided sovereignty – significant differences still persist. For example, the member states acquire EU membership by their own volition (contrary to the international community, where all belong "automatically" to and where the sanctions can be imposed on a state, even though – or sometimes because – it does not recognise the validity of certain international rules).

In the case of the EU, if a state decides to withdraw from the structure no sanctions could be imposed by other states. Sanctions (of certain kind) can be imposed only if the state remains in the EU. This in turn might contradict Kelsen's view that international law is valid regardless of the recognition of its effectiveness and binding force by the particular state (see Kelsen, 1967, 333). However it should not be a controversial issue in the EU's case where membership is voluntary. Furthermore the analogy provided by Kelsen and described above can be also used here. If states have an analogical position to individuals the situation would be equivalent to emigrating to another country. In consequence – metaphorically – the law binding for such person is the law of their new "homeland" especially if they renounced previous citizenship.

To conclude, Kelsen's vision does not conform totally to the structures of the EU that are neither based on the model of national legal order nor on the international one. However this idea can be valued not as an exclusive alternative but as a different model matching only to some degree (including two extreme versions presented by Kelsen). Thus his distinction would be quite correct. Hence the EU's legal order with its divided sovereignty is a hybrid of both models.

However such a solution creates a new problem related to the issue of the basic norm. If the EU escapes the dualist division with regard to supremacy of national or international order then what basic norm holds validity for a unified system? Is the basic norm of a national, international, or another nature?

Three possible answers can be considered: national norms, international norms, or both. The integrating and unifying purpose of the EU contradicts consideration of "purely" national norms. Such a possibility would deny the EU's coordinating function. A specific European basic norm at the top of the whole system would lead back to the concept of supremacy of international law. But the EU law separates itself from the order of international law. Thus a possibility remains that a basic norm combines international and domestic meta-norms. While the EU's basic norm would concern all the regulations regarding competences of the EU, the national basic norm would provide for a law making process independent from the EU's supremacy.

In addition, independent of Kelsen's thought, the contemporary jurisprudence puts the emphasis on the mixed (hybrid) nature of the European legal order. Hence in terms of the law making process the basic norm for the EU has a mixed origin due to the establishment of the mechanism by the EC (former European Community). As in any other international organisation the grounds came from international law but incorporating European law into domestic legal orders was conducted due to national law.

Moreover the European values (see Moorhead, 2014, pp. 66–107) are derived from both the general principles of law recognised by civilised nations and the constitutional traditions common to the EU's member states.[3] Such considerations seem to outreach Kelsen's concept of law. Kelsen did not deny some content to the particular basic norm (for example: Kelsen, 1967, 198).

Nowadays it seems that Kelsen was unrealistic and possibly wrong about universal *legal order* and world state (see Kelsen, 1967, 328), since the multicentric legal systems are less broad in scope, but more complex. His work is a great reference point for any discussion about the place of national states in a multicentric legal order and may serve as an efficient tool to explain the complexity of a multicentric legal reality. His concepts and models allow for creating further classifications providing additional answers for complicated issues such as the relation between law and state. Thus Kelsen's ideas are able to face contemporary challenges.

Therefore no contradiction is present between Kelsen's thought and *Multicentrism*. What is more, Multicentrism may be gradable (present in different legal systems to different extent) and it does not exclude the hierarchy of legal norms. Hierarchical and multicentric relations coexist within legal systems in a mutually complementary or conflicting manner.

Hans Kelsen himself did not reject the possibility of various *legal orders* coexisting simultaneously. One can anticipate his possible answers to the main issue: the coexistence of various systems of law may be regarded as an analogy to the phenomena of decentralisation (internal aspect of *Multicentrism*).

Thus it seems that also no contradiction between stateless law doctrine and Kelsen's doctrine of a state transpires. Moreover his idea of international law has potential for being coherent with the EU's legal concept.

3 E.g. art. 6.3. The Treaty of European Union (*"Fundamental rights, as guaranteed by the European Convention for the Protection of Human Rights and Fundamental Freedoms and as they result from the constitutional traditions common to the Member States, shall constitute general principles of the Union's law"*) linking the international, supranational, and national legal levels.

4. Complexity of Multicentric Legal World – Concluding Remarks

To sum up, this article demonstrates that Kelsen's concept is not only agreeable to the concept of *Multicentrism*, but potentially can provide theoretical support for such an idea. Three notions reinforce this belief: "state within law" construction, properly constructed dynamic structure of law, and unity of international and national legal order. Thereby that corresponds with further issues linked with globalisation and a European reply to it, such as the difficult and sometimes controversial or even questionable integration process. Unarguably within Europe there are needs to negotiate responses to problems that affect more than one state but European integration causes more detailed legal questions on results, matter, and quality of European governance. It also makes inquiries on the modification of the concept of sovereignty and liaisons between law and state.

Returning to the question stated in the introduction whether Kelsen's theory concerns legal system or legal order, it can be argued that although at first glance Kelsen's *Pure Theory of Law* refers only to legal systems, if properly interpreted it applies to some extent to legal order as well. However some elements of the legal order related to the factual sphere (e.g. decision making process) needs to be excluded due to the scientific and formal character of the theory. It does not seem that Kelsen is against the concept of legal order. To some extent he supports and provides elements that are in conformity to the idea of Multicentrism. Some restrictions imposed by Kelsen, such as formal character or duality of *Is* and *Ought*, the same as in the case of Multicentrism, cannot explain all aspects of legal order. However, Kelsen's theory can provide a framework for the main ideas of Multicentrism. Thereby he bases the concept of legal order on the unity of law and state and of national and international law mentioned above. Nevertheless when Kelsen mentions legal order, he implies something different than the contemporary understanding of the expression.

To address the possible reconciliation between *Pure Theory of Law* and *Multicentrism*, obvious objections to the former can be balanced by appropriate interpretation of Hans Kelsen's theory. However his concepts are unable to explain the entire complexity of the multicentric world. Neither can it be explained by *Pure Theory of Law* alone. Hans Kelsen's *Pure Theory of Law* does not contradict the multicentric concept (or vice-versa). However it cannot provide sufficient explanation for complex processes as exemplified by the EU.

The purpose of the *Pure Theory* was to establish valid conditions for legal science and to build a theory of law as general as possible. In the context of European governance in which issues such as legal standard-setting by non-state actors and the increasing importance of the judicial practice and of its effects on the separation of powers arise a new theory which operates on another factual level must be built. Such a theory needs to be less general and related to the content of law and cannot exclude facts from its scope.

References

Brunkhorst, Hauke. 2014. Critical Theory of Legal Revolutions: Evolutionary Perspectives. London: Bloomsbury.

Dedek, Helge; Van Praagh, Shauna (eds). 2015. Stateless Law. Evolving Boundaries of a Discipline, Ashgate Publishing Group.

Jovanović, Miodrag. 2013. Revisiting the Concept of International Law – On Methodological Aspects (Paper presented at the international conference *Methodology of Legal Theory*. Zagreb, on file with the Author).

Kelsen, Hans. 1967. The Pure Theory of Law. The Lawbook Exchange, Ltd. New Jersey.

Kelsen, Hans. 2014. Pure Theory of Law, translated from the Second (Enlarged and Revised) German Edition by M. Knight, Lawbook Exchange Ltd., Clark New Jersey.

Moorhead Timothy. 2014. The Legal Order of the European Union: The Institutional Role of the Court of Justice, New York.

Pavel Carmen. 2014. Divided Sovereignty. International Institutions and the Limits of State Authority. Oxford: Oxford University Press.

Schütze, Robert. 2012. European Constitutional Law. Cambridge: Cambridge University Press.

Somek, Alexander. 2006. Stateless Law: Kelsen's Conception and its Limits. Oxford Journal of Legal Studies.

Triepel, Heinrich. 1899. Völkerrecht und Landesrecht. Leipzig.

Vinx, Lars. 2007. Hans Kelsen's Pure Theory of Law: Legality and Legitimacy. Oxford: Oxford University Press.

Zirk-Sadowski, Marek. 2009. Soft-kelsenism Versus Multicentrism. Some Remarks on Theoretical Foundations on European Law. eds: Golecki, Mariusz;. Wojciechowski, Bartosz; Zirk-Sadowski, Marek. Multicentrism as an Emerging Paradigm in Legal Theory. Frankfurt/Main: Peter Lang.

Zirk-Sadowski Marek; Golecki, Mariusz; Wojciechowski, Bartosz (eds). 2009. Multicentrism as an Emerging Paradigm in Legal Theory. Frankfurt/Main: Peter Lang.

Aleksander Tsekov

The Constitutional Identity of the EU Member States as a Legal Limit to the Constitutionalisation of the European Integration

Abstract

The notion of constitutional identity is *en vogue*, although the meaning seems vague and indeterminate. Constitutional identity is currently somewhat of a buzzword in constitutional studies and in recent years much scholarship has emerged on the issue. However the idea of the protection of national constitutional identity is not new. It is complicated to define it – emphasising the conceptual vagueness that characterises it. The notion and the concept of constitutional identity has mostly been approached from a realistic i.e. judicial perspective because the notion is increasingly making appearances in case law.

This paper aims to investigate constitutional identity from a new perspective, which does not focus only on the contribution of judicial actors to the definition of the concept. In order to deal with this issue I will approach the constitutional text as the source out of which it might be possible to determine a state's constitutional identity as a legal limit to the ideal of legal constitutionalisation of the European Union.

1. Introduction

The notion of constitutional identity is *en vogue*, although the meaning seems vague and indeterminate. As it has been pointed by Michel Troper "one of the main virtues of the notion is its vagueness that would allow the courts to fill it with whatever content might be needed" (see Troper, 2010, 196). Constitutional identity is currently somewhat of a buzzword in constitutional studies and in recent years much scholarship has emerged on the issue.

However the idea of the protection of national constitutional identity is not new. During the long process of European integration the member states were expected to transfer various competences but at the same time they enshrined the respect for their national constitutional identities in the founding Treaties. The national identity clause made its entry in the founding treaties in 1992 with article F (1) of the Treaty of Maastricht according to which "the Union shall respect the national identities of its member states, whose system of government are founded on the principles of democracy." The Lisbon Treaty is the first EU Treaty (apart from the Treaty on the Constitution of Europe that has never come into force) that codifies the national *constitutional* identity in art. 4 (2):

> The Union shall respect the equality of Member States before the Treaties as well as their national identities, inherent in their fundamental structures, political and constitutional, inclusive of regional and local self-government. It shall respect their essential state functions, including ensuring the territorial integrity of the state, maintaining law and order and safeguarding national security. In particular, national security remains the sole responsibility of each Member State.

The concept of constitutional identity is fashionable. It is however complicated to define it – emphasising the conceptual vagueness that characterises it. The concept has been approached most frequently from a realistic i.e. judicial perspective because the notion is increasingly making appearances in case law. This approach can be explained by the fact that the notion of *identity* is not mentioned in the constitution of any member state, but can be found in the case law of the CJEU and a number of member states' constitutional courts.

This paper aims at investigating constitutional identity from a new perspective that does not focus on the contribution only of judicial actors to the definition of the concept. In order to deal with this issue I will approach the constitutional text as the source out of which it might be possible to identify the state's constitutional identity (Section 2). Although the term *constitutional identity* cannot be found in the Constitution, the concept exists as a legal limit to the ideal of constitutionalisation of the EU (Section 3). The debate about the definition and the functions of the concept of constitutional identity within the EU's legal order leads us to various questions.

First of all we ought to survey what identity is at stake. Are we discussing the identity of a constitution that we can find in the constitution or rather the constitutional identity could be found only behind or above the constitution? Discussing the issue of constitutional identity presupposes clarity about the object. In the expression *constitutional identity* we face two different but interrelated concepts: *constitution* and *identity*. So, what exactly may be defined as "constitution" and "identity" in a legal system is an ontological problem.[1] In order to reduce the

1 In order to deal with these issues I will adopt positivist normativism as a methodology i.e. a theory aimed at explaining legal orders as self-referential with the following specificity : First, legal orders are set by human beings and are organised dynamically i.e. the step form a more general provision to a more concrete one requires a particular normative act; Second, the legal norms are identified as belonging to a certain legal order through another set of legal rules, that are already valid i.e. belong to the system; Third, legal orders are relatively efficient.

complexity and uncertainty, I shall begin with a clarification on the meaning of the concepts of constitution and identity, before moving to the identification of the meaning and elements of the constitutional identity I want to suggest.

1.1 The Concept of Constitution

Very often constitutions are identified according to subjective or purely empirical criteria and standards. Many scholars define the constitution as the most important and highest norm or the rule that regulates the exercise of public power, organises the form of government and the protection of fundamental rights or the constitution is defined as a "frame" and a "mirror" to the society (see Grimm, 2010; Henkin, 1994; Mathieu, 2014). The legal problem with these intuitively credible functional definitions is that they refer to non-legal concepts.

The *legal importance* of the constitution could be identified with the fact that the constitution in the material sense is a collection of rules that organises the creation and modification of rules. In its formal meaning the constitution could be defined as a set of norms enacted according to a more complicated and exigent procedure than "ordinary" legislation (see Favoreu et al., 2005). Formal constitutional law could be created either by the revolutionary i.e. the non-legal or extra-legal exercise of the constituent power or by the instituted in the constitution set of determined procedural acts for its own amendment (see ibid). Only the latter has a legal nature.

1.2 The Concepts of Identity

What is *identity*? It is a question that occupies an important place in philosophy, sociology, psychology, anthropology, history, and even in literature. Entire libraries could be filled with books and articles on the definition, scope, and meaning of identity. *Identity* is a widespread term. In recent years the term has found its place also in the legal discourse. Although it is an unclear concept, it plays a central role in the on going debates on the European integration. The *term* identity refers to two different but interrelated *concepts* of identity (see Ricoeur, 1992).

First, the term identity refers to the concept of *ipse* or self, selfhood. "Identity in the sense of *ipse* implies no assertion concerning some unchanging core of the personality" (see ibid., 2). The characteristic of self-identity is such that it continues even if the subject in question has totally changed i.e. as much as I have changed over the years, today I am the same as I was when I was a child. Even though none of the characteristics that defined me when I was a child was maintained neither the size nor the shape of the body, or hair colour, or face shape, etc.[2]

Second, identity derives from the *idem*, meaning in Latin sameness, continuity, similarity. As should be obvious, sameness has to be asserted in opposition to difference or otherness, its *idem* is the unchanging core of the personality. The *idem* identity implies that there are some fundamental features of *identity*, i.e. "identity in the sense of *idem* unfolds an entire hierarchy of significations [...] In this hierarchy, permanence in time constitutes the highest order, to which will be opposed that which differs, in the sense of changing or variable" (see Ricouer, 1992, 2). The *idem* identity is then defined by the maintenance and preservation of an essential element that remains the same over time and allows us to recognise something as the same.

My thesis is that most of the legal difficulties which obscure the question of constitutional identity result from not distinguishing between these two usages of the notion of identity. The result of this research is the identification of certain methods that can contribute to discover the constituting elements of the constitutional identity. The definition of what encompasses constitutional identity under member state's constitutions and the founding treaties is crucial in terms of primacy and the resulting application of EU law.

The fact that the concept of constitutional identity has suddenly began to be *très à la mode* tends to make us a little bit suspicious. We ought to ask if we are really confronted with an absolutely new concept or should the member state's constitutional identity discourse rather be *nihil novi*.

It seems to be certain that the respect for the constitutional identity of the member states is part of the European integration since its very origin (see Saiz Arnaiz, 2011; Burgorgue-Larsen, 2014; Guastaferro, 2012). Nevertheless if not

2 This idea of *ipse* identity might be seen as overlapping with Locke's conception of personal identity (the self) that is founded on consciousness, and not on the substance of either the soul or the body i.e. it "*depends on consciousness, not on substance.*" According to his argument we are the same person to the extent that we are conscious of the past and future thoughts and actions in the same way as we are conscious of present thoughts and actions. If consciousness is this "*thought*" which "*goes along with the substance ... which makes the same person,*" then personal identity is only founded on the repeated act of consciousness: "*This may show us wherein personal identity consists: not in the identity of substance, but... in the identity of consciousness.*" Neither is self-identity founded on the body substance, argues Locke, as the body may change while the person remains the same (Locke, 1689, Book II Chapter XXVII).

the concept at least the growing use of identity discourse in legal scholarship and jurisprudential practice seems to be a rather recent phenomenon.

Many scholars explain the emergence of the use of the concept of identity in the debate on the relationship between the European and national legal orders by the decline of the discourse on sovereignty (see Weiler, 2002; Toniatti, 2013; Walker, 2006) because of the existence of the so-called "constitutional pluralism" within the EU. According to Neil Walker, we encounter ourselves in a "late sovereign moment" that still presents some continuity with the traditional sovereignty narrative. However it has lost its grip under the on going changes due to globalisation and multi-dimensionality.

Constitutional pluralism accepts that "states are no longer the sole *locus* of constitutional authority and [...] are now joined by other sites or putative sites of constitutional authority" (see Walker, 2006, 4). Neil Walker recognises that: "we cannot [...] ignore the objective reality of globalisation and multi-dimensionality which has caused many at the meta-level to forsake the claims of sovereignty" (see ibid., 18). In the frame of this late "sovereignty moment" the EU, which found its origins as a creature of state-based international law, did not restrain itself to be a derivative, sovereign-based polity construction, but rather made a claim for an "ultimate authority and [...] does so through a complex of institutions which, however and wherever derived, comes to claim to be representative of the polity in question" (see ibid., 21). Walker considers that the replacement of the state-derived authority with the original authority could be seen in the early CJEU jurisprudence, Van Gen den Loos[3] (the EC as autonomous polity) and Costa v. ENEL[4] as well Internationale Handelsgesellschaft[5] (EC law as the supreme law of the land) (see ibid.).

2. Identification of the Constitutional Identity of the Member States

How are the *ipse* and *idem* parts of the concept of identity are transposed in the legal realm and more specifically within the legal analysis of the European integration? In other words, which are the elements constituting the constitutional

3 Case 26/62, *NV Algemene Transporten Expeditie Onderneming van Gend en Loos v Nederlandse Administratis der Belastingen*(1963).

4 Case 6/64, Flaminio Costa v. ENEL (1964).

5 Case 11/70, *Internationale Handelsgesellschaft mbH v Einfuhr- und Vorratsstelle für Getreide und Futtermittel* (1970).

identity (2.2.) and where are they found: only in the constitution or above the constitution (2.1.).

2.1 The Identity in the Constitution: Rejection of the Supra-Constitutional Nature of the Constitutional Identity

The idea that the constitutional identity should be found above the constitution is widespread and it may cover several overlapping hypotheses.

First, it may concern some elements of the ideological and factual context in which constitutions are adopted. Some scholars claim that the constitutional identity could and should be identified in certain elements of the historical context. These political decisions serve as a basis for the adoption of the constitution and override and predetermine the content of the formally written text. Some authors admit that the constitutional identity should be found in the changing political, economic, and social context around which the constitutions evolve. Examples of this approach are shown by Gary Jeffrey Jacobson who admits that:

> a constitution acquires an identity through experience, that this identity exists neither as a discrete object of invention nor as a heavily encrusted essence embedded in a society's culture, requiring only to be discovered. Rather, identity emerges *dialogically* and represents a mix of political aspirations and commitments that are expressive of a nation's past, as well as the determination of those within the society who seek in some ways to transcend that past (see Jacobson, 2010, 7).

Nevertheless this *prima facie* credible stance faces several problems. This argument rejects the impossibility of deriving normative propositions and conclusions exclusively from a non-normative premise, i.e. that the historical facts do not produce legal norms (Hume's law) except to the extent that norms so ordain. Without pre-existing normative procedures of norm production, no norm can appear which would belong to the legal system (see Pfersmann, 2012, pp. 489–496).[6]

Second, the constitutional identity may concern as well some normative standards related to the constitution without being formalised and contained in it, but which determine the constitution "core" content or some of its application. One may think of the existence of some "supra-constitutional" principles, i.e. the superiority of certain rules to the content of the constitution (see Dubout, 2010).

6 The "revolutionary" adoption of a new constitution i.e. the "revision" of the actual constitution not following the set of determined procedural acts for its own amendment might be seen as an exception.

The argument about the supra-constitutional character of the constitutional identity is highly attractive but it faces one (among others[7]) very important difficulty. If the constitution is the "constitution," i.e. the legal act that determines norm-production at first and highest level, then there can be nothing else having the same normative function in the legal order. Otherwise "this other thing" would be the constitution and there can be nothing above with a superior normative force. Most of the present-day valid constitutions either distinguish between different revision procedures (every provision can be modified, but not in the same way) or exclude some provisions form any revision, i.e. some elements may be amended, but not others. It would be incorrect to consider these provisions as supra-constitutional, they constitute simply the formal constitutional *idem* identity as the highest level within the constitution, not above it.

2.2 The Elements of the Identity in the Constitution

Identifying the constituting elements of the constitutional identity to some extent overlaps with the distinction elaborated by Carl Schmitt between the constitution and the constitutional laws (see Grewe, 2013; Mayer, 2011). The constitution is the polity's fundamental political decisions i.e. constitutional identity, which cannot be amended, and constitutional laws regulate inferior issues (see Schmitt, 2008). Thereby Schmitt considers that an amendment cannot annihilate or eliminate the constitution.

The problem of constitutional identity within the European integration constitutes, in my opinion, the privileged place of confrontation between the two major uses of the concept of identity, which I have evoked above. Placed in their legal setting conceptions of constitutional identity range from a focus on the structural *ipse* identity of the constitution to the formal *idem* identity.

2.2.1 The Structural Ipse *Constitutional Identity*

Identity in the sense of *ipse* implies no assertion concerning some unchanging core of the personality (see Ricoeur, 1992, 2). The characteristic of self-identity is such that it continues even if the subject i.e. the state in question has totally changed. Every state structure of a legal system implies certain elements that, if they disappear, this structure disappears as well. These elements constitute the constitutional *ipse* identity.

7 I will not repeat the old arguments about the existence of natural law and its relationship to positive law

A legal order is structurally defined by the way it distributes competences at the constitutional level (see Favoreu et al., 2005, pp. 35–40). The state legal order is conceptually linked to the constitution which is identified by its supremacy that generates the autonomy of the state legal order, that is to say, the impossibility to deduce its validity form another positive legal norm (see Troper, 2002). In its purely legal sense, a constitution is identified as being, for any legal order, the set of rules determining the legal validity of other rules without being themselves determined by other rules of the order (because as it has been stressed about the problem of the supra-constitutionality, those other norms would be the constitution).

This autonomy corresponds to the sovereignty of the state legal order i.e. the sovereignty is expressed only at the constitutional level. Thus, the determining element of the formal constitution will be the organ(s) empowered to modify it, i.e. the organ that holds the constitutional competence to distribute competences.

Therefore, to be defined from a purely normative point of view, sovereignty must be perceived in terms of production and validity of legal norms. A legal system is sovereign if it is not subject to any other legal standard. Sovereignty corresponds to the first and most important of the all normative powers which is also called "competence-competence" and derives directly from the supreme nature of the constitution (see Vahlas, 2005). Consequently from a legal point of view sovereignty is indivisible and it is governed by the constitution in general and the procedural settings that regulate the methods for constitutional revision in particular. Moreover, it is indivisible: it is a specific and unique competence, not a set of competences that should belong, "by nature," to the state.

Above all, it is not possible to transfer sovereignty to another legal system because it would be the equivalent to destroying the constitution itself, which is legally impossible. Indeed, the destruction of the constitution would be tantamount to its repeal, which can only result of another legal norm: the derogation is the repeal of the validity of an already valid norm by *another norm* (see Kelsen, 1991, pp. 106–108). A norm repealing another norm cannot base its own validity in the norm it repeals, as it would deprive it with a valid basis from the moment it enters into force. To admit constitutional validity, without reference to another positive constitutional norm, engenders a break in the constitutional continuity and corresponds to a legal revolution (see Derosier, 2015).

The constitutional *ipse* identity could be identified in the fact that the member states' constitutions safeguard the sovereign statehood and not only presupposes it. The principle of structural *ipse* constitutional identity can be mainly related to some structural character of the state legal system itself i.e. to the existence of the state. The obligation under European law to respect the "equality of member states before the Treaties" (art. 4–2 TEU) i.e. the constitutional *ipse* identity of the Member States as the "masters of the Treaties" corresponds also to the non-transferable *idem* identity of the constitution which is not open to integration in this respect. To some extent the *ipse* and *idem* identity overlaps.

2.2.2 The Formal Idem *Constitutional Identity: The Limits for Constitutional Revision*

The *idem* identity is defined by the maintenance and preservation of an essential element that remains the same over time and allows us to recognise something as the same. The importance of certain elements of the constitution could be identified through the existence of the hierarchical differentiation within the formal constitutional law (see Favoreu et al., 2005; Magnon, 2004), i.e. the polymorphic conception of formal constitutional law (see Pfersmann, 2012). The content of formal *idem* constitutional identity depends on the political will to ensure extra stability to certain principles. This kind of hierarchical differentiation may cover two hypotheses.

First, it may constitute the *hard constitutional core*: certain elements of the constitution may be modified, but not others. These "other" provisions i.e. the substantive limitations to amendment power the constitution constitute the formal hard *idem* constitutional identity. This kind of identity is intangible[8]. This kind of hard constitutional core could be amended only by unconstitutional i.e. revolutionary means (in the legal sense). Nevertheless the constitutional *ipse* identity doesn't change.

Second, the hierarchical differentiation within the formal constitutional law may constitute the *flexible constitutional core*: every constitutional provision can be amended, but not in the same way i.e. there are complementary procedural obstacles to amend certain elements (see Grewe, 2013, 42). This kind of differentiation within the formal constitutional law seems to have first been adopted in

---

8 Overall among the Member States of the EU, eight prohibit certain amendments: France, Germany, Greece, Italy, Portugal, Romania, Cyprus, and the Czech Republic. The content of these limits for constitutional revision varies. In order to prevent a return to Monarchy this method has been adopted in France already in 1884 and remains in the art. 89 para 5 of the Constitution of 1958: "The Republican form of government cannot be the object of revision." After the Second World War, Italy followed France adopting the same provision (art. 139 of the constitution of 1947) this model had been developed in Germany in order to sanctify the principles of federalism, the protection of fundamental rights, and representative democracy (art. 79 (3)).

Switzerland in 1875, where the constitution distinguishes between partial and total revision.[9] This method has been adopted by Austria,[10] Spain,[11] and Bulgaria.[12] This content[13] of the formal *idem* constitutional identity may be seen as corresponding to the member states "fundamental structures, political and constitutional, inclusive of regional and local self-government" – art. 4 (2) TEU.

Founding their argument on the concepts of constitutional *ipse* and *idem* identity is a trend used by constitutional courts to resist the absolute primacy of European law. The new provision of art. 4 (2) is seen as:

> Integrating the thrust of the jurisprudence of numerous domestic constitutional courts on the relationship between EU law and national constitutional law. The revised identity clause in Article 4 (2) TEU not only demands the respect for national constitutional identity, but is understood as permitting domestic constitutional courts to invoke, under certain limited circumstances, constitutional limits to the primacy of EU law (see Bogdandy & Schill, 2011, 1419).

The most notorious example is the German Constitutional Tribunal, whose case law evolved from a human rights protection to a constitutional identity test (see Tomuschat, 2013; Mayer 2011). The French Conseil Constitutionnel could be seen a precursor with respect to the last of these "contro-limiti."[14] Nonetheless, national constitutional identity does not function only as a member states' trump card, but structures and inspires the ECJ adapting his jurisprudence in order to avoid a "frontal conflict" (see Simon, 2011, 42) between the European and national constitutional orders.[15]

The concept of "constitutional identity" might be analysed and would be of most benefit within the topical issue of the relationship between legal systems and in particular the relationship between national constitutional law and EU law. The

9 See articles 138–140 of Swiss constitution of 1875. In the present Swiss constitution – art. 192–195. The main difference is the addition of the requirement to respect *jus cogens*.

10 See articles 44–46 of the Federal Constitutional Law.

11 See articles 166–169 of the Spanish Constitution.

12 See articles Chapter 9 of the Bulgarian Constitution.

13 The constitutional elements subject of the more complicated procedure for amendment varies from the changes in the form of State structure or form of government to provision on the Fundamental Rights and Public Liberties.

14 Conseil constitutionnel, Decision № 2006–540 DC of 24 July 2006.

15 Case C-208/09,*Sayn-Wittgenstein*, judgment of 22 Dec. 2010; Case C-391/09 *Runevič-Vardyn and Wardyn* [2011] ECR I-3787. Case C-51/08*Commission v Luxembourg*, [2011] ECR I-4231; Case C-151/12*Commission v Spain*, [2013].

use of the terms of constitution and constitutional identity in recent academic writings has caused a great confusion about the legal nature of the EU.

3. The Impossible Constitutionalisation of the European Integration

With the process of more enhanced integration, many analysts of the relationship between EU law and national legal systems emphasise on the transformations of state sovereignty in global society concluding that the relations between legal systems cannot be analysed in the old categories of hierarchy and "monism" – "dualism" and we are in the era of "constitutional pluralism" in which sovereignty loses its "classic" meaning. The global society coincides with unorthodox conceptualisations, such as "constitutionalisation without the state" (see Teubner 2004, 7) or "post-constituent constitutionalism" (see Walker, 2007) (3.1.). However this stance seems inaccurate, for one reason – the existence of constitutional identity of the member states of the EU (3.2.).

3.1 The EU as a Post-Sovereign Globalised Society: The Ideal of Constitutional Pluralism

The concept of constitutional pluralism emerged in the context of the legal philosophy of the European integration in the aftermath of the German Federal Constitutional Court's *Maastricht* decision[16] under the influence of Neil MacCormick. In his comment (see MacCormick, 1995) of the German jurisprudence he concluded that the decision had a "sound basis in legal theory" (see ibid., 265) following which:

> the most appropriate analysis of the relations of legal systems is pluralistic rather than monistic, and interactive rather than hierarchical. The legal system of Member States and their common legal system of EC law are distinct but interacting systems of law, and hierarchical relationships of validity within criteria of validity proper to distinct systems do not add up to any sort of all-purpose superiority of one system over another (see ibid., 264).

MacCormick portrayed the "constitutional pluralism" as

> a situation of plurality of institutional normative orders, each with a functioning constitution (at least in the sense of a body of higher-order norms establishing and conditioning relevant governmental powers), it is possible that each acknowledge the legitimacy of

16 Case 2 BvR 2134, 2159/92 *Maastricht* [1993] BVerfGE 89, 155, published in English as [1994] 1 CMLR 57.

> every other within its own sphere, while none asserts or acknowledges constitutional superiority over another (see MacCormick, 2002, 104).

Instead of depending on the will of one constitutional sovereign, transnational and supranational systems, such as the EU, constitute their stability through a network of legal and constitutional institutions and practices of cooperation and conflict resolution (see ibid., 119). Where there is a plurality of institutional normative orders, each with a functioning constitution, "it is possible that each acknowledge the legitimacy of every other within its own sphere, while none asserts or acknowledges the constitutional superiority over another." In this situation, constitutional pluralism prevails. MacCormick's essential claim is that there exists a number of non hierarchical legal orders that intersect with one another in various ways that he calls "radical pluralism" (see ibid., 118). All that is offered by way of resolution is the acceptance that "radical pluralism entails that not every legal problem can be solved legally." It requires "political judgment" (see ibid., 119).

For MacCormick, once the supremacy of EU law is established by the Court of Justice and recognised by national courts, there would no longer to be a need for an elaborate theory about interaction of distinct systems. As he would prefer to express it, there are national legal orders and the legal order of the EU, neither of which is to be conceived as a subsystem of the other but both cohere "within a common legal universe governed by the norms of international law." This is a pluralistic relationship within a monistic framework of international law; this is "pluralism under international law" (see ibid., 117).

Within the European integration's legal debate constitutional pluralism *has* grown in popularity, but in so doing it has also become a more heterogeneous concept (see Avbelj & Komárek, 2012).

One important family of European legal theories concerned with the complexity of its structure consists in saying that European and member state law are interacting at different levels without there being a "hierarchy" but a "multilevel constitutionalism." A representative example of this position has been offered by Ingolf Pernice. He considers Dieter Grimm's question, "Does Europe need a Constitution?" (see Grimm, 1995) as :

> not relevant, because Europe already has a 'multi-level constitution': a constitution made up of the constitutions of the member states bound together by a complementary constitutional body consisting of the European Treaties (Verfassungsverbund) (see Pernice, 1999, 707).

Judicial review would be again neither superior nor inferior, but would unfold in a "dialogue" between European and national courts i.e the constitutional reasoning by both European and member state's courts should be "constructively engaged with one another" (see Maduro, 2009, 2012). Finally, the relation of state-law and Union-law would not be hierarchical but a coordinative link within a global system. Pernice vigorously developed and argued that:

> the Member States' constitutions and the treaties constituting the European Union, despite their formal distinction as a unity in substance and as a coherent institutional system, within which competence for action, public authority or, as one may also say, the power to exercise sovereign rights is divided among two or more levels (see Pernice, 1999, 706).

In order to sustain the claim of the coordinative link between member states law and Union law, Pernice considers that the ultimate foundation of validity of the respective legal orders would be the "will of the citizens" and the reason for primacy would be the exigency of equal application which is also the foundation of its acceptance (see Pernice, 2002, 2009). The authors' proponents of the ideal of constitutional pluralism within the EU seems to accept literally the claim of the "autonomous legal order" made by the ECJ in Van Gend en Loos and of the EU treaties as the "*constitutional charter of the Community.*"[17]

3.2 The Constitutional Identity as a Legal Limit to the Formal Constitutionalisation of the EU Integration

The critical issue is where exactly to place the boundaries between what still belongs to European law and what belongs to the domestic law of a state. In the case of the EU, this borderline would be crossed, when the member states would be deprived of their *ipse* identity i.e. their power to decide on the distribution of competencies.

It is important to see that this is a structural, not a material issue. It's an issue of centralisation and decentralisation of the legal systems (see Kelsen, 1961). The centralisation and decentralisation can have consequences for European integration (see Derosier, 2009). Indeed, this integration is a gradual centralisation of the legal order of the EU that is manifested by the constant shift of competences from the member states to the EU. It is possible to imagine a threshold where the member states would have lost the exclusive competence for any materially significant domain, but could still retain their *ipse* identity, i.e. the capacity to modify the global dynamics of European integration. The federal states very often belong to the opposite hypothesis, i.e. the member states would have been attributed substantially significant competences but have lost their constitutional competence i.e. *ipse* constitutional identity.

17 Case 294/83, Parti Ecologiste 'Les Verts' v. Parliament. (1986) ECR 1339.

Within the European integration seen as a global or "total" (in Kelsenian terms) legal system composed of partial legal systems, i.e. the member states become on the whole materially weaker, but remain powerful at the constitutional level. Therefore the critical question is who is empowered to distribute these competencies and to modify this distribution.

The rules that set this frame are contained in provisions of the founding treaties in art. 48 TEU. The competence of distributing competencies is still a state competence because the *amendments shall enter into force after being ratified by all the member states in accordance with their respective constitutional requirements.* All treaty revisions throughout the history of European integration maintained this same requirement. The primary law of the EU i.e. its material constitution is to be modified only through an amendment of the treaties according to the norms of public international law concerning the law of treaties. Therefore the "Master of the Treaties"[18] i.e. those who are competent to exercise the "original authority" within the EU legal order and to enact such changes are exclusively the member states whose constitutions contains also the *idem* constitutional identity.

Ultimately, the transfer of constitutional *ipse* identity would nullify the supreme character of the state constitution by stating that the constitutional competence is no longer regulated by the constitution but by another higher norm, and this character is an intrinsic quality of the constitution, his disappearance causes destruction of the constitution. This destruction is legally impossible, it is not possible to consider the transfer of sovereignty: structurally related to the state law and the constitution on which it is based, the constitutional *ipse* identity is a constitutional limit to European integration.

4. Conclusion

The *term* "constitutional identity" is fashionable and it covers two overlapping concepts. First the constitutional *ipse* identity as the structural elements of the constitutional order which, if they disappear, this structure i.e. the constitution disappears as well. Second the constitutional *idem* identity as the more important elements of the constitution that could be identified through the existence of the hierarchical differentiation within the formal constitutional law. Whereas constitutional *idem* identity has different content in the various constitutions of

18 German constitutional court *Kloppenburg*, 3 C.M.L.R. at 18, BVerfGE 75, 242. The Court reiterates this term in *Maastrichtcase*. at 188–190.; see also Lisbon Treaty case, para 231, 235, 298, 334.

the member states, the constitutional *ipse* identity of all states has the same nature and shape.

The concept of sovereignty is not lost. It has been just renamed constitutional *ipse* identity. The concept of constitutional identity exists and has always existed even without being formally canonised in the primary law of the EU or the case law of the national constitutional courts and the European Court of Justice. The material constitution of the European Union is still to be found in a set of international treaties and it still determines that the revisions of these founding treaties have to respect the proceedings of international treaty ratification. The constitutional *ipse* identity is not a competence of the Union itself but of the member states.

The democratic political domain is undoubtedly made up of a plurality of institutional arrangements and a plurality of values. The fallacy of the constitutional globalists and pluralists is to consider that the empirical existence of pluralism and convergence of political values or institutions and the political idea of the "will of citizens" (which are undoubtedly very important politically) can be considered also as a legal pluralism of foundations. In the frame of the most of the constitutionalist theories of Europe the relations within the EU become entirely unexplainable if not in terms of some contingent and strictly empirical facts such the "will of the citizens" or "judicial dialogues" instead of organised procedures. They try to promote a vision of the legal integration in Europe as an already accomplished ideal. The legal theories of Europe and the legal concepts of constitutional identity may give a new impulse for more political discussions about the present and future of the European integration.

References

Avbelj, Matej; Komárek, Jan. 2012. Constitutional Pluralism in the European Union and Beyond. Oxford: Hart.

Bogdandy, Armin; von Schill, Stephan. 2011. Overcoming absolute primacy: respect for national identity under the Lisbon Treaty, In Common Market Law Review 48: 1419.

Burgorgue-Larsen, Laurence. 2014. Les origines de l'identité constitutionnelle. In Revue Générale de Droit International Public 3: 483–499.

Derosier, Jean-Philippe. 2009. Constitutionnalisation ? Réflexions sur le degré de centralisation et de décentralisation de l'Union européenne In: Union de droit, Union des droits. Mélanges en l'honneur de Philippe Manin, 95–107. Pédone: Paris.

Derosier.Jean-Philippe. 2015. Qu'est-ce qu'une révolution juridique? Le point de vue de la théorie générale du droit. In Revue française de droit constitutionnel, 2 /102: 391–404.

Dubout, Édouard. 2010. « Les règles ou principes inhérents à l'identité constitutionnelle de la France » : une supra-constitutionnalité ? In Revue française de droit constitutionnel 83: 451–482.

Favoreu, Louis; Gaïa, Patrick; Ghevontian, Richard; Pfersmann, Otto; Roux, André; Scoffoni, Guy; Mestre, Jean-Louis. 2005. Droit constitutionnel. Paris: Dalloz.

Grewe, Constance. 2013. Methods of Identification of National Constitutional Identity. In National Constitutional Identity and European Integration, edited by Alejandro Saiz Arnaiz and Carina Alcoberro Llivina, 37–48, Intersentia Publishing.

Grimm, Dieter. 1995. Does Europe Need a Constitution? In European Law Journal 1/3: 282–302.

Grimm, Dieter. 2010. The Achievement of Constitutionalism and its Prospects in a Changed World. In The Twilight of Constitutionalism, edited by Petra Dobner and Martin Loughlin, pp. 3–22, Oxford University Press.

Guastaferro, Barbara. 2012. Beyond the Exceptionalism of Constitutional Conflicts: The ordinary Functions of the Identity Clause. In Yearbook of European Law 1/31: 263–318.

Henkin, Louis. 1994. A New Birth of Constitutionalism: Genetic Influence and Genetic Defects. In Constitutionalism, Identity, Difference and Legitimacy, edited by Michel Rosenfeld, pp. 39–53, Duke University Press.

Jacobson, Gary Jeffrey. 2010. Constitutional Identity, Harvard University Press.

Kelsen, Hans. 1945. General Theory of Law and Slate. Cambridge, Massachusetts: Harvard University Press.

Kelsen, Hans. 1991. General Theory of Norms. Oxford University Press.

Locke, John. 1689. On Identity and Diversity in An Essay Concerning Human Understanding, Book II Chapter XXVII.

MacCormick, Neil. 1995. The Maastricht Urteil: Sovereignty Now. In European Law Journal 1/3: 259–266.

MacCormick, Neil. 2002. Questioning Sovereignty: Law, State and Nation in the European Commonwealth. Oxford: Oxford University Press.

Maduro, Miguel Poiares. 2012. Three Claims of Constitutional Pluralism, in Constitutional Pluralism in the European Union and Beyond, edited by Matej Avbelj and Jan Kom6rek, Oxford: Hart.

Maduro, Miguel Poiares. 2009. Courts and Pluralism: Essay on a Theory of Judicial Adjudication in the Context of Legal and Constitutional Pluralism, In Ruling the World? Constitutionalism, International Law, and Global Governance, edited by Jeffrey Dunoff and Joel Trachtman, 356–379, Cambridge University Press.

Magnon, Xavier. 2004. Quelques maux encore à propos des lois de révision constitutionnelle: limites, contrôle, efficacité, caractère opératoire et existence. In Revue française de droit constitutionnel, 3/59: 595–617.

Mathieu, Bertrand. 2014. La Constitution cadre et miroir des mutations de la société. In Revue française de droit constitutionnel 100: 1011–1019.

Mayer, Franz C. 2011. L'identité constitutionnelle dans la jurisprudence constitutionnelle allemande. In L'identité constitutionnelle saisie par les juges en Europe, edited by Laurence Burgorgue-Larsen, 63–87, Paris: Pedone.

Pernice, Inglof. 2002. Multilevel Constitutionalism in the European Union. In European Law Review 27: 511–529.

Pernice, Inglolf. 2009. The Treaty of Lisbon: Multilevel Constitutionalism in Action. In Columbia Journal of European Law, 3/15: 349–407.

Pernice, Ingolf; Mayer, Franz C. 2000. De la constitution composée de l'Europe. In Revue Trimestrielle de Droit Européen 36: 623–647.

Pernice, Ingolf. 1999. Multilevel Constitutionalism and the Treaty of Amsterdam: European Constitution-Making Revisited In Common Market Law Review 36: 703–750.

Pfersmann, Otto. 2012. La production des normes : production des normes et hiérarchie des normes. In Traité international de droit constitutionnel, La distribution des pouvoirs, edited by Dominique Chagnollaud, Michel Troper, 483–528, Paris:Dalloz.

Ricoeur, Paul. 1992. Oneself as Another. Translated by K. Blamey. Chicago: The University ofChicago Press.

Saiz Arnaiz, Alejandro. 2011. L'identité nationale et le droit de l'Union européenne dans la jurisprudence constitutionnelle espagnole. In L'identité constitutionnelle saisie par les juges en Europe, edited by Laurence Burgorgue-Larsen, Paris: Pedone.

Schmitt, Carl. 2008. Constitutional Theory. Duke University Press.

Simon, Denys. 2011. L'identité constitutionnelle dans la jurisprudence de l'Union européenne. In: L'identité constitutionnelle saisie par les juges en Europe, edited by Burgorgue-Larsen, Laurence Paris: Pedone.

Teubner, Gunter. 2004. Societal Constitutionalism: Alternatives to State-Centred Constitutional Theory? In: Transnational Governance and Constitutionalism, edited by Joerges, Christian; Sand, Inger-Johanne; Teubner, Gunther. 3–28, Oxford: Hart.

Tomuschat, Christian. 2013. The Defence of National Identity by the German Constitutional Court, In: National Constitutional Identity and European Integration, edited by Saiz, Alejandro Arnaiz and Alcoberro Llivina, Carina. 205–220 Intersentia Publishing.

Toniatti, Roberto. 2013. Sovereignty lost, identity regained. In National Constitutional Identity and European Integration, edited by Saiz Arnaiz, Alejandro and Alcoberro Llivina, Carina. 49–74, Intersentia Publishing.

Troper, Michel. 2002. La Constitutioncomme système juridique autonome. In: Droits 35: 63–78.

Troper, Michel. 2010. Behind the Constitution? The Principle of Constitutional Identity in France. In: Constitutional Topography: Values and Constitutions, edited by Sajó, András & Uitz, Renáta: 187–203. Eleven International Publishing.

Vahlas, Alexis. 2005. Souveraineté et droit de retrait au sein de l'Union européenne. In: Revue du Droit Public. 6: 1574–1581.

Walker, Neil. 2006. Late Sovereignty in the European Union. In: Sovereignty in Transition, edited by Walker, Neil, 3–32, Oxford: Hart.

Walker, Neil. 2007. Post-Constituent Constitutionalism? The Case of the EuropeanUnion. In: The Paradox of Constitutionalism: Constituent Power and Constitutional Form, edited by: Laughlin, Martin and Walker, Neil. 247–67, Oxford: Oxford University Press.

Weiler, Joseph. H.H. 2002. A Constitution for Europe? Some Hard Choses. In: Journal of Common Market Studies 40: 563–580.

Part IV. Global Governance and its Effects on Human Rights

Christoph Good

Corporate Human Rights Initiatives – From International Law to Global Governance and Back?

Abstract
In recent years, promising new legal approaches to tackle the business and human rights nexus evolved within the international law arena. Especially the UN Guiding Principles on Business and Human Rights – the current regulative core within the respective field – took the role of a game changer by introducing new governance approaches into international law discussions. The central element of the changes is a (re-)definition of the corporate sector's role within the relevant norm-creating and norm-shaping process and the granting of regulative agency to corporations. Results are a large number of corporate driven human rights initiatives. The aim of the paper is to clarify the interdependent linkages between these initiatives and the existing international human rights law framework from a theoretical viewpoint and to outline the specific challenges for the existing international law theory in general.

1. Introduction

That the realities of economic globalisation challenges the classic notion of international law theory is a commonplace argument (see e.g. Koroma, 2009). The rising of new categories of actors such as transnational corporations (TNCs) and the de-territorialisation of economic relations and supply chains questions central fundamental principles of international law. Obvious examples are the restrictive actors paradigm (see e.g. Alvarez, 2011; Hansen, 2015)[1] as well as common concepts of state sovereignty and territoriality-centred jurisdiction (see e.g. Augenstein, 2015). Recent regulative attempts to tackle these new developments pragmatically, which have at the same time an eminent practical influence on international law making as such, often ignore the underlying dogmatic questions.

This can be demonstrated by referring to the regulative consequences of the heated debate on the missing accountability of corporations for their involvement in human rights violations. The deadlocked regulative history on an international level from the 1970's onwards until the first decade of the new millennium

1 According to international law doctrine, only states and to a certain extent international organisations are recognised as duty bearers and right holders in international law.

(see Weissbrodt & Kruger, 2005, pp. 318–321) and the related failing of the *Draft United Nations Code of Conduct on Transnational Corporations* (UN Doc E/1988/39/Add.1) and the *Norms on the Responsibilities of Transnational Corporations and Other Business Enterprises with Regard to Human Rights* (UN Doc E/CN.4/Sub.2/2003/12/Rev.2), clearly evince the shortcomings of international law to tackle theses changed realities (see e.g. Arnold, 2010, pp. 373–376).

Strongly influenced by these developments and fostered by the creation of the *UN Global Compact* (Mares, 2009, pp. 386–390), a new regulative type entered the international human rights arena in the beginning of the 21st century: the individual and collective corporate human rights initiatives (e.g. Preuss & Brown, 2012, 291). These initiatives took their starting point in the emerging Corporate Social Responsibility debate (see Wettstein, 2012, pp. 745–751; Santoro 2015, pp. 157–158) and can be described as the global governance driven private corporate answer to the deadlocked discussion of the (international) law makers.

Whereas these initiatives were initially relegated by the international law community to an existence in a dark vault – often seen as purely window dressing public relations measures of corporations with no traction in the (international) legal system – the endorsement of the *UN Guiding Principles on Business and Human Rights* (UN Doc A/HRC/17/31) by the Human Rights Council in 2011 changed this attitude fundamentally. Due to the fostering of the corporate obligation to respect human rights, corporate human rights initiatives became a respectable instrument in practice, to operationalise the international law based human rights framework.

The aim of this paper is to sketch current interdependencies of these governance driven corporate human rights standards with the *classical* legal human rights framework and to highlight synergies and challenges with respect to the legislative agency and the underlying dogmatic fundaments. To clarify the object of investigation, the analysis will start by outlining the emergence of corporate human rights initiatives in practice (Part 2). In a second step, the regulative interplay between these governance driven standards and the legal sphere will be shown, to demonstrate the oscillation between global governance and legal approaches in the realm of the business and human rights nexus (Part 3). Based on these findings a critical assessment of the theoretical consequences and challenges of these practical developments will be carried out (Part 4).

2. Setting the Scene – The Emergence of Corporate Human Rights Initiatives

The emergence of corporate human rights initiatives – understood in a rather broad sense (including codes of conduct, corporate human rights frameworks and business policies with references to international human rights law) – can be traced back to the late 1980's and the first orchestrated uproars by NGOs in the global press regarding the working conditions in developing countries (see Wettstein, 2012, pp. 746–748; Ramasastry, 2015, pp. 239–243). Some corporations responded with individual or collective, in any case selective and voluntary policy-adjustments to tackle certain human rights issues like child labour and work safety requirements in their supply-chains. The addressee of the corporate's discourse was mainly the consumer and only in a subordinate role the lawmakers. Nevertheless, given the fact that these normative self-regulation standards contributed to the solution of global "co-ordination and co-operation problems" and the promotion of global welfare, these voluntary standards can easily be qualified as global governance instruments (see Benvenisti, 2014, 60). Following Benvenisti's typology of different forms of global governance, these corporate standards can furthermore be characterised as "informal procedures" by "private bodies" (see ibid., 67).

Nevertheless, this "first generation" of corporate human rights rules-set is not really yielding for the purpose of this paper, since these undertakings can – slightly exaggerated – be interpreted as purely philanthropic attempts without any serious traction in law. Traction is thereby understood as the momentum, where national or international legal systems explicitly refer to these standards and therefore take to a certain extent their content over in the classical legal realm. The manifestation of traction implies at the same time a certain legalisation of voluntary standards.

The absence of legal traction with regard to those first generational corporate human rights standards is obvious. The non-compliance had no legal consequences whatsoever and no cross-fertilisations with the general (human) rights framework took place. In that sense they can be compared with the first self-taming projects in corporate environmental approaches and the implementation of voluntary corporate sustainability goals in the late 1980's and early 1990's (see Morrison & Roht-Arriaza, 2008, pp. 500–501, 506–511).

The independency between corporate driven *private* global governance mechanisms and state driven *public* global governance mechanisms via national and international legal systems changed dramatically in the last couple of years: Initiated by the welcoming of the *Protect, Respect and Remedy-Framework* (UN Doc A/HRC/8/5) the surprising regulative breakthrough on the international level finally took place in 2011 with the unanimous endorsement of the *UN Guiding Principles on Business and Human Rights* (UN Doc A/HRC/17/31) by the Human Rights Council. This set of 31 soft law rules (provided with a wide authoritative commentary by its authors), rests on three pillars: (1) The state duty to protect human rights, (2) the corporate responsibility to respect human rights and (3) the improvement of victims' access to remedy (see e.g. Addo, 2014, pp. 134–136).

An essential factor for the success of the new framework was the tacit ignoring of fundamental principles of international law making (e.g. breaking the primacy role of states in the creation process) and the paradigmatic turn towards new polycentric governance approaches (see Ruggie, 2014, pp. 8–10), initiated by the UN Special Representative John Ruggie and his team (see e.g. Buhmann, 2012, pp. 101–104). Especially the strong and formalised involvement of all main stakeholder categories in the norm-shaping process itself (*multistakeholderism*), characterised a blurring momentum between public and private approaches in global governance (see Addo, 2014, 135).

But not only the formal creation of this expanding soft law instrument was strongly influenced by non-legal governance approaches. The same can be said on a substantive level with regard to the paradigmatic turn towards the foundation of the *corporate responsibility to respect*. This corporate obligation is not based in law, but rather grounded on "societal expectations" (see e.g. Jägers, 2013, 298; Nolan, 2013, pp. 154–160). Furthermore, the Guideline's eminent uptake on the international, regional, and national levels manifests a unique turn towards global governance approaches to regulate the downsides of economic globalisation within the legal sphere (see Ruggie, 2014, pp. 11–12). To formulate it in slightly exaggerated terms, it opens a responsive and procedural playing field, where – within the framework's broad frontiers – the different actors (states, corporations as well as civil society organisations) are free to test individually as well as collectively regulative models without bothering too much about the limiting principles of international law making. In the result, one could argue that the *UN Guiding Principles on Business and Human Rights* itself are thought of as an interactive global governance instrument camouflaged by its jargon and form as a classical international law regulation.

Not surprisingly, corporations broadly replied to this unique opportunity of almost free-floating co-regulating powers by fostering or improving in no time dozens of new standards, either alone or in cooperation with other stakeholder groups.[2] Already the corporations' motivation to do so would be an interesting object of research in the triangle of good corporate citizenship, binding law avoidance strategies, and the potential business case validity of corporate human rights engagement.

Meanwhile it is obvious, that these standards vary immensely in their normative quality and with regard to their effectiveness on the ground (see Jägers, 2013, pp. 304–306). One of the main differences between these new initiatives and the abovementioned "first generation" initiatives is that they definitely show traction in international and national law. In general – as will be demonstrated in the following chapter by referring to two practical examples – situations of independent parallel development, of concurrence as well as fruitful interaction between private standards and legal framework are conceivable.

3. Back and Forth and In Between – The Practical Interplay of Global Governance and International Law

The practical interplay of corporate driven *private* global governance mechanisms and state driven *public* legal mechanisms with regard to legislative measures shall be contextualised by referring to two different collective corporate human rights initiatives from different economic sectors. The first example – the *Extractive Industries Transparency Initiative (EITI)* – tackles transparency issues in the extractive industries sector as an indirect pre-condition for the realisation of an effective human rights protection framework in resource-rich, but weak government zones. The second example – the *International Code of Conduct for Private Security Service Providers (ICoC)* – refers to the realisation of minimal human rights standards in the "mercenary"-business. Both initiatives have in common, that they try to regulate sectors that are prone to corporate involvement in human rights violations[3] and that both had explicit traction in law. Nevertheless they differ fundamentally in their functional interplay with the national and international legal system.

---

2 A sector-specific overview can be found on http://business-humanrights.org/en/company-action-platform (accessed on 23.08.2015).

3 In 2008, a report by the UN Special Representative on Business and Human Rights showed, that 28% of all allegations of corporate involvement in human rights violations were related to the extractive industries sector (UN Doc A/HRC/8/5/Add.2, para. 8). Given the fact that most of the allegations were related to the (excessive) use of force by the security providers at the extractive industries sites, the amalgamation of extractive industries and private security services providers is obvious.

Example I: Corporate norm-shaping with legal consequences – The EITI

At first glance, it may irritate to qualify the *EITI* as a corporate human rights initiative at all. According to its self-description EITI is "a global coalition of governments, companies and civil society working together to improve openness and accountable management of revenues from natural resources."[4] Therefore corporations are not the only actor and human rights are not directly addressed by the self-description.

But looking at its general aim – to support resource-rich developing countries in avoiding the risks of the resource curse and creating at the same time a level playing field for the involved corporations (see Aaronson, 2011, 50) – the connection to human rights protection becomes clearer. Thinking of examples like Democratic Republic of Congo, Nigeria or Myanmar, obvious human rights risks of the resource curse are the non-existence of labour protection, severe health risks and an exceptionally low level of economic, social and cultural rights due to the malfunctioning of state institutions. The fostered transparency of revenues from the exploitation of natural resources contributes directly to the elaboration of these rights by strengthening state building capacities.[5]

The initiative – launched by the UK Government and later explicitly backed by the UN General Assembly (UN Doc A/Res/62/274 para. 4) – started by the definition of a set of *core principles* in 2003, which were translated into *rules* in 2009. At the EITI Global Conference in Sydney in 2013, the EITI Board adopted the new *EITI Standard*, containing a set of minimal requirements that implementing states have to fulfil.[6] Central aspects are *inter alia* the creation of an effective

---

4 http://eiti.org/eiti (accessed on 23.08.2015).

5 EITI's human rights dimension becomes clear by the discussion between the Human Rights Watch (HRW) and the EITI Board on this issue [https://eiti.org/document/new-accountability-agenda-human-rights-and-eiti (accessed on 23.08.2015]. In 2013 the HRW published its report *A new Accountability Agenda – Human Rights and the Extractive Industries Transparency Initiative* [available at: https://eiti.org/files/A%20New%20Accountability%20Agenda%2C%20Human%20Rights%20and%20the%20EITI.pdf (accessed on 23.08.2015)] and requests the EITI to better address human rights. In his response *Jonas Moberg*, the head of the EITI Secretariat, acknowledges the HRW report and stresses that the EITI already explicitly tackles minimal human rights guarantees as a precondition of the realisation of transparency [https://eiti.org/blog/open-letter-new-hrw-report-jonas-moberg-writes-human-rights-watch (accessed on 23.08.2014)].

6 EITI, *The Extractive Industries Transparency Standard*, 11/07/2013 [hereafter EITI (2013)], http://eiti.org/files/English_EITI%20STANDARD_11July_0.pdf (accessed on 23.08.215).

oversight-mechanism by establishing a correlated multi-stakeholder dialogue[7] and clearly defined reporting requirements "that include full government disclosure of extractive industry revenues, and disclosure of all material payments to government by oil, gas and mining companies."[8] Furthermore, the reports are subjects to an external validation process.[9]

From an organisational perspective, corporations do not take a dominant role within the EITI structures. The executive organ of the initiative is the EITI Board, where the implementing states, supporting states, civil society organisations as well as corporations and investors are equally represented. Yet contrary to the multi-stakeholder approach of the existing standard governing body, main driving force in the standard's original norm-shaping process were the corporate representatives and investors, mainly motivated by the idea of a competitive level economic playing field in the resource-rich developing countries. In contrast, the originally involved supporting states, like the UK, saw their role more as a facilitator of the standard-setting process.[10]

Coming back to the initial subject of this chapter, the interplay of independent global governance standards and the legal systems, the question that has to be raised is, whether the EITI has *legal* traction or not, and therefore reaches a new *legal quality* of corporate human rights standards? The legal uptake of the EITI is quite impressive and follows two different avenues. On one hand and rather not surprising, the standard directly affects the legal systems of the states that want to become EITI compliant countries. Becoming a member state of the EITI is voluntary, but once a state applied for membership – this has to happen by giving an unequivocal public statement of its intention to implement the EITI. The statement has to be issued by the head of state or government[11] – non-compliance with the EITI Standard and especially with the reporting obligations can lead to suspension or delisting from the initiative.[12] Next to the reporting obligations, mainly the provisions regarding the establishment of national multi-stakeholder bodies can comprise concrete legal obligations for the member states.[13] Therefore, designated member states have to transfer the content of the standard in their

7 EITI (2013), Requirement 1.
8 EITI (2013), Requirement 4.
9 EITI (2013), Validation Guide.
10 See https://eiti.org/eiti/history (accessed on 23.08.2015).
11 EITI (2013), Requirement 1.1.
12 EITI (2013), Requirement 1.6.
13 EITI (2013), Requirement 1.3.

national legislation. Currently 31 compliant countries are members of the initiative and 16 candidate countries are in the process of becoming members.[14]

Furthermore the standard's legal traction can be demonstrated by referring to a second – more surprising – avenue that has no direct connection with the member states but affects national legislation with regards to corporate reporting obligations. In 2013 the EU legally ennobled the initiative in its *Financial Statement Directive*[15], by stating that:

> "In order to provide for enhanced transparency of payments made to governments, large undertakings and public-interest entities which are active in the extractive industry (…) should disclose material payments made to governments in the countries in which they operate in a separate report, on an annual basis. (…) The report should include types of payments comparable to those disclosed by an undertaking participating in the Extractive Industries Transparency Initiative (EITI)" (para 44.).

In the result, the *Financial Statement Directive* legally mainstreams the content of the EITI governance standard within the borders of the EU. Furthermore the *Directive* obliges the member states to take legislative steps in order to comply with EITI-norms, even though most of the addressees are not member countries of the EITI. Referring to the general remarks in part 2 above, the EITI standard is therefore an illustrative example of how existing gaps in legal systems are closed by transplanting the regulative outputs of corporate driven global governance instruments in the legal sphere.

Example II: Corporate norm-shaping vs. legal norm-shaping – The ICoC

A further example of an industry-driven global governance standard from a different field but with similar features regarding the role of corporations within the norm shaping process is the 2010 established *ICoC*. The ICoC initiative goes back on a campaign by the Swiss government and the International Committee of the Red Cross (ICRC) to clarify the role and obligations of states related operations of private military and security companies during armed conflicts (provided by the so called *Montreux Document*[16]). Simultaneously, the initiative is strongly

14 See https://eiti.org/countries (accessed on 23.08.2015).

15 Directive 2013/34/EU of the European Parliament and of the Council (26 June 2013) on the annual financial statements, consolidated financial statements, and related reports of certain types of undertakings.

16 https://www.icrc.org/eng/assets/files/other/icrc_002_0996.pdf. In December 2014, the participants of the Montreux-Document established the so called "Montreux Document Forum," co-chaired by Switzerland and the ICRC with the aim to "support national implementation of the Montreux Document and the development of

influenced by the earlier mentioned *Protect, Respect and Remedy-Framework* (see Jägers, 2013, pp. 311–313). Whereas the *Montreux Document* is a state-driven, non-binding, interpretative comment on existing states obligations regarding the use of private security providers by states,[17] the ICoC is the voluntary corporate answer on operational grounds (see Richemond-Barak, 2014, 783). Signatory companies of the ICoC commit to the responsible provision on security services so as to "support the rule of law, respect the human rights of all persons, and protect the interests of their clients."[18] The central aim of the ICoC is the creation of better governance, compliance, and accountability mechanisms for private security companies (see ibid., 783).

The code of conduct was drafted by business-representatives in several stakeholder-workshops, supported by civil society organisations and academics.[19] The multi-stakeholder-approach was professionalised in the post-drafting structure of the ICoC Association by appointing the equal number of states-, civil society- and business-representatives for the ICoC Steering Committee and within all working groups.[20] Currently, more than 700 private security companies (PSCs) have signed the ICoC[21] and the 2013 established ICoC Association is engaged with the creation of an independent governance and oversight mechanism (certification model) and a complementary, individual complaint mechanism (see Richemond-Barak, 2014, pp. 784–786).

---

implementation tools, as well as to bring more states to actively support it. The Forum further aims to strengthen dialogue on lessons-learned, good practices and challenges related to the regulation of PMSCs." see https://www.icrc.org/en/document/private-military-and-security-companies-implementation-montreux-document#.VJRHuUAOBtw.

17 Seventeen governments have been involved in the development of the *Montreux Document*: Afghanistan, Angola, Australia, Austria, Canada, China, France, Germany, Iraq, Poland, Sierra Leone, South Africa, Sweden, Switzerland, the United Kingdom of Great Britain and Northern Ireland, the Ukraine and the United States of America.

18 ICoC, *International Code of Conduct for Private Security Service Providers*, 09 November 2010, para 3, http://www.icoca.ch/en/the_icoc (accessed on 30.08.2015).

19 Regarding the drafting history see http://www.dcaf.ch/Project/International-Code-of-Conduct-for-Private-Security-Service-Providers (accessed on 30.08.2015).

20 ICoC (2010), para 11.

21 http://www.dcaf.ch/Project/International-Code-of-Conduct-for-Private-Security-Service-Providers (accessed on 30.08.2015). Only 88 companies are currently members of the ICoC-Association [see http://www.icoca.ch/en/membership?private_security_companies=companies&op=Search&view_type=list&form_id=_search_for_members_filter_form (accessed on 30.08.2015)].

Regarding the question of legal traction, the ICoC shows – similar to the EITI standard – direct implications in national legislations. A recent example is the 2014 adopted Swiss *Federal Law about Private Security Services provided Abroad.*[22] Its article 31 para 1 lit. b makes the membership and the compliance with the ICoC a mandatory precondition for private security companies to receive a public contract. Similar transferals can be found in the UK and other states.[23]

This development demonstrates once more the possible fruitful interrelations between originally governance driven multi-stakeholder norm shaping initiatives and their uptake in government driven classical legal norm-shaping processes. At the same time the ICoC is an illustrative example of partly concurring approaches of *private* governance-driven multi-stakeholder initiatives and *state-based* legislative procedures in international law. The topic of regulating private security providers is already since the late 1980's a hot discussed issue within several UN institutions. Especially with regard to the human rights compliance of these corporations, the 2005 established the *UN Working Group on the Use of Mercenaries as a Means of violating Human Rights and impeding the Exercise of the Right of Peoples to Self-Determination* as a clear signal of the regulative ownership of the UN.

The working group's mandate includes next to its monitor function *inter alia* the task "to elaborate and present concrete proposals on possible complementary and new standards aimed at filling existing gaps, as well as general guidelines or basic principles encouraging the further protection of human rights" as well as "to seek opinions and contributions from Governments and intergovernmental and non-governmental organisations on questions relating to its mandate" (UN Doc E/CN.4/RES/2005/2 para 12). Corporations are not mentioned as stakeholders of the process at all.

Up to now, the Working Group did not produce any regulative output with regard to its human rights related task, except a concept note on a possible legally

22 http://www.admin.ch/opc/de/federal-gazette/2013/7353.pdf.

23 Within its *National Action Plan* regarding the implementation of the *UN Guiding Principles on Business and Human Rights*, the UK government commits to "engage with state and non-state clients to urge them to commit to contracting only with PSCs that are pursuing certification against recognised standards by accredited certifying bodies, and membership of the ICOC Association" [see HM Government (2013), *Good Business – Implementing the UN Guiding Principles on Business and Human Rights*, 11 lit. ii (online available at: https://www.gov.uk/government/uploads/system/uploads/attachment_data/file/236901/BHR_Action_Plan_-_final_online_version_1_.pdf].

binding instrument for the regulation of private military security companies.[24] Comparing these non-developments in the UN-Framework with the practical legal success of the corresponding corporate ICoC-Initiative, the concrete example of regulating private security companies demonstrates perfectly, how private actors overtook the complete norm-shaping and -setting agency.

4. The Devil Takes the Hindmost – Theoretical Challenges

Whereas it seems quite easy to describe these phenomena of coexisting, overlapping, and mutually reinforcing regulative approaches in general governance terms, mainstream international law scholarship misses already the right vocabulary to tackle the trend in the first place, since these developments obviously are taking place outside their self-defined classical disciplinary arena. New actors are involved that do not fit in the existing "subjects" categories of international law and new norm-reservoirs are approached that question the canon of accepted "sources" of the discipline.

In recent years different attempts were undertaken in the candy shop of legal theory to change that. One can think of the discussion on global legal pluralism as represented by Paul Schiff Berman and others (see e.g. Berman, 2012), the suggestion of informal international law making by Joost Pauwelyn, Ramses Wessel and Jan Wouters (see Pauwelyn, Wessel, & Wouters, 2012), Fabrizio Cafaggi's project on the enforcement of transnational private regulations (see Cafaggi, 2012), the theory of regulatory hybridisation in the global sphere by Puol Kjaer and others (see Jurčys, Kjaer, & Yatsunami, 2013) or the discourse on global law without a state as argued by Gunter Teubner and his followers (see Teubner, 1997; Teubner, 2012). A common denominator of these theories is that they try to make the alternative regulative approaches fruitful for the international law discourse itself by blurring the dogmatic frontiers.

Nevertheless, the dominant community of international law scholars is quite stranded and defensive towards this emerging regulative phenomenon. Keeping in mind, that the amalgamation of private global governance standards and legal approaches is already broadly taking place in the legal reality on national and international level, the dogmatic ostrich tactic does not seem to be a promising solution to the problem. Particularly, since these changes affect (international) law-making in general as well as the norm-shaping and -enforcement of human rights norms in particular (see e.g. Augenstein, 2013, pp. 59–63).

24 http://www.ohchr.org/EN/Issues/Mercenaries/WGMercenaries/Pages/IssuesFocus.aspx (accessed on 15.09.2015).

Only an intensified dialogue between the mainly political science driven global governance scholarship and international law scholarship could help to better bridge the practical problems. The ironic thing about it is, that – with a few exceptions (see e.g. de Búrca, Keohane, & Sabel, 2014, 477) – the community of international law scholars seems to miss the fact that international law itself is – whether they want it or not – already an important research object within the global governance discourse.

Even though the practical consequences of these transplants of new governance approaches especially in the human rights arena are eminent and promising, since they seem to close existing implementation gaps, a thorough analysis of the relationship and interdependencies of these new regulative approaches to classical legal approaches of norm-shaping and regulation in international human rights law is not done yet.

One has to distinguish between the material and the formal dimension of this new development. Regarding the material content of these norms, the entailed cognitive learning processes of enhanced cooperation are definitely to be welcomed since it opens up an opportunity for the legal system to integrate available practical knowledge from its surrounding social structures (see e.g. Weber, 2014, pp. 5–10). At the same time – as demonstrated in the two practical examples above – the formal legislators are buying into not only the material norms but also procedural aspects with regard to reporting and grievance mechanisms that are entailed in most of the standards.

In particular unsolved is the problem, how these parallel grievance mechanisms – as they are for example foreseen in the planned individual complaint procedure of the ICoC Association – are related to state driven court procedures. Or to put it a little more frankly, do we trust the cat to keep the cream? Furthermore it is not clear, what should happen, if private human rights standards – on which national and international legislators are referring to (as in the example of the EITI) – change with regard to their content.

And last but not least one has to raise the questions of procedural legitimacy, transparency and participation in the relevant norm-creating and -shaping process itself. Even though the idea of multi-stakeholder norm-shaping is hyped as *the* truly effective norm-creating procedure, at least within legal scholarship not much thoughts are made about procedural preconditions of such processes, even though in legal practice the results of these private processes are already widely implemented.[25]

5. Conclusions

This short analysis of the nature and evolution of corporate human rights standards in the human rights arena highlights their tremendous influences on the current norm-shaping and norm-setting process on the national as well as the international level. Furthermore it exemplifies roughly the oscillating movement between private global governance initiatives and the public international law framework as well as the struggle of legal scholarship to tackle the dogmatic problems raised by these new instruments. In general, these initiatives can be read as a reasonable material expansion of the human rights framework on new categories of actors (such as corporations), which was initially intended by the *UN Guiding Principles on Business and Human Rights.*

However, the self-reflecting reshaping and interpretation of human rights norms by private actors and the unchecked reintroduction of these standards in the legal realm – as was illustrated in the two practical examples (EITI & ICoC) – can bear eminent risks. Most obvious examples are cases where such private initiatives tame or substitute classical legal regulation by states.

This shall not be read as a plea for an exclusive state-driven approach to the realisation of an effective human rights protection framework. But due to the fact that the heavy load of the legal responsibility to realise a functioning protection framework still rests exclusively on the shoulders of the states, they should at least be aware of the potential negative influences by the legal implementation of private standards.

Therefore, a more thorough analysis with regard to the current outsourcing of international norm-shaping and enforcement in the human rights arena seems to be appropriate. A promising way to minimise the risks of conflicts could be to resolve the existing lack of control over private global governance initiatives by developing legal procedural safeguards, as for example the definition of minimal requirements regarding the institutional dimension of private human rights standards and the related norm-shaping processes.

25 For minimal requirements of experimental global governance mechanisms see e.g. de Búrca/Keohane/Sabel, 2014, pp. 478–480. Regarding the concrete case of the ICoC Initiative see Jägers, 2013, pp. 306–314 (regarding the need for transparency) and Richemond-Barak, 2014, pp. 802–815 (regarding legitimacy, participation and monitoring).

References

Aaronson, Susan Ariel. 2011. Limited Partnership: Business, Government, Civil Society, and the Public in the Extractive Industries Transparency Initiative (EITI), *Public Administration and Development* 31:1, 50–63.

Addo, Michael. 2014. The Reality of the United Nations Guiding Principles on Business and Human Rights. *Human Rights Law Review* 14, 133–147.

Alvarez, Jose E. 2011. Are Corporations "Subjects" of International Law? *Santa Clara Journal of International Law* 9:1, 1–35.

Arnold, Denis G. 2010. Transnational Corporations and the Duty to Respect Basic Human Rights. *Business Ethics Quarterly* 20:3, 371–399.

Augenstein, Daniel. 2013. The Crisis of International Human Rights Law in the Global Market Economy. *Netherlands Yearbook of International Law* 44:3, 41–64.

Benvenisti, Eyal. 2014. The Law of Global Governance (= Collected Courses of the Hague Academy of International Law 2013, Vol. 368). Leiden/Boston: Martinus Nijhoff Publishers.

Berman, Paul Schiff. 2012. Global legal pluralism: a jurisprudence of law beyond borders. Cambridge/New York: Cambridge University Press.

Buhmann, Karin. 2012. The Development of the UN Framework: A Pragmatic Process Towards a Pragmatic Output. In: The UN Guiding Principles on Business and Human Rights: Foundations and Implementation, edited by Mares, Radu. 85–105. Leiden/Boston: Martinus Nijhoff Publishers.

Cafaggi, Fabrizio. 2012. Introduction: The transformation of transnational private regulation – enforcement gaps and governance design. In: Enforcement of Transnational Regulation – Ensuring Compliance in a Global World, edited by Cafaggi, Fabrizio. 1–38. Cheltenham/Northhampton: Edward Elgar.

de Búrca, Gráinne; Keohane, Robert O. and Sabel, Charles. 2014. Global Experimentalist Governance. *British Journal of Political Science* 44:3, 477–486.

Hansen, Robin F. 2015. MNEs as Enterprises in International Law. In: Responsibilities of the Non-State Actors in Armed Conflicts and the Market Place – Theoretical Considerations and Empirical Findings, edited by Gal-Or, Noemi, Ryngaert, Cedric and Noortmann, Math, 127–153. Leiden/Boston: Brill Nijhoff.

Jägers, Nicola. 2013. Will transnational private regulation close the governance gap? In: Human Rights Obligations of Business – Beyond the Corporate Responsibility to Respect? edited by Deva, Surya and Bilchitz, David. 295–328. Cambridge: Cambridge University Press.

Jurčys, Paulius, Kjaer, Poul F. and Yatsunami, Ren 2013. Regulatory Hybridization in the Transnational Sphere. Leiden/Boston: Martinus Nijhoff Publishers.

Koroma, Abdul G. 2009. The Effects of Globalization on the Development of International Law. In: Globalisation – the State and International Law, edited by Hobe, Stephan. 25–33. Stuttgart: Franz Steiner.

Mares, Radu. 2009. Voluntary Reporting: The Global Compact. In: International Human Rights Monitoring Mechanisms. Essays in Honour of Jakob Th. Möller, edited by Alfredsson, Gudmundur; Grimheden, Jonas; Ramcharan, Bertrand G. and Zayas Alfred. 385–398. 2. Ed. Leiden: Nijhoff.

Morrison, Jason and Roht-Arriaza, Naomi. 2008. Private and Quasi-Private Standard Setting. In: The Oxford Handbook of International Environmental Law, edited by Bodansky, Daniel; Brunnée, Jutta and Hey, Ellen, 498–527. Oxford: Oxford University Press.

Nolan, Justine. 2013. The corporate responsibility to respect human rights: soft law or not law? In: Human Rights Obligations of Business – Beyond the Corporate Responsibility to Respect? edited by Deva, Surya and Bilchitz, David. 138–161. Cambridge: Cambridge University Press.

Pauwelyn, Joost; Wessel, Ramses and Wouters, Jan. 2012. An Introduction to Informal International Lawmaking. In: Informal International Law Making, edited by Pauwelyn, Joost, Wessel Ramses and Wouters, Jan. 1–10. Oxford: Oxford University Press.

Preuss, Lutz and Brown, Donna 2012. Business Policies on Human Rights: An Analysis of Their Content and Prevalence among FTSE 100 Firms. *Journal of Business Ethics* 109:3, 289–299.

Ramasastry, Anita. 2015. Corporate Social Responsibility versus Business and Human Rights: Bridging the Gap between Responsibility and Accountability. *Journal of Human Rights* 14:2, 237–259.

Riechemond-Barak, Daphné. 2014. Can Self-Regulation Work? Lessons from the Private Security and Military Industry. *Michigan Journal of International Law* 35:4, 773–826.

Ruggie John Gerard. 2014. Global Governance and "New Governance Theory": Lessons from Business and Human Rights. In *Global Governance* 20: 5–17.

Santoro, Michael A. 2015. Business and Human Rights in Historical Perspective. *Journal of Human Rights* 14:2, 155–161.

Teubner, Gunter. 1997. Global Law without a State. Aldershot: Dartmouth.

Teubner, Gunter. 2012. Constitutional Fragments – societal constitutionalism and globalization. Oxford: Oxford University Press.

Weber, Rolf H. 2014. Multilayer Governance as a Theoretical Foundation of Enhanced Cooperation [http://www.internetsociety.org/doc/multilayer-governance-theoretical-foundation-enhanced-cooperation-rolf-h-weber, accessed on 30.08.2015]

Weissbrodt, David and Kruger, Muria. 2005. Human Rights Responsibilities of Businesses as Non-State Actors. In: Non-State Actors and Human Rights, edited by Philip Alston, 315–351. Oxford: Oxford University Press.

Wettstein, Florian 2012. CSR and the Debate on Business and Human Rights: Bridging the Great Divide. *Business Ethics Quarterly* 22:4, 739–770.

Axelle Reiter

State Responsibility for Private Breaches of International Law and the Horizontal Application of Human Rights

Abstract
The privileged position of human rights in the international legal system has led to their horizontal application to interpersonal relations between private actors in order to integrate the relevant international rules in all spheres of society. This paper analyses the invocation of human rights and humanitarian law against private actors at three levels: the direct effect of international norms in interpersonal conflicts before domestic courts; the indirect effect of international norms between private actors by invocation of states' international responsibility before international courts; and the direct applicability of international norms to non-state actors in international trials or domestic trials based on universal jurisdiction.

1. Introduction

The privileged position of human rights in the international legal system has led to their horizontal application to interpersonal relations between private actors. Universal rules have revolutionised the conception of normativity at the international level. The Charter of the United Nations recognises the emergence of community interests that supersede bilateralism and it entrenches the ideas of international public order and core normative values, shared by all humanity with an aim to protect each and every single human being against instances of aggression and abuse. In this perspective, it is important to integrate the relevant international rules in all spheres of society, to "prioritise the rights of [the individual] over those of the traditionally defined community" and to have them sanctioned by national legal orders (see Hossain, 1994, pp. 486–487), to pronounce the state liable when it enables or fails to prevent private abuses (Cook, 1994), and to entitle the victims to file lawsuits in front of domestic or international institutions (Knop, 1994, 159).

This paper studies the role played by global governance and multilevel constitutionalism in the horizontalisation of fundamental freedoms and entitlements and examines the methods available to apply human rights in interpersonal relations. It analyses the shared responsibility of states and non-state actors for private breaches of international norms, focusing on the accountability of states parties to human rights and humanitarian treaties, as the perfect illustration of the materialisation of the international legal integration process through a normative hierarchy and of a universal substantive law.[1]

Only states parties to supranational instruments are required to respect their provisions. However, various dispositions of these international agreements imply an absolute application of their terms to interpersonal relations and their supervisory organs increasingly refer to states' positive obligations. The responsibility of states can be invoked on account of their failure to legislate or take other preventive measures against private violations of international norms and by reason of the judgements of domestic courts and tribunals that legitimise these infringements or refuse to compensate their victims.

The invocation of human rights and humanitarian rules against private actors plays at three levels, which this paper explores in turn. First, it raises the question of the direct effect of public international law in interpersonal conflicts in front of domestic courts and tribunals. Second, the international condemnation of public authorities for violations of individual rights by private actors entails that international documents have indirect effects on private relations. Third, the fast growth of international criminal law over the last two decades contributes to the direct applicability of international dispositions to non-state actors, be it in front of supranational or municipal courts and tribunals.

The following analysis mostly focuses on the dispositions implemented at the level of the Council of Europe, and related case law, because of the specific position they occupy in the legal systems of its member states and the comparative strength of the mechanisms controlling their respect. Without possessing the same force as EU regulations, the European Convention on Human Rights benefits from a particular supra-contractual status in international law, similar to that of constitutional instruments and grounded in the peremptory nature of

---

1 As the founding text of this organisation, the UN Charter applies immediately and without exceptions or reservations to all its members. It obliges states worldwide to abide by its provisions and is effectively analogous to an actual social contract. The transfer of competences from the domestic to the supranational level and the devolution of traditional state prerogatives to the international community are irreversible, providing legitimacy for a universal legal order and its institutions. This constitutionalisation process and the higher rank assigned to the basic principles entrenched in the UN Charter ground the notion of *ius cogens* or peremptory norms of general international law at the basis of the substantive unity of the international system. Peremptory norms create a normative hierarchy and function as a Hartian rule of recognition for the international legal system (see Reiter, 2012); namely, they serve as criteria for the validity of legal provisions at the international level.

its provisions. It consecrates the evolution from the classical vision of state sovereignty towards a liberal conception of international sovereignty. International sovereignty ultimately takes its roots in an inalienable liberal right to liberty and self-determination of all individuals. International human rights law constitutes the personal rights of each and every individual into universal absolute obligations that the international community owes to her because of her humanity.

This peculiarity has been confirmed by the European Court of Human Rights, in 1978, in the interstate case opposing the Republic of Ireland to the UK. Called "to clarify the nature of the engagements placed under its supervision" by an argument of the Irish government, the Court declared that, "unlike international treaties of the classic kind, the Convention comprises more than mere reciprocal engagements between contracting states" and that it creates a set of "objective obligations which [...] benefit from a collective enforcement." Furthermore, it touched upon the problem of its applicability to third parties, by adding that "the Convention does not merely oblige the higher authorities of the contracting states to respect for their own part the rights and freedoms it embodies" but "also has the consequence that, in order to secure the enjoyment of those rights and freedoms, those authorities must prevent or remedy any breach at subordinate levels."[2]

2. Horizontal Application of Human Rights Norms in Domestic Law

The applicability of human rights conventions to interpersonal relations is primarily a concern at the national level, where they are normally raised. This practice coincides with the general approach to the question in public international law. National courts and tribunals are the primary organs entrusted with the competence and power to enforce international dispositions on a daily basis (see *e.g.* Conforti, 1993). More specifically, the protection of international human rights provisions falls first under the control of the national judiciary of the country exercising jurisdiction over the holders of fundamental freedoms and entitlements.

It has been put forward that the sole secure way to safeguard the respect of human rights instruments is to delegate the oversight of their domestic application to municipal organs (Sciotti, 1997, pp. 15–16). Although the frequent breaches of individual rights by public authorities undermine this claim, monitoring their respect at the national level facilitates the elimination of private abuses and should be welcomed. In any case, national courts and tribunals are bound to secure

2 ECHR, *Ireland v. UK*, 18 Jan. 1978, § 239.

human rights in their interpretation of domestic rules and their assessment of divergent legal solutions, in order to dodge engaging the state's responsibility under international law.

Several dispositions of the European Convention on Human Rights offer a sound foundation for the direct effect of this document between private persons. First, the English text of Article 1 declares that "the high contracting parties shall secure to everyone within their jurisdiction the rights and freedoms defined in [...] this convention." The choice of the words "shall secure" rather than "protect" or "respect" translates an idea of absolute effect of the liberties listed.

Secondly, Article 13 stipulates that "everyone whose rights and freedoms as set forth in this convention are violated shall have an effective remedy before a national authority notwithstanding that the violation has been committed by persons acting in an official capacity." Thereby, it indicates that international law is equally concerned with infractions perpetrated by other agents than public officials. In addition, the notion of effective remedy imposes on states to provide domestic redress to all victims of public or private abuses.

Thirdly, the availability of remedies against breaches of human rights is not only entrenched in Article 13 but also in the core of each particular provision. In this light, the European Court of Human Rights judges that the failure to investigate individual claims concerning violations of Articles 2 and 3 of the Convention or to condemn the culprits constitutes in itself a breach of the Convention, independent of the actual role and involvement of state actors.[3]

Fourthly, Article 17 of the European Convention pleads even more fervently for its direct application between private persons. By stating that "nothing in this convention may be interpreted as implying for any state, group or person any right to engage in any activity or perform any act aimed at the destruction of any of the rights and freedoms" or "their limitation to a greater extent than is provided for in the Convention," Article 17 bans *expressis verbis* the infringement of protected freedoms and entitlements by public and private actors alike. It outlaws "liberticidal" or freedom-curtailing activities, constrains private agents to respect the basic rights of other people, creates positive obligations for states to safeguard personal autonomy and self-determination to everyone, and grants a right of action to wronged right-holders.

Fifthly, Articles 6 § 1, 8, 9, 10 and 11 of the Convention, Article 2 § 3 of the Fourth Protocol and Article 5 of the Seventh Protocol admit particular limitations in order to protect the rights of others. Subsequently, the rights to public trial,

3 See *infra*, section III.

privacy and family life, religion, expression, association and assembly, free movement, and equality of spouses in relation to their children can solely be exercised in full consideration of other persons' liberties and entitlements.

Sixthly, the wording of the articles that consecrate individual rights decisively argues in favour of an interpersonal application of the European Convention, by specifying either that "everyone has the right" or "shall be entitled to" something, or that "no one shall be" the object of a given abuse. This choice of formulation accentuates the idea of subjective claims *in rem* opposable *erga omnes*.

A similar application of human rights provisions in interpersonal relations can be deduced from the text of other conventions approved in the frame of the Council of Europe, the UN and the Organisation of American States, as well as from the positions expressed by the organs in charge of monitoring their respect. In 1992, the United Nations Committee competent to protect women's rights issued a general recommendation on violence against women, which explicitly proscribes such acts, independently of their public or private character.[4] At the level of the Council of Europe, Article 6 § 2 of the 1995 Framework Convention for the Protection of National Minorities engages states parties "to take appropriate measures to protect persons who may be subject to threats or acts of discrimination, hostility or violence as a result of their ethnic, cultural, linguistic or religious identity." Article 6 has a broad personal scope, in the sense that it protects against discrimination and hatred of all people residing in states parties and not just the members of minority groups, and it consecrates the negative and penalising aspect of complementary dispositions. The Advisory Committee controlling the respect of the relevant provisions demands that states prosecute and punish discriminatory actions and hate crimes (see Gilbert, 2005, pp. 187–191). The 2011 Istanbul Convention on Preventing and Combating Violence against Women and Domestic Violence goes beyond and provides for changes in the perceptions and prejudices of private individuals.

From the standpoint of the horizontal application of human rights law in interpersonal relations, the International Convention on the Elimination of All Forms of Discrimination Against Women constitutes the most activist instrument espoused in the UN's framework. The Preamble of the Convention pleads for a transformation of the existing society and out-dated gender roles. This progressive program is confirmed in the core of the document. Article 2 stipulates that "states parties condemn discrimination against women in all its forms" and

4 CEDAW, *General Recommendation No 19 (11) on Violence against Women*, 29 Jan. 1992.

"agree to pursue by all appropriate means and without delay a policy of eliminating discrimination against women;" an obligation reinforced by Articles 3 and 24.

States are bound to use all avenues at their disposition to suppress discrimination by private actors. They are responsible for the offences of individuals, groups or organisations, and are supposed to punish them. In practice, states should compensate the victims of discrimination and penalise the offenders. Article 5 prescribes the elimination of prejudices and stereotypes, even if they are culturally or religiously rooted. Therefore, reliance on established customs and practices cannot be accepted any longer as an excuse for failing to defend human rights and non-interference with the "personal affairs" of a community violates the text of the agreement. Then again, this last requirement would benefit from being qualified, taking into consideration the actual experiences, views, and perceptions of the women living in the targeted communities.

3. Indirect Effect Between Private Persons at the International Level

Third party application of international law is not restricted solely to domestic courts and tribunals. On the contrary, it is much discussed at the international level. Whereas individuals cannot be called and tried in front of the human rights oversight mechanisms for violation of other persons' rights, their breaches of international law receive an indirect sanction by summoning the state involved.

A double question arises at this level: the obligation of individuals to respect human rights, and the corollary issue of states' international liability for private acts attributable to their citizens or other people residing on their national territory. This second part of the question would then allow, indirectly, the horizontal application of human rights provisions, by putting pressure on states and forcing them to adopt legislation or judgements protecting private persons from each other. The extent of states' accountability for the deeds of non-public authorities needs to be assessed carefully, though, since the conduct of some private actors, like terrorist organisations, may prove extremely difficult to control, deter, or influence.

First and foremost, in general public international law, states' responsibility may be engaged both for actions and for omissions, as recognised by several decisions of the International Court of Justice.[5] As a result of their accountability

---

5 ICJ, *Corfu Channel*, 9 Apr. 1949, p. 23; ICJ, *United States Diplomatic and Consular Staff in Tehran*, 24 May 1980, p. 31-ff.; ICJ, *Application of the Convention on the Prevention and Punishment of the Crime of Genocide*, 11 July 1996, p. 615-ff.

for omissions, states may be penalised for not taking all appropriate measures to prevent or repress international offences and for failing to provide satisfactory compensation to the victims. As soon as their responsibility is confirmed, states themselves are presumed guilty for the infringements.

Along these lines, the organs of the Council of Europe have repetitively affirmed that states are not exclusively supposed to abstain from violating fundamental freedoms and entitlements. They are additionally compelled to put in place positive measures for them to be successfully protected, some of which relate to the conduct of private persons (see e.g. Warbrick, 1983, 95).[6] In particular, Article 2 of the European Convention "may also imply in certain well-defined circumstances a positive obligation on the authorities to take preventive operational measures to protect an individual whose life is at risk from the criminal acts of another individual." The European Court of Human Rights interprets this requisite "in a way which does not impose an impossible or disproportionate burden on the authorities"[7] and is usually reluctant to condemn states on the basis of their positive duties under Article 2.

Second, aside from the recognition of states' international responsibility for omissions, plaintiffs may invoke the doctrinal theory of "state complicity" and call for the attribution of private attacks to the state in case of public complicity or official complaisance. For example, states are accomplices and thus accountable whenever their domestic courts and tribunals tolerate the execution of a contract that includes discriminatory clauses (see Lauterpacht, 1950, pp. 154–160, 340–341).

Third, due to the wording of the international rules protecting the right to an effective remedy, states cannot escape liability by claiming that it was a private person that perpetrated the infraction.

Fourth, the European Court of Human Rights judges that Articles 2 and 3 of the European Convention protect rights so important that the respect of these provisions encompasses implicit procedural commitments in supplement to states explicit substantive duties. It is more willing to find a breach of states' substantive undertakings in the absence of an adequate inquest. Moreover, procedural duties benefit from the same absolute character as states' negative obligations under

6 ECommissionHR, *National Union of Belgian Police v. Belgium*, 27 May 1974, § 59; ECommissionHR, *De Geillustreerdre Pers NV v. Netherlands*, 6 July 1976; ECommissionHR, *Young, James and Webster v. UK*, 14 Dec. 1979, §§ 168–169; ECHR, *X and Y v. Netherlands*, 26 Mar. 1985, § 23; ECHR, *Plattform 'Ärtzte für das Leben' v. Austria*, 21 June 1988, § 32.

7 ECHR, *Osman v. UK*, 28 Oct. 1998, §§ 115–116.

Articles 2 and 3.[8] Lastly, the Court considers that the prominence of inalienable rights justifies increased constraints under Article 13.

The procedural branch of Articles 2 and 3 obliges states to organise efficient enquiries and to criminalise and prosecute any infringement of the rights to life and physical integrity, whether public or private. In such cases, the award of damages to the victims of violations or their families does not meet the prerequisites of an effective remedy. For instance, the European Court of Human Rights has condemned the UK under Article 3 for having left unpunished the private mistreatment of children.[9] Likewise, it has applied proactive judicial developments elaborated to penalise systemic acts of violence, by the police forces of several states parties to the European Convention against members of the Roma minority, to cases of unsanctioned hate crimes.[10]

This jurisprudence has been praised for its creativity and its acknowledgement of the pre-eminence of an evaluation *in concreto* of the protection of fundamental rights. The assertion that "some human rights violations should properly be the subject of criminal proceedings against the individuals involved, as opposed to simply civil action against the state which they represent" (see Livingstone, 1999, 74), coupled with the necessity to investigate and punish private offences, implies that basic rights ought to be fully horizontalised and respected by public and private persons alike.

4. Direct Effect Between Private Persons at the International Level

At the international level, direct applicability of human rights rules against third parties would require a modification of the existing agreements or new additional protocols. The necessity of either option remains questionable due to the backlog created by the high number of applications introduced against states parties. Whereas human rights conventions do not foresee actively any punishment for private actors who violate the rights of others, international monitoring bodies have dismissed these people's claims to protection by declaring their applications

8 ECHR, *Aksoy v. Turkey*, 18 Dec. 1996, §§ 97–99.

9 ECHR, *A v. UK*, req. No 25599/94, 23 Sept. 1998; ECHR, *Z et al. v. UK*, req. No 29392/95, 10 May 2001.

10 ECHR, *Šečić v. Croatia*, 31 May 2007, §§ 52–59 and 66–70; ECHR, *Angelova and Iliev v. Bulgaria*, 26 July 2007, §§ 93–105 and 116; ECHR, *Koky et al. v. Slovakia*, 12 June 2012, §§ 213–215 and 239–240; ECHR, *Fedorchenko and Lozenko v. Ukraine*, 20 Sept. 2012, § 41.

inadmissible, under Article 35 § 3 of the European Convention, Article 3 of the Optional Protocol to the International Covenant on Civil and Political Rights and Article 47 of the Inter-American Convention, on grounds of incompatibility with the provisions of these treaties or of abuse of the right to petition.[11] Otherwise, they reject them as abusive under Article 17 of the European Convention, Article 5 § 1 of the Covenant and Article 29 (a) of the Inter-American Convention.[12] Besides, they interpret the scope of protected freedoms and entitlements in a manner compatible with the respect of other people's rights. So, the European Court of Human Rights considers that, to qualify as such, "philosophical convictions" must be worthy of protection in a democratic society and, hence, respectful of human dignity.[13] In comparison to the now well-established indirect application of human rights to private relations, their direct effect between individuals and other non-state actors in the international sphere still remains largely inexistent.

Human rights instruments have been applied directly between private persons in front of domestic courts and indirectly through the invocation of state responsibility before international supervisory organs. The combination of existing control methods allows international judges to press domestic authorities to apply international human rights norms in interpersonal disputes, by condemning states whose judiciary does not recognise them such direct effect. In contrast, it is usually assumed that they may not receive any direct horizontal application at the international level. This affirmation needs to be seriously qualified and elaborated upon, in view of the creeping expansion of supranational criminal enforcement mechanisms; including the extensive case law of the two *ad hoc* International Criminal Tribunals for the former Yugoslavia and Rwanda, the creation of the International Criminal Court, and the elaboration of so-called "hybrid" alternatives to domestic trials in transitional settings. Another question to be considered in this view is the universal jurisdiction of municipal courts and tribunals over international crimes, including grave human rights violations that qualify as crimes against humanity.

11 EComHR, *Ilse Koch v. FRG*, 8 Mar. 1962, pp. 134–137; ECHR, *Volkmer v. FRG*, 22 Nov. 2001; ECHR, *Petersen v. FRG*, 22 Nov. 2001.

12 ECHR, *Witzsch v. FRG*, 20 Apr. 1999; ECHR, *Schimanek v. Austria*, 1 Feb. 2000; ECHR, *Garaudy v. France*, 24 June 2003; ECHR, *WP et al. v. Poland*, req. No 42264/98, 2 Sept. 2004; ECHR, *Norwood v. UK*, 16 Nov. 2004; ECHR, *Witzsch v. FRG (2nd case)*, 13 Dec. 2005; HR Committee, *JRT and the Western Guard Party v. Canada*, 6 Apr. 1983; HR Committee, *MA v. Italy*, req. No 117/1981, 10 Apr. 1984.

13 ECHR, *Campbell and Cosans v. UK*, 25 Feb. 1982, §§ 36–37; ECHR, *Refah Partisi v. Turkey*, 31 July 2001, § 52.

Owing to these parallel trends, the prospects for a direct application of human rights dispositions in private interactions have significantly improved.

Some international conventions already have a direct horizontal effect and allow bringing individuals on trial either before international bodies or before domestic courts and tribunals, by relying on universal jurisdiction clauses. The Inter-American Court of Human Rights addressed this question in its advisory opinion concerning states' liability for laws that violate the Inter-American Convention. The Court recognises that "international law may grant rights to individuals and, conversely, may also determine that certain acts or omissions on their part could make them criminally liable under that law." Yet, it concedes that "at the present time individual responsibility may only be invoked for violations that are defined in international instruments as crimes under international law, such as crimes against peace, war crimes, and crimes against humanity or genocide." What regards those crimes, "it is of no consequence that they are committed by enforcing a law of the state to which the agent or official belongs," since "the fact that the action complies with domestic law is no justification from the point of view of international law." The Court concludes that, "as far as concerns the human rights protected by the Convention, the jurisdiction of the organs established thereunder refer exclusively to the international responsibility of states and not to that of individuals." But it judiciously observes that, "if these violations were also to constitute international crimes, they would, in addition, give rise to individual responsibility."[14]

The International Criminal Court has a purely complementary or subsidiary jurisdiction over international crimes, in the event of domestic reluctance to put on trial their authors. Prosecution on the basis of universal jurisdiction, which is not submitted to the principle of subsidiarity, might thus take precedence over it. It has been defended that permissive universal jurisdiction applies whenever the offence is universally condemned in the international legal order and that *ius cogens* violations entail mandatory universal jurisdiction and the inapplicability of all immunities, including heads of state immunities.[15] Incidentally, if such a view was accepted, the prescription to punish the authors of grave breaches of human rights would have to be considered a peremptory norm of international law; just like the prosecution of suspects of crimes against humanity is sometimes conceived to be (see Cassese, 2000, 623). In the present state of public international

---

14 ACHR, *International Responsibility for the Promulgation and Enforcement of Laws in Violation of the Convention*, 9 Dec. 1994, §§ 51–57.

15 ICTY, *Furundžija (Lašva Valley)*, IT-95–17/1-T, Judgement, 10 Dec. 1998, § 156.

law, both claims remain highly contentious. By opposition, the consolidation of international criminal justice has led to an increase in the number of international crimes tried by national judiciaries, be it through penal avenues or by means of civil liability and corrective justice. These solutions could be extended to cover human rights violations by private actors. Concerning this last point, it is important to keep in mind that the primary purpose of human rights treaties is the protection of fundamental freedoms and entitlements *ex ante*, rather than the punishment *ex post* of the culprits.

5. Conclusion

Private violations of individual rights present a challenge for the international legal order and its traditional focus on state actions. The main function of international human rights law is to effectively safeguard individual freedoms and entitlements, by regulating the behaviour of state actors and delineating the limits of interpersonal relations. Public authorities are bound to take them into account when they judge interpersonal disputes and adjudicate conflicting claims. In the absence of domestic control over the respect of fundamental freedoms and entitlements, states may be held internationally accountable for the private abuses that the lack of enforcement of their positive obligations under international law has facilitated. On top of this, international organs stigmatise the failure to properly investigate grave human rights abuses and offer redress to their victims as distinct violations of these provisions. Finally, most of the gravest violations of individual liberties are directly sanctioned at the supranational level. Universal jurisdiction clauses have been inserted in numerous international agreements, while human rights supervisory organs consider that international treaties protect basic rights on the condition that they are not exercised in a detrimental fashion and reject other claims as if they were out of their scope or declare them inadmissible. These legal advances provide evidence of the direct application of human rights as side constraints on all actions, independent of the public or private character of the agent, and the evolution of the international legal system away from the classical Westphalian model towards global governance and transnational constitutionalism.

References

Cassese, Antonio. 2000. La répression des infractions internationales. In: Droit international pénal, edited by Ascenscio, Hervé; Decaux, Emmanuel and Pellet, Alain. 621–631. Paris: Pedone.

Conforti, Benedetto. 1993. International Law and the Role of Domestic Legal Systems. Dordrecht: Nijhoff.

Cook, Rebecca. J. 1994. State Accountability under the Convention on the Elimination of All Forms of Discrimination against Women. In: Human Rights of Women: National and International Perspectives, edited by Cook, Rebecca J. 228–256. Philadelphia: University of Pennsylvania.

Gilbert Geoff. 2005. Article 6. In: The Rights of Minorities in Europe: A Commentary on the European Framework Convention for the Protection of National Minorities. edited by Weller, Marc. 177–191. Oxford: Oxford University Press.

Hossain, Sara. 1994. Equality in the Home: Women's Rights and Personal Laws in South Asia. In: Human Rights of Women: National and International Perspectives, edited by Cook, Rebecca J., 465–494. Philadelphia: University of Pennsylvania.

Knop, Karen. 1994. Why Rethinking the Sovereign State Is Important for Women's International Human Rights Law. In: Human Rights of Women: National and International Perspectives, edited by Cook, Rebecca J. 153–164. Philadelphia: University of Pennsylvania.

Lauterpacht, Hersch. 1950. International Law and Human Rights. London: Steven.

Livingstone, Stephen. 1999. Non-Derogable Rights, the Interests of the Nation and International Order. In: Dignité humaine et hiérarchie des valeurs: Les limites irréductibles, edited by S. Marcus-Helmons, 59–85. Brussels: Bruylant.

Reiter, Axelle. 2012. Hedgehogs, Foxes and Hart's Rule of Recognition: The Concept of Law in the post-Westphalian International Legal Order. Central and Eastern European Forum Yearbook.

Sciotti, Claudia. 1997. La concurrence des traités relatifs aux droits de l'homme devant le juge national. Brussels: Bruylant.

Warbrick, Colin. 1983. The European Convention on Human Rights and the Prevention of Terrorism. International and Comparative Law Quarterly 32: 82–119.

Part V. Global Governance, Transgeneration Justice, and Rights of the Future Generations

Miklós Könczöl

Future-Related Interests: What and How to Represent?

Abstract
This paper is part of a larger project that seeks to examine the potential of rights-based argumentation in future-related political decision making. Since future persons cannot be regarded as holders of actual rights of interests, what can (and should) be represented are present people's rights and interests with regard to their posterity. In terms of the possible forms of representation, the main requirement is that concerns regarding posterity be directly formulated in most public discourses possible. The paper concludes by looking at this form of representation at the European and global levels.

1. Introduction

The idea that future generations, their rights and interests, should be represented in present decision making is an answer to the unquestionable insight that present decisions can heavily influence the life circumstances of future people. This has become particularly apparent in terms of environmental deterioration due to the fact that technological development was not (or at least not always) accompanied by an increase in the ability to foresee the consequences of industrial and other human activity (see Jonas, 1984). But even if present people knew all the consequences of present policies with near-complete certainty, the problem of generational egoism would remain. To try to cater for future needs may require the adoption of policies that lead to sub-optimal results, or indeed serious sacrifices, in terms of the fulfilment of present needs. Therefore, it seems that future people's interests tend to be largely disregarded unless they are "given a voice" in present debates.

It may be for this reason that those trying to advocate sustainable environmental (and other) policies usually speak of the interests and rights of future people in the same way as we speak of rights and interests of present people (adding, to be sure, that these rights are possible rather than actual, see e.g. Elliot, 1989). In legal and political debates, rights can only be counterbalanced by rights, interests by interests: a voice for posterity will be only heard if it speaks a language decision-makers can understand.

There is, however, also a good deal of scepticism against this way of formulating the duty of the present generation to care for its posterity (see e.g. Gosseries, 2008; Tattay, in the present volume). While political positions in general may not be particularly sensitive to such theoretical problems as the concepts of rights and interests, a position that is formulated in order to change the now dominant character of decision making may be less plausible if it rests on questionable theoretical grounds.

It is for this reason that in the present paper I shall start by suggesting another, maybe less counter-intuitive approach: one that relies on the psychological fact that future generations do matter for members of the present generation. What can, and should, be represented is, I argue, present people's rights and interests in respect of their posterity. As for the form of political representation of future-related interests, I shall first examine some recent proposals and formulate another one myself, based on the insight that concerns regarding posterity should be directly formulated in most public discourses possible. In the final part of the paper, I look at this form of representation at the European and global levels.

2. Future and Rights

Rights and interests of future people are generally opposed to those of present persons, in order to protect the former from the harmful consequences of the latter's imminent actions. Future persons are by definition unknown to us. Indeed, the very basis of the concept is the separation of future generations from the present one. This separation can be interpreted in various ways, according to our understanding of "present" and "future."[1] As for the present generation, it can be conveniently defined as the sum of persons living at a certain point of time. It is the future that makes for the puzzle.

Focusing on time, we may oppose to the present moment a series of future moments. In this sense, the major part of people living in the present is also going to be the major part of those living in the immediate future: a change of generations comes about gradually, according to the pace of human life cycle. If, however, it is the generation that we take as the starting point of our distinction, we have to take a look at the more remote future: at least as remote as the moment where no one of the currently living persons will be alive any more, but rather to the life time of the generation whose members will be all born after the death of all those persons living in the present, which means that their generation does not overlap with the present one.

Our choice among the possible definition of future generations obviously has certain consequences in terms of the interpretation and justification of rights.

1 For some conceptual distinctions concerning future generations, see Gosseries (2004).

Now, however, we have to examine on what conditions one can speak of rights of future generations at all.

The first problem is that of the subjects of these rights. Generally speaking, the rights usually attributed to future generations or individuals belonging to them are not specifically tailored to future persons, but are the same ones which currently living people are thought to have. The consequence of this is that the subjects of these rights cannot be defined in a positive way, by referring to a certain situation or characteristic, only through their lack of present existence. Thus, the group of subjects is not simply too narrow or too broad: it is infinite and non-existent at the same time. The problem is not due to any requirement of legal or moral theory according to which subjects of rights have to exist in the present: law and morals – like human existence itself – are directed towards the future. What is problematic here is that in this case we are speaking of present rights of those not-yet-existing persons and, furthermore, the latter is the only (negative) characteristic we know of them for sure.

And even if we accept that not-yet-existing persons can have rights, we still have to face uncertainty in terms of the content of these rights and the obligations they determine. This is all the more problematic, as the rights of future generations are apparently meant to provide the grounds for obligations of presently living people. For it seems clear in the case of such rights that they are not exerted in any sense: there is no pleading of claims, as it would not be possible with non-existing subjects of rights.[2] If we concentrate, in turn, on the (potential) future existence of future people, then their rights will be the rights of then existing persons, who exert their rights and base their claims on them in their lifetime – and not the rights of the then future generations. We reach the same conclusion, only on a shorter run, if we consider all persons who will live in any moment after the present one as members of the future generations: in exchange for certainty we have to sacrifice the possibility of saying something about the rights of the ever future generations.

Basically, there are two ways to circumvent these problems. It may be suggested – as it was done by George W. Rainbolt, who opposed his own ideas to both the will- and the interest-based concepts of rights – that instead of these "substantive" concepts that contain more or less justification, one should be content with a

2 Feinberg (1981, 147) claims that "[o]ur remote descendants are not yet present to claim a livable world as their right, but there are plenty of proxies to speak now in their behalf. These spokesmen, far from being mere custodians, are genuine representatives of future interests." It is difficult, however, to see how contingent future interests could have genuine representatives.

purely "conceptual" one. According to this, the meaning of "right" suggested by Rainbolt is limited to the notion that "a person has a right if and only if a feature of that person is a *reason* for others to have an obligation or impossibility. A person has a right if and only if a feature of that person is the justification of the obligations or impossibilities of others" (see Rainbolt, 2006, xiii, emphasis in the original).

Although this undeniably corresponds to our previous observation, i.e. that the rights of (the members of) future generations are not intended to be exerted, and although Rainbolt convincingly shows that his concept of justified constraint may be smoothly applied for the rights of persons already dead or who do not yet exist, his suggestion seems to fail with the most sensitive question, that of justification. Or, more precisely, he eliminates it from the concept of rights, relegating it to the field of substantive moral views. As a consequence, we either accept that our concept of rights allows for nothing more than explaining what we exactly mean by saying that "the (members of) future generations have rights," but does not help to decide *whether* they have any right or if we *ought* to attribute rights to them – or we have to face a number of similarly puzzling problems.

Another way is relying on certain assumptions concerning both the existence and the identity (in the most general sense) of future persons. Indeed, it is not counter-intuitive to assume with Joel Feinberg "that there will still be a world five hundred years from now and that it will contain human beings who are very much like us" (see Feinberg, 1981, 139). What follows from this is that we may reasonably assume that future people are going to have largely the same interests as we do,[3] which may allow for "the coherence of present talk about their rights" (see ibid., 148). These rights, however, are merely contingent ones. In the unlikely case all present people decide not to have children, "[n]o one can complain on behalf of presently non-existent future generations that their future interests which give them a contingent right of protection have been violated since they will never come into existence to be wronged" (see ibid.).

In addition to their existence, the identity (this time in a stricter sense) of future persons also seems to be contingent on present actions. In a way analogous to Feinberg's claim concerning the impossibility of harming people who are not going to exist, Derek Parfit pointed out some cases where it is not possible to speak of harming people who are actually going to exist, either. What he calls "the Non-Identity Problem" arises, he explains, "because the identities of people

3 See also Kavka (1978, sect. III), speaking of "relative ignorance" but "a high degree of certainty" in terms of future people's needs.

in the further future can be easily affected. [...] When we are choosing between two social or economic policies, of the kind I described [i.e. whether to deplete or conserve certain kinds of resources], it is *not true* that, in the further future, the same people will exist whatever we choose. It is therefore *not true* that a choice like Depletion will be against the interests of future people" (see Parfit, 1987, 363, emphasis in the original).

The basis of this claim is the mere fact that "[i]f any particular person had not been conceived within a month of time when he was in fact conceived, he would in fact never existed" (see ibid., 352). If different policies influence people's decisions about marriage and having children differently, "[w]e can plausibly assume that, after one or two centuries, there would be no one living in our community who would have been born whichever policy we chose" (see ibid., 361). As it is not the same persons who will exist in the two cases, it cannot be said that opting for one policy rather than the other is going to harm future persons, even if our choice means that those existing in one case will be worse off than those existing in the other case. The Non-Identity Problem makes clear that "we need a new theory of beneficence." Unfortunately, however, Parfit does not provide such a theory. What we are left with in this case is the less than comforting advice that "we should conceal this problem from those who will decide whether we increase our use of nuclear energy" (see ibid., 451).

3. What to Represent?

In theories focusing on future people's rights and interests, as we have seen, it is the present and the future generations that are opposed with at least the present generation being regarded as homogeneous. A different approach should try to avoid the pitfalls of that opposition by recognising the internal division of the present generation on the one hand, and the continuity between generations on the other. This approach could then, at least to some extent, rely on ideas such as the trans-generational character of human projects and, consequently, of communities.[4]

4 In terms of political communities, see the often quoted statement of Burke (1790, pp. 143–144): "Society is indeed a contract. [...] It is a partnership in all science; a partnership in all art; a partnership in every virtue, and in all perfection. As the ends of such a partnership cannot be obtained in many generations, it becomes a partnership not only between those who are living, but between those who are to be born."

While these ideas are usually attributed to the philosophical current known as communitarianism,[5] they are not irreconcilable with liberalism either.[6] Whether one emphasises the importance of communities for the shaping of human self, or the freedom to revise allegiances, it may be reasonably held that people do have identities composed of memberships in various communities and that therefore people have a legitimate interest in the continuity of their respective communities.

If present members of a community have an interest in their past, it is this interest that can be referred to in order to protect the life stories (or narrative selves) of past members of the same community from malicious slander (see cf. Thompson, 2009, pp. 39–40). Someone already deceased cannot continue his or her own story even if (s)he had an interest in its good continuation while (s)he was alive. Presently living persons, however, can do so and if they share the values of their predecessor, they will be interested in the adequate continuation, and consequently their interests will be harmed by any present action aimed at the contrary.

The same applies to the interests present people have in the future of their community. If any action jeopardises the well being of potential future members of a community, it necessarily harms present members of the same community. Moreover, present interests in respect of a community's future include interests in being able to do something for posterity and to attempt, in the words of John O'Neill, "to ensure that future generations do belong to a community with ourselves" (see O'Neill, 1993, 34), i.e. to maintain the values of one's community by way of passing them on to subsequent generations. It is these latter interests that form the basis of "collective" rights, like e.g. the right of using minority languages.

Members of the community, who share the interest in its future, have the right to participate in such debates and deliberation, and their lifetime-transcending interests have to be considered as legitimate reasons. Moreover, all members of the community who share its values and consider membership as their good, have

---

5 One of the starting points of communitarianism in the 1980's was the criticism of the liberal conception of the self, see e.g. Sandel (1981), Taylor (1989). On the transgenerational self and political communities, see e.g. O'Neill (1993) and Thompson (2009).

6 A liberal example may be John Rawls' motivational assumption, according to which the parties of his "original contract" may be regarded as "heads of families," who care about the well-being of their children and grandchildren (Rawls, 1999, 111). Cf. Hubin (1976), focusing on family ties but speaking about obligations between contemporaries with regard to future generations rather than inter-generational ones, and Könczöl (2012), seeking to accommodate other community identities within the framework of Rawls' "original contract."

to contribute to maintaining of these values. Since, at least according to the fundamental doctrine of communitarianism, membership *per definitionem* implies that members of a community share the interest in its future and also share its values and consider membership as their good, those not taking the well-being of future members into account at all must be failing to do so because of ignorance in terms of the nature of their community. The best way to persuade these people, as others, is through democratic deliberation.

4. How to Represent?

In an essay published some twenty years ago, Andrew Dobson (1996) proposed a model for the representation of future generations in democratic decision making. Focusing on legislation, he suggested that a certain number of members of the legislative assembly should function as dedicated representatives of future generations. These representatives would be elected by a group of citizens functioning as a proxy for future generations, and also the candidates running for these seats in the assembly could only come from the same group. Members of the proxy would thus have two votes each, one to cast on "ordinary" representatives and one on those of future generations, but Dobson also contemplates the possibility of maintaining equality by giving the proxy generation only one vote for future generations (see ibid., 134).

A modified version of Dobson's model was offered more recently by Kristian Skagen Ekeli (2005). Rather than letting citizens vote for one sort of representatives only, Ekeli seeks to preserve equality by giving two votes to each member of the electorate, thus having the entire present generation act as a proxy for future generations and elect its own rep "the environmental sustainability lobby," but have to be nominated by dedicated political parties (who could not nominate "ordinary" candidates, as "ordinary" parties could not nominate candidates for the seats reserved for representatives of future generations). The right to form such parties, however, should be restricted to people and organisations that can be expected to genuinely represent future interests.[7] While these representatives could participate in legislation in the same way as their "ordinary" colleagues, they would also have the right to "demand that the final decision about a law proposal should be delayed—either for 2 years or until a new election has been held," provided their qualified majority supports the motion (see Ekeli, 2005, 434).

---

7 E.g. labour unions and employers' organisations could be excluded (see Ekeli, 2005, 438).

As is the case with most advocates of the representation of future generations, both Dobson and Ekeli take it for granted that future people can be represented.[8] Ekeli makes this assumption explicit: while he is aware that there may be theoretical objections to this kind of representation, he finds comfort in the fact that acknowledging the moral standing of future people is now the *communis opinio* (see ibid., 444).

The suggestion according to which present rights and interests regarding posterity, rather than those of future people, should be represented in democratic decision making, has by necessity some consequences in terms of the form of representation. Given that the persons represented in this model are not separate from but identical with the present members of the political community, having a group of dedicated representatives in the legislative assembly would seem pointless.

While this apparently contradicts the models proposed by Dobson and Ekeli, it does not question what may be called the "discursive aim" of representation. Alongside the principle of *Quod omnes tangit ab omnibus approbetur*, there are at least two further aspects of the justification Ekeli provides for his model, all related to the nature of deliberative democracy.[9] On the one hand, representation of posterity can bring in a perspective otherwise (at least potentially) absent from public deliberation. On the other hand, the representatives "can make relevant information […] available to the participants" of the deliberative process. Drawing on the distinction originally made by Robert E. Goodin (2000), Ekeli claims that the "communicative presence" of representatives can contribute to the "imaginative presence" of future generations (see Ekeli, 2005, 447). This seems to be an important insight that deserves consideration when looking at the possible forms of representation.

As said above, present rights and interests may not need dedicated representatives in legislation, yet they need to be represented. Moreover, as political debates in a properly working deliberative democracy are not confined to the legislative assembly, also the representative(s) need to be present in other discursive spaces as well. It may, of course, be open to question whether this kind of presence really needs to be achieved by way of a state organ (rather than NGOs for instance). At any rate, Ekeli is certainly right in claiming that a formalised presence is of key importance in influencing democratic deliberation.

8 See also the caveats of O'Neill (2001).

9 See, however, Beckman (2013), emphasising that "justice and democracy may conflict" here.

Still focusing on legislation, an alternative to the members of the assembly may be a spokesperson in the strict sense, who does not participate in legislation through voting but who can contribute to the preceding debate, either directly, by way of adding his or her *ceterum censeo* to the discussion of proposals (s)he finds relevant from the perspective of sustainability, or indirectly, by providing background information for the representatives that allow for a well-informed decision. Between the walls of the parliament, this task might as well be fulfilled by a standing committee comprising members of the assembly, who in this respect would work as a proxy for future generations; but an effective representation also requires presence outside these walls.

These considerations point towards an alternative model, which may be called the "ombudsman model," following the way such spokespersons are often referred to in practice.[10] Ombudsmen are usually appointed to represent public interests threatened by the violation of rights. A particularly important domain of such activity is those aspects of human life where citizens are likely to be unable to vindicate their own rights.[11] In terms of rights related to future generations this may be due to two things: either the lack of information, or the lack of motivation. As in the case of other specialised ombudsmen, a speaker of posterity-related rights has to deal with both problems, by providing information on the circumstances of individual decision as well as by making people aware of their rights and interests through education.

Finally, a possible objection and a question need to be considered. What makes Ekeli's model of parliamentary representatives appealing from the perspective of deliberative democracy is partly that the plurality of views concerning future interests may be better expressed by a plurality of representatives. A single spokesperson (or a strict limitation of the organisations that can nominate candidates, as in the case of Dobson's model) would necessarily fall short of that ideal. This is certainly true if we assume that it is only these representatives who care for posterity. Yet if we look at the spokesperson as representing everyone's posterity-related rights and interests (as opposed to other rights and interests) rather than future people's rights and interests (as opposed to the rights and interests of the present generation), then it may be more reasonable to think that the spokesperson only has to make the members of the legislative assembly (as well as the participants

10 For essays on the implementation of the political representation of future generations and documents related to the Israeli and Hungarian ombudsmen (Parliamentary Commissioners), see Jávor and Rácz (eds. 2006), Fitzmaurice (2009, pp. 148–153).

11 E.g. children's rights, information rights, or the rights of ethnic or religious minorities.

of other public debates) aware of their interests and leave it to them to advocate their own competing views in terms of these interests.

While ombudsmen normally work with a team of experts and other assistants, just as members of the legislation do, they have the advantage that they represent the respective rights and interests in their own person, which allows for an efficient communication. Thus, if the spokesperson feels it necessary to take a definite position on a certain issue, rather than just bringing it up as a question for public deliberation, then (s)he is much better situated to do so than a number of representatives who may even disagree among themselves.

A related question is how the spokesperson should be selected. Ombudsmen are usually elected by the legislative assembly or appointed by the government, but other ways can be imagined as well. It may be worthwhile considering a regulation that provides for at least a mandatory consultation with what Dobson calls the "environmental sustainability lobby," and also establishing certain incompatibility rules for candidates.

5. Representation at Supra-National Levels

Proposals for a democratic representation of future-related interests are usually meant to work within a nation-state context. My above proposal, I have to admit, is no exception in that respect. By way of conclusion, I briefly consider the problems raised by different contexts. This needs to be done, since it would be difficult to deny that decisions influencing the life circumstances of future people are not necessarily made at the national level. But even if they are, their effects may well go beyond national borders, and it is therefore necessary to address these at a supra-national level.

Beginning with the European context, the main problem here may be identified as the "democratic deficit" of the EU. Today, that means not so much the absence of an elected legislative body with real powers as the lack of a common public political discourse (see cf. Jakab, forthcoming, pt. II.9). It is therefore not too difficult to establish an ombudsman-like position for a speaker of the future generations. The problem is, rather, that the ombudsman may not find the discourse (s)he is meant to participate in.

In that sense, a European ombudsman either has the possibility to communicate with the governments of the member states concerned, and perhaps with NGOs working in those countries, or (s)he has to establish the discourse needed for the proper functioning of the office. In other words, we have to face the well-known dilemma of a "Europe of nations" versus a higher level of integration. As in other cases, the former (to which I shall come back presently) may lack efficiency, while the latter may be difficult to achieve as it may conflict with the interests (or sensitivity) of national political actors.[12]

Having a common European political discourse on future interests may not be without problems in itself. A caveat formulated by Andrew Moravcsik in terms of referenda seems worth considering in that context, too. According to Moravcsik (2008, 340), "[i]n the context of low-salience issues, any future effort to induce greater participation is inherently condemned to generate (at best) continued apathy and (at worst) another explosion of plebiscitary populism." What follows from that is that discursive efforts should be aimed at provoking informed interest among European citizens (e.g. by making sustainability a salient issue while avoiding moral panic) rather than just making them participate by any means. Seen in this light, the second option, i.e. seeking to just bring some important messages to several national discourses, seems not so much an alternative to the former as an inevitable first step. Moreover, it is what happens (or what can happen) at the global level.

Throughout the paper, I have been referring to individual rights and interests, although I assumed that present people can be argued to have rights with respect to their posterity *qua* bearers of community identities (see cf. also Könczöl, 2012, pp. 134–135). It is important to see, however, that in discourses at supra-national levels, rights are often attributed to nation-states as well. While collective rights may be acknowledged by national legal systems, too, at the supra-national stage states (and sometimes other communities) are regarded as the actors *par excellence*: those making treaties, having disputes, etc.

In such a case, representation has a twofold meaning. On the one hand, it is the states who are primarily taken to represent their citizens' rights. Here, then, their internal, national discourses will determine what and how the state is going to represent. On the other hand, states' "rights" and "interests" may need to be represented, too, in international organisations or supra-national decision making bodies. Spokespersons dealing with future-related interests can have a key role in both cases. In terms of the national discourse, they can act as a corrective, by raising concerns not (or not adequately) considered by national political actors. Among international actors, in turn, they can do the job of a "national" ombudsman, reminding the parties, as it were, of their own interests.

12 Even though seeking to establish a common discourse may seem less "imperialistic" than a new institution with decision making powers, such as the European "economic constitutional court" suggested recently by Jakab (2015).

Recent research on international organisations has emphasised "the general shift from intergovernmental politics to global governance, and the increasing functional differentiation of international decision making, including the emergence of environmental policy as a distinct field of international politics" (see Biermann, Siebenhüner, & Schreyögg, 2009, 1). Given these developments, it seems that the possibility of a global representation of future-related interests can be meaningfully considered. I shall conclude by doing so, looking at the United Nations Environmental Programme (UNEP), which seems to be the most promising candidate for this kind of representation. Indeed, the UNEP has been in the focus of debates and plans concerning a possible reform of the global environmental governance system.

In a study published in 2009, Maria Ivanova analysed the strengths and weaknesses of the UNEP as the "anchor organisation" of global environmental governance (see Ivanova, 2009). While the UNEP was established exactly in order to serve as the centre of international efforts at providing institutionalised protection for the environment,[13] it did not fulfil that expectation in every aspect of its work. Ivanova identified four factors responsible for that limited success. These were the UNEP's legal status (programme instead of an agency), the structure of its governance and financing (the role of individual states), and its location (Nairobi, Kenya). Their constellation has led to a fragmentation of environment-related functions within the UN. In conclusion, Ivanova suggested that instead of trying to re-centralise environmental governance in the hands of the UNEP, "[a] more strategic, prioritised and long-term capacity development approach, drawing on UNEP's comparative advantage as an information clearing-house and a policy forum, rather than an operational agency, could facilitate the implementation of multilateral environmental agreements" (see ibid., 168).

What seems the most important point for us here is that according to Ivanova's analysis, one of the main challenges an international organisation has to face is that of communicative presence. The UNEP's perceived inefficacy was at least partly due to the fact that it did not "have a voice" (see cf. ibid., 162) within the UN (due to its form), or that it did not have *one* voice (governance), or that the voice it had was sometimes not regarded as its own (financing), or, finally, that its voice came from a distance (location). This realisation seems to underlie most of the provisions of the document *The Future We Want* (see United Nations, 2012), and particularly those of paragraph 88, aimed at "strengthening and upgrading

13 See also the overview of the UNEP's history in Ivanova (2007).

UNEP."[14] Whether or not the UNEP is going to be more efficient due to these changes is a question for the next years and decades. It seems clear, however, that discursive representation is at least one of the ways in which we should try to protect our posterity from ourselves.

Acknowledgements

Research for this paper took place within the framework of a research project funded by the Hungarian Scientific Research Fund OTKA (K 112900). I am grateful to all participants of the discussion at the Forum 2015 conference, and to Kinga Debisso, Ákos Szalay, Szilárd Tattay, and Martin Belov for their helpful comments and advice.

References

Beckman, Ludvig. 2013. Democracy and Future Generations: Should the Unborn Have a Voice? In Spheres of Global Justice, vol. 2: Fair Distribution – Global Economic, Social, and Intergenerational Justice, edited by Merle, Jean-Christophe, 775–788. Dordrecht: Springer.

Biermann, Frank; Siebenhüner, Bernd; Schreyögg, Anna. 2009. Global Environmental Governance and International Organizations: Setting the Stage. In International Organizations in Global Environmental Governance, edited by Biermann, Frank; Siebenhüner, Bernd; Schreyögg, Anna. 1–16. London and New York: Routledge.

Burke, Edmund. 1790. Reflections on the French Revolution. Dodsley: London.

Dobson, Andrew. 1996. Representative Democracy and the Environment. In: Democracy and the Environment: Problems and Prospects, edited by Lafferty, William and Meadowcroft, James. 124–139. Cheltenham: Edward Elgar.

Ekeli, Kristian Skagen. 2005. Giving a Voice to Posterity – Deliberative Democracy and Representation of Future people. *Journal of Agricultural and Environmental Ethics* 18: 429–450.

Elliot, Robert. 1989. The Rights of Future People. *Journal of Applied Philosophy* 6.2: 159–170.

Feinberg, Joel. 1981. The Rights of Animals and Unborn Generations. In: Responsibilities to Future Generations: Environmental Ethics, edited by Partridge, Ernest. 139–150. Buffalo (NY): Prometheus Books. [Originally published in:

14 Para. 88 (c) actually uses the phrase "enhance the voice of UNEP."

Philosophy and Environmental Crisis, edited by Blackstone, William. 43–68. Athens (GA): The University of Georgia Press.]

Fitzmaurice, Malgosia. 2009. Contemporary Issues in International Environmental Law. Cheltenham: Edward Elgar.

Goodin, Robert E. 2000. Democratic Deliberation Within. *Philosophy and Public Affairs* 29.1: 81–109.

Gosseries, Axel. 2004. Penser la justice entre générations: De l'affaire Perruche à la réforme des retraites. Paris: Aubier.

Gosseries, Axel. 2008. On Future Generations' Future Rights. *The Journal of Political Philosophy* 16.4: 446–474.

Hubin, D. Clayton. 1976. Justice and Future Generations. *Philosophy and Public Affairs* 6: 70–83.

Ivanova, Maria. 2007. Designing the United Nations Environmental Programme: A Story of Compromise and Confrontation. International Environmental Agreements: Politics, Law, and Economics 7.3: 337–361.

Ivanova, Maria. 2009. UNEP as Anchor Organization for the Global Environment. In: International Organizations in Global Environmental Governance, edited by Biermann, Frank; Siebenhüner, Bernd and Schreyögg, Anna. 151–173. London and New York: Routledge.

Jakab, András. 2015. Sustainability in European Constitutional Law. [Available at SSRN: http://ssrn.com/abstract=2593371].

Jakab, András. Forthcoming. European Constitutional Language. Cambridge: Cambridge University Press.

Jávor, Benedek, and Rácz, Judit (eds). 2006. Do We Owe Them a Future? The Opportunities of a Representation for Future Generations in Europe. Budapest: Védegylet.

Jonas, Hans. 1984. The Imperative of Responsibility: In Search of an Ethics for the Technological Age. Chicago: The University of Chicago Press.

Kavka, Gregory. 1978. The Futurity Problem. In: Obligations to Future Generations, edited by Sikora, Richard I. and Barry, Brian. 186–203. Philadelphia: Temple University Press.

Könczöl, Miklós. 2012. Future Generations: An Almost Rawlsian Perspective. In: Jurisprudence and Political Philosophy in the 21st Century: Reassessing Legacies, edited by Jovanović, Miodrag A. and Spaić, Bojan. 130–136. Frankfurt: Peter Lang.

Moravcsik, Andrew. 2008. The Myth of Europe's 'Democratic Deficit.' *Intereconomics: Journal of European Public Policy* 43.6: 331–340.

O'Neill, John. 1993. Ecology, Policy and Politics: Human Well-Being and the Natural World. London: Routledge.

O'Neill, John. 2001. Representing People, Representing Nature, Representing the World. *Environment and Planning C: Government and Policy* 19.4: 483–500.

Parfit, Derek. 1987. Reasons and Persons [1984], repr. with corrections. Oxford: Oxford University Press.

Rawls, John. 1999. A Theory of Justice, 2d ed. Cambridge (MA): Harvard University Press.

Sandel, Michael. 1981. Liberalism and the Limits of Justice. Cambridge, Cambridge University Press.

Taylor, Charles. 1989. Sources of the Self: The Making of the Modern Identity. Cambridge: Cambridge University Press.

Thompson, Janna. 2009. Identity and Obligation in a Transgenerational Polity. In: Intergenerational Justice, edited by Gosseries, Axel and Meyer, Lukas H. 25–49. Oxford: Oxford University Press.

United Nations. 2012. *The Future We Want: Outcome Document of the United Nations Conference on Sustainable Development, Rio de Janeiro, Brazil, 20–22 June 2012* [A/RES/66/288].

Szilárd Tattay

Making Sense of a Nonsense: Representation of the "Rights" of Future Generations

Abstract

The legal conceptualisation of unborn generations and their specific rights raises important theoretical issues, and constitutes a special challenge to jurisprudence in general and legal philosophy in particular. Even the most fundamental and essential questions regarding the legal situation of upcoming generations are not settled yet. Are future generations capable of being holders of rights or not? And if they are, how can we conceptualise their rights? Can we use the conventional modern rights theories, either the "benefit" or "interest," or the "choice" or "will" theory of rights for that purpose? What does it mean and how is it possible to "represent" the rights or interests of future generations? And so forth. In my paper I will endeavour to address some of these theoretical questions and make an attempt to offer an adequate conceptual framework for their analysis.

1. Introduction

One of the most pressing global problems nowadays is environmental pollution. As pollution itself transcends national boundaries, the protection of the environment for the future inevitably raises the question of global governance, and invites a deliberate reconsideration of the relationship between the state and the international community.

Owing to the perception and continually growing consciousness of the responsibility of humankind for the natural resources of the earth, as well as for its own descendants, in the last decades the idea of sustainability and particularly the conception of sustainable development has received wide acknowledgement and acceptance both by the scientific community and the lay public. However, even though the fact that the notion of sustainable development seems closely interwoven within the concept of intergenerational justice and the protection and representation of the "rights" of future generations, until the present day apparently no universal consensus and generally accepted theoretical model was formed concerning these commonly evoked ideas.

As a consequence, the legal conceptualisation of unborn generations and their specific rights still raises important theoretical issues, and constitutes a special challenge to jurisprudence in general and legal philosophy in particular. Even the most fundamental and essential questions regarding the legal situation of upcoming generations are not settled yet. Are future generations capable of being holders of rights or not? And if they are, how can we conceptualise their rights? Can we use the conventional (nineteenth century rooted) modern rights theories, either the "benefit" or "interest," or the "choice" or "will" theory of rights for that purpose? What does it mean and how is it possible to "represent" the rights or interests of future generations? What kind of rights or interests can be attributed at all to not yet existing people? Can we identify the interests of future generations, and if yes, how can we specify them? What exactly do ombudspersons and other guardians, e.g. parliamentary representatives of future generations represent, and on which grounds can such a representation be based? And so forth.

In my paper, I will endeavour to address some of these theoretical questions and make an attempt to offer an adequate conceptual framework for their analysis. As I will focus chiefly on the problem of the conceptualisation of the rights of future generations, I will treat questions concerning representation only briefly and indirectly.

2. Much Ado About Nothing?

The principal, crucial problem related to the representation of future generations lies within the legal status of future persons: notwithstanding the recognition of the potential existence of future generations, no consensus is emerging as to whether future generations can possess rights or (international) legal personality, or they have only hypothetical interests to be represented.

There exists much – and various kinds of – scepticism about the conceptualisation of the "rights of future generations," and these doubts come up among theoreticians of sustainable development and intergenerational justice, too. Joerg Chet Tremmel, for example, considers it a sterile effort to seek to determine the exact meaning of the concept of "rights," on the grounds that words can and often do change their meanings over time, and, consequently, qualifies the controversy as to whether future persons are capable of having "rights" or merely "needs" or "interests" as "quite futile" (see Tremmel, 2006, pp. 51–52). Or, it is often argued that the phrase "representation of the rights of unborn generations" can become intelligible and useful only if taken as a manifestation of purely "figurative" or "metaphorical" language.[1] There might be an element of truth in these statements, but I cannot scrutinise them now in detail. At any rate, for my present purposes it suffices to note that I start out from the methodological presupposition that legal

1 See e.g. the Decision 28 of 1994 of the Hungarian Constitutional Court and Saward (2006).

systems should be based on a coherent conceptual framework, and legal thinking cannot be built on wholly arbitrary metaphors. Either lawyers are able to make "legal" sense of a notion, or they cannot...

Furthermore, according to some critics, to found our obligations towards future generations upon their correlative rights is to jeopardise the whole project of intergenerational justice and equity (see Beckerman & Pasek, 2001, pp. 13–14).[2] This objection is easily answerable by saying that those obligations are self-sufficient so that they can exist without any corresponding rights. This reply, however, while solving one issue, raises another, perhaps even more serious theoretical challenge. If this is so, then – just as in the case of animals or plants (let alone rocks and rivers) – we do not necessarily need to "bestow" rights on future people to defend present obligations concerning them (see Gosseries, 2008, pp. 450–452). It may be asked, why is it worth undertaking such a doubtful and difficult conceptual manoeuvre? What do we – our succeeding generations – gain in exchange for further inflating the notion and value of "rights" by postulating future generations' rights?

Richard Dagger calls attention to two opposite risks that the proliferation of human rights rhetoric carries: it threatens to overwhelm other concepts and considerations on the one hand, and to rob the appeal to rights of much of its power on the other (see Dagger, 2006, 207). In other Dworkinian words: "Rights are trumps and if we have more and more trumps then we inflate the old (traditional) ones" (see Jakab, 2015, 16).

It is absolutely clear, nevertheless, what future persons would gain if "conferred" with rights. The theoretical added value of rights lies in the fact, stresses Axel Gosseries, that they serve as a "label of significance:" "Upgrading an interest to the status of right is a sign of its special *importance*" (see Gosseries, 2008, 453). This is because rights are usually deemed to carry much greater moral force than do non-rights-based obligations (see Brown Weiss, 1989, 101).

As for the practical significance of ascribing rights to unborn generations, trump cards with an inflated value are still valuable and stronger than "ordinary" cards, either in legal procedures or in political and moral argumentation. While rights are able to impose constraint on present people's behaviour, "claims" or "interests" not clothed in the form of a "right" could look frivolous compared to them. But is this extension of rights conceptually possible and plausible?

---

2 Robert E. Goodin, though highly sympathetic with both ideas, also perceives this danger: "Casting the question in those terms gives the opponents of intergenerational justice an argumentative advantage. They need simply to deny the possibility of purely potential people's having any claims in terms of rights" (see Goodin, 1985, 169).

3. An Old Debate: Will or Interest?

The aim of this paper does not extend to taking sides in the traditional debate between the "will" or "choice" theory and the "interest" or "benefit" conception of rights. However, the problem of the rights of future generations might be approached not exclusively from the perspective of the question whether we can meaningfully predicate rights of potential persons; not only is it possible to test the very concept of the "rights of future generations" but also to use those rights as a test case for examining classical theories of rights. Perhaps most famously, Neil MacCormick tested – and rejected – the "will theory" in this way with children's rights (see MacCormick, 1976). There is a huge difference, though, between children's and future persons' rights: while both our moral and theoretical intuitions tend to dictate, I guess, that children do have rights, at least prima facie, it sounds paradoxical to say that non-existent human beings can have them.

The choice between the "will" and the "interest" theory can surely influence the range of potential right-holders. While it seems self-evident that rights can be predicated of "competent" adult human beings but not of rocks, between these two "clear cases" there is a large spectrum of "borderline cases," including e.g. infants, fetuses, dead persons, madmen, and animals (see Feinberg, 1974, 44). For the sake of the argument, let us start out from the working hypothesis that choice theory is more persuasive in relation to the paradigmatic cases of rights, requiring an autonomous decision from the rights-holder, while the interest theory appears more convincing in regard to the borderline cases (see Győrfi, 2009, pp. 53–56). Now it remains to be verified whether this assumption proves to be true in connection with the rights of future generations, which, of course, falls under the latter category. That would suggest that the interest theory of rights is more suitable for grounding and justifying those rights.

Certainly, at first glance the will theory does not seem to be at all favourable to the rights of unborn generations. According to Hart's classic formulation of the choice conception of rights, the right-holder is a "small-scale sovereign" possessing "exclusive control, more or less extensive, over another's person's duty" (see Hart, 1982, 183). Consequently, being a moral agent able to make free choices is a necessary precondition for the possession of a right, argues Carl Wellman, and as the essential function of rights is to determine the morally justified distribution of dominion, freedom and control, the ascription of a moral right to any being incapable of exercising dominion is idle and inappropriate. It is idle because there could be no moral purpose in allocating dominion to those completely incapable of taking advantage of it in any way; it is inappropriate because it would mislead us into imagining that freedom and control belong morally to those incapable of acting freely or exercising control (see Wellman, 1995, 107).

On this view, beings incapable of making rational and free decisions, including animals, dead persons, future people, fetuses, and even infants, cannot be said to have rights (see Ekeli, 2006, 401). As Hart warns us:

If common usage sanctions talk of the rights of animals or babies it makes an idle use of the expression "a right," which will confuse the situation with other different moral situations where the expression 'a right' has a specific force and cannot be replaced by […] other moral expressions' (see Hart, 1955, 181).

If this is so in the case of newborn infants, it is *a fortiori* true of merely potential persons who will become moral agents at an even later date – if at all. As future people are of necessity incapable of either demanding or waiving present persons' performance of correlative duties, they cannot be holders of rights (see Steiner, 1994, 261).

Although such uncompromising concern for "semantic hygiene" on the part of many proponents of will theory may be, to a certain extent, justified and understandable, it might be suspected that it entails, literally, throwing the baby out with the bathwater. If one is willing to affirm children's rights, but at the same time is reluctant to draw the same conclusion as MacCormick, namely, that moral considerations provide reasons strong enough to repudiate altogether the choice conception of rights on this ground (see MacCormick, 1976, 309), then virtually the only way out left open is to have recourse to the principle of potentiality. Nevertheless, as we will see below, this principle cannot be extended to the case of future generations.

Joel Feinberg combines, somewhat surprisingly, a will theory of the nature of rights with an interest theory of the capacity to possess rights. While defining "right" as a valid claim to something against someone (see Feinberg, 1970, pp. 253, 256–257; Feinberg, 1974, 43), Feinberg identifies the class of potential rights-holders with those beings "who have (or can have) interests" (see Feinberg, 1974, 51).[3] He gives two reasons for this: because a right holder must be capable of being represented and it is impossible to represent a being that has no interests, and because a right holder must be capable of being a beneficiary in his own person, and a being without interests is a being that is incapable of being harmed or benefitted, having no good or "sake" of its own (see ibid.).

3 On the question whether this is a contradiction, and if yes, whether and how it can be resolved, see particularly Wellman (2005).

In this theoretical perspective, future generations, fetuses, infants, dead persons, and animals all fall under the category of beings that "can have rights" (see ibid., passim). However persuading this line of argument may appear, it gives rise to some perplexing questions. First of all, it leaves room for the objection that in order to have a right, it is not sufficient to have potential interests (to "can have" interests) but to "have" *actual* interests. It is not an accident that standard formulations of the benefit theory usually require that "right-holders are creatures who *have* interests" (see Raz, 1984a, 204, my emphasis).

Secondly, although a superficial reading might suggest that Feinberg unnecessarily complicates the first argument when he arrives to the concept of interest-ownership through the notion of representation, in reality, this latter turns out to be a crucial link in his overall argumentation. He must place so much emphasis on the representation of rights because while "paradigmatic" rights-holders are able to claim their own rights, beings that lack moral agency do not have this capacity (see Wellman, 1995, 117). This is why Feinberg insists on the point that all that is needed for the existence of a right is that someone be able to press the claim on behalf of the rights-bearer – not that this someone personally be the rights-bearer (see Dagger, 2006, 208).[4]

Now the basic problem with this approach is that the notion of representation is itself ambiguous. As Wellman highlights, the term "representation" can denote a principal–agent relationship where the agent is representing the agency – autonomous will – of the principal, and it can also refer to a relation between trustee and beneficiary in which the trustee is representing the interests of the beneficiary (see Wellman, 1995, pp. 114–116; Wellman, 1997, 18).

"Representation of agency" is perfectly suitable for representing rights, but it is, by definition, not applicable to beings not possessing moral agency, whereas "representation of interests" does not necessarily imply rights (see Wellman, 1995, pp. 118, 120). Moreover, this view is at odds with Feinberg's own concept of right as a "valid claim" that appears evidently to entail, as a logical corollary, that only a person capable of making claims can become a right-holder. As Feinberg (1970, 251) himself underlines: "The legal power to claim (performatively) one's right or the things to which one has a right seems to be essential to the very notion of a right."

4 A similar argument is presented by Robert E. Goodin: "After all, court-appointed guardians exercise the rights of infants and idiots even though these are just as incapable as future generations of exercising choices themselves" (see Goodin, 1985, 170 n. 36).

Perhaps the most influential theory of the rights of future generations has been developed by Edith Brown Weiss. More precisely, she speaks of "planetary" rights that are held by all generations as groups in relation to other generations (intergenerational level), as well as by individual members of the present generation (intragenerational level) (see Brown Weiss, 1989, pp. 96–97). She founds the rights of future generations on Joseph Raz's thoroughgoing interest conception of rights according to which an individual or a group has a right if and only if an interest (i.e., an aspect of the well-being) of his, her or its is a sufficient reason for holding another to be under a duty (see Raz, 1984a, 195; Raz, 1984b, pp. 1, 5). Brown Weiss offers a general definition of rights as follows:

> "A right is an interest that is juridically protected. It is always associated with a duty or obligation. If a person has a right, he or she has an interest that is sufficient ground for holding another subject to a duty" (see Brown Weiss, 1989, 99).

By bringing the notions of interest and well being into prominence, Brown Weiss is able to argue that every human being who has or will have interests in the future can be a rights-holder (see Ekeli, 2006, 399).

So far so good. We can reach a temporary conclusion that seems to reinforce our initial presupposition, viz. that the interest theory of rights is more likely to provide a solid foundation for the rights of future generations. We will return to this matter later. Now let us continue our conceptual analysis with a discussion of the philosophical problems inherent in attributing rights to future persons.

4. Philosophical Problems

To ascribe rights to future people is not without danger. As Feinberg acknowledges, one easily incurs the charge of "falling into obscure metaphysics, by granting rights to remote and unidentifiable beings who are not yet even in existence" (see Feinberg, 1974, 65). Within this charge, two separate issues should be differentiated, which are usually discussed in the literature on future generations under the rubric of "non-existence problem" and "non-identity problem," respectively. We shall examine each of them in turn.

4.1 The Non-Existence Problem

The so-called "non-existence problem" is related to the simple fact that "future persons, qua future, do not exist now" (see Partridge 2001, 378). Possible persons, however, it is objected, cannot be said to have actual rights, for it is meaningless to confer rights on persons who do not exist (see Macklin, 1981, 151). As Richard De George categorically puts it:

Future generations by definition do not now exist. They cannot now, therefore, be the present bearer or subject of anything, including rights. Hence they cannot be said to have rights in the same sense that presently existing entities can be said to have them. This follows from the briefest analysis of the present tense form of the verb "to have" (see De George, 1981, 159)

In a similar vein, Beckerman declares that "properties, such as being green or wealthy or having rights, can be predicated only of some subject that exists" (see Beckerman, 2006, 55). Stanley I. Benn even contends that it is a logical error to deduce actual rights from merely potential qualification for those rights.

For if *A* has rights only because he satisfies some condition *P*, it does not follow that *B* has the same rights now because he *could* have property *P* at some time in the future. It only follows that he *will* have rights *when* he has *P*. He is a potential bearer of rights, as he is a potential bearer of *P*. A potential president of the US is not on that account Commander-in-Chief (see Benn, 1984, 143).[5]

The absence of a certain property may arguably be overcome by means of the principle of potentiality. For instance, in the normal course of events, a human fetus or infant will sooner or later presumably acquire the capacity of rational and autonomous decision making (see e.g. Dagger, 2006, 208). Yet in the case of future generations we are dealing with a "two-level potentiality" which seems to present an insurmountable theoretical difficulty: a future person, as a merely potential being, first has to be conceived, and only then can obtain moral agency. The rights of future people, if they exist, are thus wholly contingent upon their coming into being (see Feinberg, 1974, 66; Elliot, 1989, pp. 161–162). As Daniel Callahan writes: "The claim of future generations against us is a conditional claim, in the sense that it depends upon their existing to make the claim" (see Callahan, 1981, 82).

Two questions can be posed here. First, cannot we say that although there is no present holder of a right, but nevertheless, the right itself does exist now? According to Robert Elliot, it is not impossible that there be present rights which do not have present bearers (see Elliot, 1989, 161). Gosseries, however, convincingly demonstrates that this is an absurd hypothesis: it is inconsistent to maintain simultaneously that, on the one hand, a right exists now and that, on the other hand, the existence of this right depends upon the existence of someone in the future (see Gosseries, 2008, 453).

The second question is purely rhetorical: what guarantees that future generations will come into being? Nothing, of course. Right now, their future existence is at best a "realistic assumption" (see Gosseries, 2004, 10) or a "well-based belief"

5 For a similar argumentation, see Warren (1977).

(see Baier, 1981, 174). Certainly, we do have a moral obligation to care for the existence and well-being of posterity, but it would be logically and conceptually untenable to grant the right to come into being to future persons on this ground, since their existence is a prerequisite for their having rights (see Feinberg, 1974, 66; De-Shalit, 1995, 116).

4.2 The non-identity problem

The "non-identity problem" presents another fundamental philosophical challenge to the notion of the rights of future generations. The term itself was coined by Derek Parfit and it was he who gave its classical formulation. Parfit distinguished between different kinds of choices that can be made with respect to future persons. If we are making "same people choices," the same future people will exist whatever we choose (see Parfit, 1984, 356). The so-called "different number choices," on the contrary, affects both the identity and number of future people. When we are choosing between two social or economic policies, e.g. whether we decide to deplete or conserve certain natural resources,

> [i]t is not true that, whichever policy we use, the same particular people will exist in the further future. […] Since the choice between our two policies would affect the timing of later conceptions, some of the people who are later born would owe their existence to our choice of one of the two policies. If we had chosen the other policy, these particular people would never have existed. […] It is therefore *not true* that a choice like Depletion will be against the interests of future people (see Parfit, 1984, pp. 361, 363).

The "non-identity" challenge has dominated the debates on intergenerational justice for several decades – perhaps, as Tremmel admits, too much (see Tremmel, 2009, 37). Contrary to the view that future persons cannot be harmed in the future by our present actions, Kristian Skagen Ekeli argues, as it seems to me rightly, that even though we may reasonably have doubts concerning some aspects of the epistemological and ontological status of unborn persons (whether we possess sufficient knowledge about the interests, needs and life-conditions of future people, and how much we influence their welfare, existence, identity, and number with our actions and policies), this does not seriously compromise the moral status of future generations or preclude the representation of their rights or interests (see Ekeli, 2005, pp. 443–444). Even such fervent opponents of the idea of the rights of future generations as Beckerman and Pasek concede readily that the objection that rights cannot be but rights of identifiable individuals is a "weak argument" (see Beckerman & Pasek, 2001, pp. 22–23). On a philosophical level, it is arguable that

> the fact that future persons cannot be individuated or counted is a bad reason for thinking that present activity cannot or need not be based on assumptions about them. Activity is

> constantly taken on the basis of quite strong assumptions about others whom we cannot individuate (see O'Neill, 1996, 115).

When owners insure their pieces of property assuming that unknown people might steal or damage them, or hotel-keepers assume that someone will book their rooms, etc., they proceed upon adequately accurate assumptions (see ibid.). It should be noted that this statement does not prove in itself that rights can be attributed to future persons, only that present people can owe obligations to them.

The legal perspective depends, at first sight at least, on our understanding of the meaning of the expression "rights of future people." If we conceive them as "collective rights," our ignorance concerning the number or kinds of future persons is completely unproblematic, inasmuch as the existence and the identity of a "community" or a "generation" is to a great extent independent from that of its individual members. As "group rights," stresses Edith Brown Weiss, intergenerational rights exist regardless of the number and identity of the individuals making up each generation (see Brown Weiss, 1990, 203): "since the rights of future generations exist only as generational rights, it does not matter who the individuals are or how many they may be" (see ibid., 205). And even granted that the rights of future persons are qualified as "individual rights," the uncertainty related to the content of those rights is not due to the non-identity problem but to other factors, viz. our limited knowledge of future people's needs and of the effects of our decisions on their life.

Therefore, in attributing rights to future persons, we can refer to them purely and simply as human beings, without regard to the question of which particular human beings they are, or to when and where they live (see Meyer, 2003, 146). This is possible because, as Annette Baier convincingly shows, the rights of future people are *not person-specific* (see Baier, 1981, 172). In general, rights and obligations are possessed by persons not owing to their unique individuality, but in virtue of the roles they fill. For example, children qua children have obligations to and rights against their parents qua parents (see ibid., 173). Likewise, Robert Elliot argues that the concern for the rights of future persons is *impersonal*:

> We are not striving to ensure that the rights of a specific set of people are not violated, rather we are striving to ensure that rights violations do not occur. Whoever comes into existence will have rights and it is the violation of the rights of individuals which we wish to avoid. (see Elliot, 1989, 163)[6]

6 Basically the same argument is deployed by Simon Caney in Caney (2009, 237).

All this implies that if there will still be human beings five centuries from now, they will have rights, even if their identity is now necessarily obscure (see Feinberg, 1974, 65).

5. Beyond the Will/Interest Controversy

Of the two philosophical challenges to the conceptualisation of the rights of future generations, the "non-existence problem" looks thus more serious. As we have seen, the conclusion seems unavoidable that future people as purely potential persons can have no *actual* rights now, for there cannot be rights whose bearers do not yet exist. Consequently, it simply does not make sense to talk about the rights of future generations *in present tense* as Feinberg (1974, pp. 65–67), Elliot (1989, pp. 160–162), Baier (1981, pp. 171–175) and Partridge (1990) occasionally do.

As Gosseries points out (see Gosseries, 2008, 454), this still leaves two options for defending rights correlative with present obligations. One consists in remaining in the present and ascribing rights to present rather than future people. I cannot and do not intend to analyse this option at length here. Nonetheless, I believe that the fundamental problem with this otherwise plausible solution is that its scope is far too narrow: as rights are linked to the existence of their bearers, it cannot handle long-term environmental effects.

The other option is to attribute future rights rather than present ones to future people. The non-existence argument does not say that *actual* future persons cannot be properly said to have rights (see cf. De George, 1981, 159; Macklin, 1981, 152), so it "is not strong enough to disprove the idea that future people, *if and when* they exist, will have rights" (see De-Shalit, 1995, 115). Gosseries differentiates between two kinds of "contemporaneity claims." While he accepts that it is reasonable to require that for a right to exist, its holder should also exist, he does not endorse as a cogent requirement that for an obligation to exist, its correlative right would already need to exist. On the basis of this distinction, he affirms that it is not inaccurate or nonsensical to speak of future persons' future rights as correlative with our present obligations (see Gosseries, 2008, 455).

Lukas H. Meyer argues along very similar lines:

> Claiming that we can violate future people's rights now does not, however, imply that future people have rights now. That implication would hold only if it were contended that presently existing rights alone constrain present action. But we can safely assume, first, that future people can be bearers of rights in the future; second, that the rights they have will be determined by the interests they have then; and, third, that our present actions and policies can effect their interests (see Meyer, 2003, 145).

This latter approach does not only appear perfectly viable, but it also brings the whole problem of the conceptualisation of the rights of future generations into new light. Up until now, when discussing the legal and moral status of future persons from the standpoint of the present, we have referred to them as merely potential human beings with at most potential rights, that is, without rights, for there do not exist purely potential rights. There can be only "conditional rights," in the sense that when and only when a person will come into existence, he or she will have rights (see Gosseries, 2008, 456). The "futurist" perspective, however, offers a completely different angle. In the future, a considerable number of present-day "potential persons" will probably become actual persons, many of them "paradigmatic" rights-holders having "real" rights.

The change of perspective to a "futurist" point of view has another important consequence as well. If we transpose our problematic into the future, the will/interest dichotomy will lose much of its force and find itself relativised.7 It can be enumerated among the basic facts we surely know about unborn generations that future persons will be sentient, self-conscious moral agents with certain biological needs and the capacity of choice (see Partridge, 2001, 385). The answer to the question of who can be a rights-bearer will thus not depend too much on whether we adopt the "choice" or the "benefit" conception of rights.

Since actual future persons, unlike non-existing potential persons, are able to make claims and free choices, it is not necessary to lean on such dubious arguments as, for instance, that which says that future generations can have rights now, for one need not make claims to have claims (see Goodin, 1985, 179 n 49). And, on the contrary, it is well-founded to assert that the present generation's obligation, grounded in the principles of intergenerational equity, to conserve options for future generations is correlative with future generations' right to free decision (see Brown Weiss, 1989, 95). Accordingly, our present actions can equally constitute a violation of rights by encroaching upon the autonomy as by infringing the interests of future people.

The relativisation of the difference between the "will" and "interest" theories manifests itself also in respect of the uncertainties concerning the representation of the rights of future generations. It would be hard to say whether the cognition of the wishes and desires or the needs and interests of future persons presents greater difficulty. Nevertheless, Gregory Kavka insists that in spite of our relative ignorance regarding future people's wishes and interests, we can foresee with a high degree of certainty their basic biological and economic needs, the satisfaction

7 I am indebted to Miklós Könczöl for suggesting this argument.

of which will surely be a prerequisite of the satisfaction of their other desires and interests – whatever they may be (see Kavka, 1981, 111). He suggests an interesting analogy between our ignorance of the wishes and interests of future persons and a young man's ignorance of the desires and interests he will have in old age:

> It is unlikely that a young adult will know in detail the goals and desires he will have in forty years: whether, for example, he will wish to spend his time travelling, doing volunteer work, or drinking beer. However, he can believe with a high degree of confidence that his important needs and interests will include good health, adequate food and shelter, and security for his loved ones (see ibid., 112).

It may even be argued, as does Callahan, that since we cannot peer into the future and divine exactly what future human beings will need and desire, or which ideals they will pursue, we should act on the assumption that their needs, desires, and ideals will not be all that dissimilar from our own: "we must use our own and present understanding of human life as the basis for any projections into the future – no other is available" (see Callahan, 1981, pp. 80, 84). This is precisely what makes the representation of the rights of future generations such an easy and difficult task at the same time.

Acknowledgements

I am grateful to Martin Belov, Péter Cserne and Miklós Könczöl for their helpful comments on this paper.

References

Baier, Annette. 1981. The Rights of Past and Future Generations. In: Responsibilities to Future Generations: Environmental Ethics, edited by Partridge, Ernest. 171–183. Buffalo (NY): Prometheus Books.

Beckerman, Wilfred. 2006. The Impossibility of a Theory of Intergenerational Justice. In: Handbook of Intergenerational Justice, edited by Tremmel, Joerg Chet. 53–71. Cheltenham – Northampton (MA): Edward Elgar.

Beckerman, Wilfred; Pasek, Joanna. 2001. Justice, Posterity, and the Environment. Oxford: Oxford University Press.

Benn, Stanley I. 1984. Abortion, Infanticide, and Respect for Persons. In: The Problem of Abortion, edited by Feinberg, Joel. 92–104. Second edition, Belmont (CA): Wadsworth.

Brown Weiss, Edith. 1989. In Fairness to Future Generations. Tokyo – New York: United Nations University – Transnational Publishers.

Brown Weiss, Edith. 1990. Our Rights and Obligations to Future Generations for the Environment. *The American Journal of International Law* 84: 198–207.

Callahan, Daniel. 1981. What Obligations Do We Have to Future Generations? In: Responsibilities to Future Generations: Environmental Ethics, edited by Partridge, Ernest. 73–85. Buffalo (NY): Prometheus Books.

Caney, Simon. 2009. Human Rights, Responsibilities, and Climate Change. In: Global Basic Rights, edited by. Beitz, Charles R and Goodin, Robert E. 227–247. Oxford: Oxford University Press.

Dagger, Richard. 2006. Freedom and Rights. In: Political Theory and the Ecological Challenge, edited by Dobson, Andrew and Eckersley, Robyn. 200–215. Cambridge: Cambridge University Press.

De George, Richard T. 1981. The Environment, Rights, and Future Generations. In: Responsibilities to Future Generations: Environmental Ethics, edited by Partridge, Ernest, 157–165. Buffalo (NY): Prometheus Books.

De-Shalit, Avner. 1995. Why Posterity Matters? Environmental Policies and Future Generations. London – New York: Routledge.

Ekeli, Kristian Skagen. 2005. Giving a Voice to Posterity – Deliberative Democracy and Representation of Future People. *Journal of Agricultural and Environmental Ethics* 18: 429–450.

Ekeli, Kristian Skagen. 2006. The Principle of Liberty and Legal Representation of Posterity. *Res Publica* 12: 385–409.

Elliot, Robert. 1989. The Rights of Future People. *Journal of Applied Philosophy* 6: 159–169.

Feinberg, Joel. 1970. The Nature and Value of Rights. *The Journal of Value Inquiry* 4: 243–257.

Feinberg, Joel. 1974. The Rights of Animals and Unborn Generations. In: *Philosophy and Environmental Crisis*, edited by Blackstone, William T., 43–68. Athens (GA): The University of Georgia Press.

Goodin, Robert E. 1985. Protecting the Vulnerable: A Reanalysis of Our Social Responsibilities. Chicago – London: University of Chicago Press.

Gosseries, Axel. 2004. Constitutionalizing Future Rights? *Intergenerational Justice Review* 4: 10–11.

Gosseries, Axel. 2008. On Future Generations' Future Rights. *The Journal of Political Philosophy* 16: 446–474.

Győrfi, Tamás. 2009. A jogosultságok önállósága és a jogalanyiság kérdése [The Independence of Rights and the Capacity to be a Right-Holder]. In: Jogosultságok – Elmélet és gyakorlat [Rights – Theory and Practice], edited by Ficsor, Krisztina; Győrfi, Tamás and Szabó, Miklós. 47–61. Miskolc: Bíbor.

Hart, Herbert. 1955. Are There any Natural Rights. *The Philosophical Review* 64: 175–191.

Hart, Herbert. 1982. Legal Rights. In Hart, Herbert. Essays on Bentham: Studies in Jurisprudence and Political Theory. 162–193. Oxford: Clarendon Press.

Jakab, András. 2015. Sustainability in European Constitutional Law [http://papers.ssrn.com/sol3/papers.cfm?abstract_id=2593371, accessed on 16. 06. 2015].

Kavka, Gregory. 1981. The Futurity Problem. In: Responsibilities to Future Generations: Environmental Ethics, edited by Partridge, Ernest. 109–122. Buffalo (NY): Prometheus Books.

Macklin, Ruth. 1981. Can Future Generations Correctly Be Said to Have Rights? In: Responsibilities to Future Generations: Environmental Ethics, edited by Partridge, Ernest, 151–155. Buffalo (NY): Prometheus Books.

MacCormick, Neil. 1976. Children's Rights: A Test-Case for Theories of Right. Archiv für Rechts- und Sozialphilosophie. 62: 305–317.

Meyer, Lukas H. 2003. Past and Future: The Case for a Threshold Notion of Harm. In: Rights, Culture, and the Law: Themes from the Legal and Political Philosophy of Joseph Raz, edited by Meyer, Lukas H.; Paulson, Stanley L. and Pogge, Thomas W. 143–159. Oxford: Oxford University Press.

O'Neill, Onora. 1996. Towards Justice and Virtue: A Constructive Account of Practical Reasoning. Cambridge: Cambridge University Press.

Parfit, Derek. 1984. Reasons and Persons. Oxford: Clarendon Press.

Partridge, Ernest. 1990. On the Rights of Future Generations. In: Upstream/Downstream: Issues in Environmental Ethics, edited by Scherer, Donald. 40–66. Philadelphia (PA): Temple University Press [republished online at http://gadfly.igc.org/papers/orfg.htm, accessed on 25. 08. 2015].

Partridge, Ernest. 2001. Future Generations. In: A Companion to Environmental Philosophy, edited by Jamieson, Dale. 377–389. Malden (MA) – Oxford: Blackwell.

Raz, Joseph. 1984a. On the Nature of Rights. Mind 93: 194–214.

Raz, Joseph. 1984b. Legal Rights. *Oxford Journal of Legal Studies* 4: 1–21.

Saward, Michael. 2006. Representation. In: Political Theory and the Ecological Challenge, edited by Dobson, Andrew and Eckersley, Robyn. 183–199. Cambridge: Cambridge University Press.

Steiner, Hillel. 1994. An Essay on Rights. Oxford: Blackwell.

Tremmel, Joerg Chet. 2006. Establishing Intergenerational Justice in National Constitutions. In: Handbook of Intergenerational Justice, edited by Tremmel, Joerg Chet. 187–214. Cheltenham – Northampton (MA): Edward Elgar.

Tremmel, Joerg Chet. 2009. A Theory of Intergenerational Justice. London – Sterling (VA): Earthscan.

Warren, Mary Anne. 1977. Do Potential People Have Moral Rights? Canadian Journal of Philosophy 7: 275–289.

Wellman, Carl. 1995. Real Rights. New York – Oxford: Oxford University Press.

Wellman, Carl. 1997. An Approach to Rights: Studies in the Philosophy of Law and Morals. Dordrecht: Kluwer.

Wellman, Christopher Heath. 2005. Feinberg's Two Concepts of Rights. *Legal Theory* 11: 213–226.

Part VI. Global Governance and its Influence on Law Application and Legal Dispute Resolution

Uroš Zdravković

Coverage and Application of the WTO Dispute Settlement Mechanism

Abstract
This article discusses issues concerning the coverage and application of the Dispute Settlement Understanding (DSU) under the WTO's legal framework. Determining the coverage and application of the WTO's dispute settlement mechanism implies determining the scope of covered agreements, especially their relationship with other sources of law both within and outside the WTO's framework. The article analyses which law ought to be applied by the WTO's judicial bodies and respectively which rights can be subject to protection. This issue is associated not only with the scope of the WTO's global power but also with the WTO's impact on global governance and globalisation. In addition, it is also important to clarify conditions for the application of special or additional rules and procedures for settlement of disputes provided in covered agreements other than the DSU. A distinction needs to be made between interpreting these rules as complementary rules, and interpreting them as replacing and prevailing rules over the DSU's rules and procedures.

1. Introduction

The WTO is a global institution comprising of 161 members around the world. Its rules constitute a common institutional and regulatory framework of the global trading system. The implementation of the WTO's regulatory function has become possible by an adequate normative framework that is supported by the mechanism of sanctions for the members that do not abide by its rules.

The multilateral system is far more powerful in the area of trade than in any other policy area (see Sbragia, 2009, 3). Today, the multilateral system of rules is centreed on the WTO, imposing rules that apply to all states and thereby create global trade order. The basic function of the WTO is to provide security and predictability of the multilateral trading system.

The WTO is based on clear rules that all members have to comply with when they create and conduct their trade policy. The fundamental aim of the WTO is trade liberalisation at the global level in order to achieve better living standard in the world.

On the one hand, the WTO's rules are a result of the inter-state negotiations and mutual concessions (intergovernmentalism). On the other hand, the WTO contains supranational nature and elements. The general assertion adopted in this article is that the WTO strives to establish a universal regulatory framework for trade that should be the legal feature of economic globalisation. The WTO can be compared with "a powerful monopolist for creating rules" that all states must apply whether they like it or not. The reason is the fact that it is more useful for most states to be part of the WTO than not to be. The interdependent structure of the world's economy does not allow for unilateral national decisions. In such conditions the WTO has become the regulator of governmental behaviour in international trade relations with a propensity to become the "world trade ministry."

The basic "device" for maintaining the WTO's supranationalism is the dispute settlement mechanism that operates independently and apart from the governments. This system was created in response to the growing need for a supranational dispute resolution mechanism in international trade. The dispute settlement system enables the WTO to be an institution of global governance that reinforces economic globalisation.

The WTO's dispute settlement system has several important supranational elements. First, the disputes are resolved by independent experts (members of panels and the Appellate Body) and not by representatives of the WTO's members. Second, the multilateral system is an obligatory dispute settlement mechanism. Initially, the disputes may be bilateral, but eventually they ought to be resolved later through multilateral forum. Third, due to the "negative consensus rule," the decisions (reports) cannot be adopted only in case all states participating at the meetings of the Dispute Settlement Body (DSB)[1] are against. Given that this could happen only in theory, decisions are adopted automatically. Therefore, the WTO's members participating in disputes have no influence on the outcome.

The first issue discussed in this article is the scope of the global governance established by the WTO's dispute settlement system. It is indisputable that it provides the global "administration" for the international trade relations, mainly due to the strong legal power that it has in that area. Nevertheless, some authors propose a broader concept of the WTO's dispute settlement system, arguing that it has to go beyond the scope of the trade-related issues. Those assertions could lead to a wider conception pertaining to the effect that the WTO's dispute settlement system has on global governance.

The central problem in this discussion is the competence of the WTO's judicial bodies (WTO panels and the Appellate Body) to resolve disputes concerning rights and obligations that are not regulated by the covered agreements. The question is whether the WTO's law allows for the application of other sources of

1 Dispute Settlement Body is a final instance in resolving disputes within the WTO.

law that are not covered by the definition provided in the *Dispute Settlement Understanding* (DSU). The article first elaborates on the difference between covered agreements and other sources within the WTO's law (intra-relationship), and then discusses the competence of panels and Appellate Body to apply non-WTO law (inter-relationship). This discussion is directly connected with the degree of influence that dispute settlement system has on the global governance and globalisation.

The second part of the article clarifies the overlapping of the DSU's norms and the special or additional rules and procedures provided in other covered agreements. In particular, the article focuses on the following question: in which cases those rules and procedures should be applied as supplement and complementary rules to the DSU's rules, and in which cases they may be used as replacing rules over the DSU's norms.

2. The WTO Dispute Settlement Mechanism: Introductory View

International trade disputes under the WTO are frequent. Since the formation of the WTO in 1995, almost 500 disputes have been filed with this organisation. Disputes were also common during the application of the General Agreement on Tariffs and Trade (GATT, 1947) that preceded the WTO and existed in the period between 1947 and 1994.

The dispute settlement mechanism under the GATT era was highly diplomatic-oriented, but it was far more efficient and rule-oriented in comparison with other international dispute settlement systems. Nevertheless, during the Uruguay round (between 1986 and 1994), the GATT's members decided to create a more efficient and more rule oriented dispute settlement system.

Hence, alongside with establishing the WTO, they established a new dispute settlement system, with the aim to preserve and protect the members' rights and expectations covered by the WTO's agreements. The negotiators of the Uruguay round drafted a subject-specific agreement for dispute settlement and called it *Understanding on Rules and Procedures Governing the Settlement of Disputes* (Annex II of Agreement Establishing the WTO) i.e., for short *Dispute Settlement Understanding* (DSU).

The DSU is, therefore, the legal basis for settling disputes between members regarding the fulfilment of prescribed obligations under the WTO's law. Each WTO member enjoys the rights provided in the WTO's agreements; yet, in case of violation of any WTO agreement by another member, the entire WTO law system would be redundant without providing for an effective access to justice.

Therefore, the dispute settlement mechanism is the most important feature within the WTO's legal framework, which has been described by many authors and academics as a *jewel in the crown* of the WTO (see Goh, 2007, 478; Khan, 2014, 90). Unlike many other international organisations, the WTO is provided with integrated, coherent, and effective dispute resolution system.

3. Covered Agreements

The concept and definition of covered agreements (CAs) is of essence in discussing access to justice and legal protection under the WTO. Hence, it is highly important to make a clear distinction between those agreements and other sources of law that may interact with a particular disputable situation.

At a glance, there should not be any uncertainty about what agreements ought to be considered CAs. Article 1.1 of the DSU in its first sentence clearly states: "The rules and procedures of this Understanding shall apply to disputes brought pursuant to the consultation and dispute settlement provisions of the agreements listed in Appendix 1 to this Understanding." The DSU marks those agreements as *covered agreements*. The all CA are listed in Appendix 1 to the DSU[2].

The given definition of CA is also followed by the WTO's judicial bodies. In the case *Brazil — Desiccated Coconut*, the Appellate Body found that the *covered agreements* "include the WTO Agreement, the Agreements in Annexes 1 and 2, as well as any Plurilateral Trade Agreement in Annex 4 where its Committee of signatories has taken a decision to apply the DSU."[3]

Although the clear definition of CAs *prima facie* seems unambiguous, there is a need to discuss and further explain the distinction and borderline between covered agreements and other agreements and documents. Firstly, distinction needs to be made within the internal structure of the WTO's system of law because CAs are not the only sources of WTO's law. Secondly, and more importantly, it is

---

2 According to the Appendix 1 to DSU covered agreements are: (A) Agreement Establishing the World Trade Organisation; (B) Multilateral Trade Agreements: Annex 1A: Multilateral Agreements on Trade in Goods; Annex 1B: General Agreement on Trade in Services; Annex 1C: Agreement on Trade-Related Aspects of Intellectual Property Rights; Annex 2: Understanding on Rules and Procedures Governing the Settlement of Disputes; (C) Plurilateral Trade Agreements: Annex 4: Agreement on Trade in Civil Aircraft; Agreement on Government Procurement; International Dairy Agreement (terminated on 1. January 1998); International Bovine Meat Agreement (terminated on 1. January 1998).

3 Appellate Body Report, Brazil – Measures Affecting Desiccated Coconut, WT/DS22/AB/R, adopted 20 March 1997, DSR 1997:I, 167, p. 13.

essential to explain whether the WTO's judicial bodies have jurisdiction to apply the sources of international law standing outside the scope of the WTO's law.

4. Other Sources within the WTO Law

The WTO's system of law is very complex and includes a vast number of sources contained in over 30,000 pages of various documents. Yet, it does not mean that a WTO member can seek legal protection of its rights and interests in accordance with any WTO document. The whole WTO's law system may be divided into two key groups: 1) the covered agreements, and 2) other agreements, documents, and legal texts. This division has been made with regard to existence or non-existence of the WTO's judicial bodies' competence to deal with the disputes arising from their application. Therefore, there is a difference between the agreements whose application can be subjected to the dispute settlement system and the agreements and documents concluded under the WTO whose application cannot be subject to examination before panels and Appellate Body (see Cvetković, 2009, 143). The CAs may be also designated as *sources of WTO law* in *a narrow sense*, while other WTO documents and legal texts can be marked as *sources of WTO law in a broader sense*, or *interpretative agreements* because they serve as a complement in the interpretation of the WTO's sources in a narrow sense (see Matsushita, Shoenbaum, & Mavroidis, 2006, 24).

Speaking of sources of the WTO's law in a broader sense, there are 27 Ministerial decisions and declarations adopted during the process of establishing the WTO. Furthermore, there are also decisions of the WTO's bodies. These sources are not CAs and they do not generate member's rights and obligations that can be protected before the WTO's judicial bodies (see Cvetković, 2010, 51).

Therefore, the legal protection is reserved only for those benefits that are granted by CAs. For example, a member can contravene some internal act or measure of another member if that specific act or measure is considered to be inconsistent with the provisions of any CA.[4] Also, if members seek redress for a violation of a CAs, the mechanism provided in the DSU is compulsory (see Graewert, 2008, 294).

4 See: Appellate Body Report, United States – Anti-Dumping Act of 1916, WT/DS136/AB/R, WT/DS162/AB/R, adopted 26 September 2000, DSR 2000:X, 4793, para. 57.

5. Extrinsic Law Sources

It has been necessary to clearly define the borderlines related to the agreements that are to be interpreted and applied by the WTO's judicial bodies. Every ambiguity regarding this fundamental question would probably create many problems, not only within the WTO mechanism but also between the WTO and other international and regional organisations. For that reason, the drafters of the DSU were precise and strict in defining the scope of the WTO's dispute settlement system. Nevertheless, a closer analysis of scholarly articles examining the relationship between the WTO's law and other international law yields a conclusion that this relationship is *clearly ambiguous*.

The question arises, however, to what extent the WTO's panels and the Appellate Body have competence to decide on legal issues which are not directly relating to CAs, i.e. whether the WTO's judicial bodies have competence to decide on all aspects of a dispute or only on the legal issues directly relating to CAs.

5.1 Strict Conception

Some scholars support a strict conception of the WTO's judicial bodies' jurisdiction pertaining only to CAs. According to Trachtman (1999, 338), "the WTO dispute resolution system is clearly not a court of general jurisdiction, competent to apply all applicable international law" and "the only law that WTO panels and the Appellate Body are authorised to apply (directly) is WTO law" (see Trachtman, 2004, 858).

To support his claim Trachtman refers to relevant provisions of the DSU. First, Article 3.2 of the DSU provides that "recommendations and rulings of the DSB cannot add to or diminish the rights and obligations provided in the covered agreements." He argues that this language "would be absurd if rights and obligations arising from other international law could be applied by the Dispute Settlement Body (DSB)." Further on, he refers to the standard panel terms of reference under Article 7 of the DSU which provides for reference only to law arising from the WTO's agreements. Finally, he points to Article 11 of the DSU which specifies the function of panels to assess the applicability of and conformity with the CA. Therefore, Trachtman concludes that "with so much specific reference to the CA as the law applicable in WTO dispute resolution, it would be odd if the members intended non-WTO law to be applicable" (see Trachtman, 1999, 342).

Some other authors refer to the DSB's rulings in supporting strict lines of coverage and application of the WTO's dispute settlement mechanism. Accordingly,

Busch (2007, 742) refers to Panel Report in the case *Mexico— Soft Drinks*. In this Report, the Panel ruled that:

> "[…] any findings made by this Panel, as well as its conclusions and recommendations in the present case, only relate to Mexico's rights and obligations under the WTO covered agreements, and not to its rights and obligations under other international agreements, such as the NAFTA, or other rules of international law."[5]

In several other cases, the WTO's judicial bodies and the DSB have also repeatedly rejected to apply the agreements and rules outside the strict lines of CAs.

In the case *EC — Commercial Vessels*, the Panel examined a bilateral agreement between the European Communities and Korea referred to as the *Agreed Minutes*. The Panel noted that the Agreed Minutes are not a *covered agreement* within the meaning of the DSU. The Panel emphasised that:

> "Its review of the text of the Agreed Minutes only serves the purpose of enabling it to decide a factual issue on which the parties disagree and that it is not interpreting the Agreed Minutes in order to determine the rights and obligations of the parties under that bilateral agreement."[6]

In the case *EC — Large Civil Aircraft*, the European Communities argued that, in its examination of the matter referred to it, the Panel should directly apply the provisions of a 1992 Agreement between the European Communities and the US. The Panel refuted the argument and stated that:

> "As the 1992 Agreement is not a covered Agreement cited by the United States, or contained in the list of covered Agreements in Appendix 1 to the DSU, or one of the instruments included in the GATT 1994, we do not have jurisdiction to determine of the rights and obligations of the parties under the 1992 Agreement."[7]

Therefore, according to the rulings of the WTO's judicial bodies, they only have jurisdiction to examine covered agreements. In other words, the WTO's law does not allow for the application of any extrinsic source of law. Thus, it does not deal with non-trade issues. Some scholars are even of the opinion that non-WTO's

5 Panel Report, Mexico – Tax Measures on Soft Drinks and Other Beverages, WT/DS308/R, adopted 24 March 2006, as modified by Appellate Body Report WT/DS308/AB/R, DSR 2006:I, 43, Para. 7.15.

6 Panel Report, European Communities – Measures Affecting Trade in Commercial Vessels, WT/DS301/R, adopted 20 June 2005, DSR 2005:XV, 7713. Para. 7.131 See also: Appellate Body Report, European Communities – Measures Affecting the Importation of Certain Poultry Products, WT/DS69/AB/R, adopted 23 July 1998, DSR 1998:V, 2031.

7 Panel Report, EC and certain member States — Large Civil Aircraft, WT/DS316/R , 30 June 2010. Para. 7.89.

law cannot be invoked at all as a defence during a WTO dispute (see Graewert, 2008, 298). That means that the international law outside the WTO's framework, such as human rights law and environmental law, cannot be applied by panels and Appellate Body in dispute settlement procedures. In any case, extrinsic law cannot be applied as applicable law to merits; in some cases, extrinsic law has been applied as an interpretation guide for clarifying some terms contained in covered agreements.[8]

At this point, we should go back to the initial discussion and make a nexus between the strict conception and the issue of the WTO's global power. The WTO is the universal trade institution and the dispute settlement system is its primary "tool" for implementation of global governance. The strict conception supports that approach, but limits the scope of the WTO's global power only to trade-related issues. Therefore, the WTO does not have "global jurisdiction" to deal with all kinds of matters that may interact with certain trade dispute.

5.2 The Need for Interaction

The strict conception was criticised by many legal scholars. There may be various disputable situations that actually combine trade issues and non-trade issues (for example, trade and human rights, or trade and environmental law). Many authors thus suggest that the WTO's judicial bodies need to take into consideration all aspects of disputes, and not just trade-related ones. If we accept the strict conception, the problem may occur when some measure complies with the WTO's obligations but concurrently implies a violation of human rights, or vice-versa. Therefore, if some state would impose trade sanctions against another state that tolerates child labour, that measure would be indisputable from the human rights' perspective but it would concurrently be against the WTO's law because it does not allow for the application of any trade sanctions. In the given example, the state that violates human rights can initiate WTO's procedure against the state that imposes trade sanctions. Consequently, the general suggestion of many authors is that the WTO's dispute settlement mechanism should be more open for other important aspects of a dispute, particularly in case of complicated disputes involving not

8 Such example can be found in the case *US-Shrimp*, where the Appellate Body used extrinsic law sources and documents to interpret the term "exhaustible natural resources" within Article XX of the GATT. See: Report of the Appellate Body in United States – Import Prohibition of Certain Shrimp and Shrimp Products, WT/DS58/AB/R, adopted 6 November 1998, DSR 1998:VII, 2755.

only trade issues but also other important aspects regulated by other branches of international law.

Some authors propose making a clear distinction between jurisdiction and the law applicable to a dispute (see Pauwelyn, 2003a, 460; Marceau, 2001, 1081). Pauwelyn views the WTO's law as a mere *branch* or a *sub-system* of Public International Law (see ibid., pp. 9, 25–26; see also Pauwelyn, 2001, 538). He argues:

> "As a branch or a sub-system, the WTO does, or must, interact with other branches or subsystems of Public International Law, such as human rights treaties and international environmental agreements. The WTO is neither a *closed legal circuit* nor a *self-contained* regime" (see Pauwelyn, 2003a, 35).

Schoenbaum (1998, 653), for example, argues that "Article 11 of the DSU resolves this question by granting panels and the Appellate Body the authority to 'make such other findings as will assist the DSB in making the recommendation or in giving the rulings provided for in the CAs'" (see Article 11 of the DSU). According to Schoenbaum (see ibid.), this is an "*implied powers* clause which should be interpreted broadly so that the panels and AB can decide all aspects of a dispute."

Graewert (2008, 295) in addition emphasises that "the fact that the jurisdiction of WTO Panels is strictly limited to WTO agreements does not mean that the applicable law before a WTO Panel has to be distinguished from all outside laws." He observes the WTO Agreement as a part of customary international law, and argues that, according to the Vienna Conventions on the Law of Treaties (VCLT), when a treaty is interpreted, "any relevant rules of international law applicable in the relations between the parties" have to be taken into account.[9] He also points to the Appellate Body Report in the case *US-Gasoline* in which it was explicitly stated that the GATT "is not to be read in clinical isolation from public international law,"[10] which is, according to Graewert (see ibid.) in conformity with Article 31.3(c) of the VCLT.

Finally, Pauwelyn (2003b, 998) distinguishes two types of cases in which non-WTO law may be applied by the WTO's panels. He argues that non-WTO law could lead a panel to decline jurisdiction, even if it had jurisdiction without the invocation of the non-WTO norm. In addition, according to Pauwelyn, non-WTO

---

9 Art. 31(3) (c) of the VCLT provides: "There shall be taken into account, together with the context: [...] (c) any relevant rules of international law in the relationship between the parties."

10 Appellate Body Report, United States – Standards for Reformulated and Conventional Gasoline, WT/DS2/AB/R, adopted 20 May 1996, DSR 1996:I, 3.

law could serve as a justification for a challenged act that would otherwise be a violation of the WTO's rules.

To which law the DSB may apply is a question left unanswered (see Lindroos & Mehling, 2006, 861), whereas the question of how far a defence based on non-WTO law could go remains controversial (see Graewert, 298), at least in theory given the fact that the WTO's judicial bodies are persistent in demonstrating the strict approach. Unlike the strict conception, the broader approach suggests the wider scope of the WTO's dispute settlement system. Nevertheless, if we accept this argumentation, the WTO's global power would become much more extensive then it should be, especially having in mind that the main principle of the WTO's dispute settlement system is protecting and maintaining security and predictability of the multilateral trading system. If the WTO judicial bodies would unconditionally allow for the application of extrinsic law sources, it would hinder that principle and endanger the achieved level of international trade integrations.

6. DSU and Special or Additional Rules and Procedures

Some CAs contain special rules and procedures for consultations and dispute settlements regarding their subject matter. Appendix 2 of the DSU identifies such rules and procedures[11] that may overlap with the DSU norms. Article 1.2 of the DSU regulates these situations and in the first and second sentence, stating:

> "The rules and procedures of this Understanding shall apply subject to such special or additional rules and procedures on dispute settlement contained in the covered agreements as are identified in Appendix 2 to this Understanding. To the extent that there is a difference between the rules and procedures of this Understanding and the special or additional rules and procedures set forth in Appendix 2, the special or additional rules and procedures in Appendix 2 shall prevail."

Therefore, the general rule under Article 1.1 of the DSU is subject to the special or additional rules and procedures identified in Appendix 2. However, two important questions arise in regard of applying the additional rules and procedures:

A) First, in which cases should these rules be considered supplement rules (i.e., rules complementary to the DSU's rules);

B) Second, when should these rules and procedures be interpreted as replacing rules over the DSU's rules.

---

11 Covered agreements which contain such special or additional rules and procedures are Agreement on the Application of Sanitary and Phytosanitary Measures, Agreement on Textiles and Clothing, Agreement on Technical Barriers to Trade, Agreement on Implementation of Article VI of GATT 1994 (Antidumping Agreement), and few others.

6.1 Special or Additional Rules as Complementary Rules

The WTO's judicial bodies have much more relied on special or additional rules and procedures as a supplement. As already referred to, Article 1.2 of the DSU provides that "special or additional rules and procedures *shall prevail* over the provisions of the DSU to the extent that there is a *difference between* the two sets of provisions." The WTO's judicial bodies established a rule according to which they need to identify a *genuine conflict* between special or additional rules and the DSU's rules. That means that special and additional rules within the meaning of Article 1.2 of the DSU apply only in the case of *inconsistency* or a *difference* between these rules and the DSU's provisions.

In the case *Guatemala — Cement I*, the Appellate Body has extensively explained the conditions for the application of special or additional rules. According to the Appellate Body, if there is no *difference*, then the rules and procedures of the DSU apply together with the special or additional provisions of the CA.[12]

In that dispute the Appellate Body discussed the relationship between Article 17 of the Anti-Dumping Agreement and Article 6.2 of the DSU. Article 6.2 of the DSU requires that both the *measure at issue* and the *legal basis for the complaint* be identified in a request for establishing a panel. However, Article 17.5 of the Anti-Dumping Agreement does not specifically require a disputant in an anti-dumping dispute to *identify the specific measures at issue* in the panel request.

In the first instance the Panel concluded that Article 17.5 of the Anti-Dumping Agreement prevails over Article 6.2 of the DSU. However, the Appellate Body considered that the Panel erred in reaching this conclusion. The Appellate Body found that Article 17.5 does not expressly require a disputant to identify the *specific measures at issue* or *to provide a brief summary of the legal basis of the complaint.* According to the Appellate Body, Article 17.5 contains none of the explicit, detailed procedural requirements that Article 6.2 of the DSU imposes on a request for the establishment of a panel. Therefore, the Appellate Body has found that these two provisions should be applied together:

> "In our view, it is only where the provisions of the DSU and the special or additional rules and procedures of a covered agreement *cannot* be read as *complementing* each other that the special or additional provisions are to *prevail*. A special or additional provision should only be found to *prevail* over a provision of the DSU in a situation where adherence to the one provision will lead to a violation of the other provision, that is, in

12 Appellate Body Report, Guatemala – Anti-Dumping Investigation Regarding Portland Cement from Mexico, WT/DS60/AB/R, adopted 25 November 1998, DSR 1998:IX, 3767, para. 65.

> the case of a *conflict* between them. An interpreter must, therefore, identify an *inconsistency* or *difference* between a provision of the DSU and a special or additional provision of a covered agreement *before* concluding that the latter *prevails* and that the provision of the DSU does not apply."[13]

According to the Appellate Body, the special or additional provisions listed in Appendix 2 of the DSU are designed to deal with the particularities of dispute settlement relating to obligations arising under a specific CA, while Article 1 of the DSU seeks to establish an integrated and comprehensive dispute settlement system for all of the CAs of the WTO Agreement as a whole. It is, therefore, only in the specific circumstance where a provision of the DSU and a special or additional provision of another CA are mutually inconsistent that the special or additional provision may be read to prevail over the provision of the DSU (See para. 66 of the Report).

The Appellate Body Report in *Guatemala — Cement I* gave enough grounds for prospective considerations concerning application of special or additional provisions. There are many subsequent cases in which the WTO's judicial bodies were on the same position.[14]

Some scholars are of the opinion that the term *conflict* should be interpreted broadly; accordingly, conflicting norms are extant not only where two obligations clash but also where a provision in one treaty permits what a provision in another treaty prohibits (see Chase, 2012, 805). Chase argues that "it can reasonably be

---

13 Para. 65 of the Report. See also: Appellate Body Report, United States - Tax Treatment for "Foreign Sales Corporations" - Second Recourse to Article 21.5 of the DSU by the European Communities, WT/DS108/AB/RW2, adopted 14 March 2006, DSR 2006:XI, 4721 para. 159.

14 See reports of the Appellate Body in following cases: United States - Sunset Review of Anti-Dumping Duties on Corrosion-Resistant Carbon Steel Flat Products from Japan, WT/DS244/AB/R, adopted 9 January 2004, DSR 2004:I, 3; United States - Anti-Dumping Measures on Certain Hot-Rolled Steel Products from Japan, WT/DS184/AB/R, adopted 23 August 2001, DSR 2001:X, 4697; United States - Measures Relating to Zeroing and Sunset Reviews, WT/DS322/AB/R, adopted 23 January 2007; United States - Tax Treatment for "Foreign Sales Corporations," WT/DS108/AB/R, adopted 20 March 2000, DSR 2000:III, 1619. See also reports of the panels in cases: Korea - Measures Affecting Trade in Commercial Vessels, WT/DS273/R, adopted 11 April 2005, DSR 2005:VII, 2749; Brazil - Export Financing Programme for Aircraft, WT/DS46/R, adopted 20 August 1999, as modified by Appellate Body Report WT/DS46/AB/R, DSR 1999:III, 1221; European Communities - Measures Affecting Asbestos and Asbestos-Containing Products, WT/DS135/R and Add.1, adopted 5 April 2001, as modified by Appellate Body Report WT/DS135/AB/R, DSR 2001:VIII, 3305.

presumed that WTO Members, by concluding a series of agreements as a single undertaking, meant for these agreements to be internally consistent" (see ibid., 803) and that the principle of *lex specialis derogat legi generali* "would be the most relevant principle that is capable of resolving a real or genuine conflict between treaty norms" (see ibid., 813.).

6.2 Special or Additional Rules as Replacing Rules: The Case of the DSU and the SCM Agreement

In discussing this issue, we will examine a case where the Panel has found that special and additional rules prevail over the DSU's rules. In Australia — Automotive Leather II (Article 21.5 — US),[15] the Panel was discussing the relationship between Article 19.1 of the DSU and Article 4.7 of the Agreement on Subsidies and Countervailing Measures (SCM). The Article 19.1 of the DSU provides in its relevant part that: "Where a panel or the Appellate Body concludes that a measure is inconsistent with a covered agreement, it shall recommend that the Member concerned *bring the measure into conformity* with that agreement." However, Article 4.7 of the SCM states: "If the measure in question is found to be a prohibited subsidy, the panel shall recommend that the subsidizing Member *withdraw the subsidy* without delay."

The US and Australia both construed Article 19.1 of the DSU as a principal element to be considered in interpreting Article 4.7 of the SCM Agreement, arguing that Article 4.7 of the SCM should be read consistently with Article 19.1 of the DSU. Furthermore, they argued that an interpretation of Article 4.7 of the SCM Agreement that would allow a retroactive remedy is inconsistent with Article 19 of the DSU.

As the parties have argued, the recommendation to *bring the measure into conformity* under Article 19.1 of the DSU is generally understood to require a Member be found to have violated a provision of the WTO Agreements to *withdraw the measure* in a prospective sense. Thus, according to these two states, it might be argued that the *withdrawal of subsidy* should also require a Member to do so only in a prospective sense.

The Panel disagreed and found the two provisions to be inconsistent, which was the ground for taking the position that the SCM's provision should prevail. As mentioned before, special and additional rules within the meaning of Article 1.2 of the DSU apply only in the case of *inconsistency* or a *difference* between these

15 Panel Report, Australia – Subsidies Provided to Producers and Exporters of Automotive Leather, WT/DS126/R, adopted 16 June 1999, DSR 1999:III, 951.

rules and the provisions of the DSU (see supra note 41 of the Report). Hence, the Panel was on the position that Article 4.7 of the SCM should prevail over the Art. 19.1 of the DSU and stated:

> "We do not believe that Article 19.1 of the DSU, even in conjunction with Article 3.7 of the DSU, requires the limitation of the specific remedy provided for in Article 4.7 of the SCM Agreement to purely prospective action. An interpretation of Article 4.7 of the SCM Agreement which would allow exclusively *prospective* action would make the recommendation to *withdraw the subsidy* under Article 4.7 indistinguishable from the recommendation to *bring the measure into conformity* under Article 19.1 of the DSU, thus rendering Article 4.7 redundant" (para. 6.31.).

Therefore, the Panel found that Article 19.1 of the DSU was not the basis for the panel recommendation in a case involving prohibited subsidies, but that Article 4.7 of the SCM must be interpreted and applied in this dispute. According to the Panel, an action of *bringing the measure into conformity* is different from the action of *withdrawal of subsidy* (which is the necessary *inconsistency* or *difference* required by Article 1.2. of the DSU); thus, that different action shall prevail.

7. Conclusion

On the basis on the foregoing analysis two basic issues in discussing the coverage and application of the WTO's dispute settlement mechanism can be identified: first, jurisdiction and competence of the WTO's judicial bodies to apply non-WTO law and second, the relationship between the DSU and special or additional rules and procedures in other CAs.

Concerning the first issue, although Article 1.1 of the DSU and Appendix 1 as well as other corresponding provisions of the DSU clearly specify the competence of the WTO's judicial bodies, some authors suggest that panels and Appellate Body should apply a broader approach in resolving disputes; thus, instead of relying exclusively on the CAs, they should also make use of other international sources of law which may be deemed relevant. The broader approach suggests the wider scope of the WTO's dispute settlement system that would enable a higher global power for the WTO. Nevertheless, the Appellate Body, and subsequently the DSB, have reasonably been rigid so far in determining their competence and jurisdiction regarding applicable law in disputes. The strict conception, which is supported by the WTO's judicial bodies, limits the scope of the WTO's global power only to trade-related issues.

As for the second issue, it is very important to distinguish when special or additional rules and procedures should be read as supplement or complementary rules, and in which cases they should be used as prevailing or replacing rules. The requirement of *genuine conflict* between the DSU and these rules must be fulfilled. It means that special and additional rules apply only in the case of *inconsistency* or a *difference* between those rules and the provisions of the DSU. Accordingly, in case there is no *difference*, then the rules and procedures of the DSU apply together with the special or additional provisions.

References

Busch, Marc L. 2007. Overlapping Institutions, Forum Shopping, and Dispute Settlement in International Trade. *International Organization* 61 (4): 735–761.

Chase, Claude. 2012. Norm Conflict between WTO Covered Agreements - Real, Apparent or Avoided? *International and Comparative Law Quarterly* 61(4): 791–821.

Cvetković, Predrag. 2010. Uvod u pravo Svetske trgovinske organizacije (english translation: Introduction to WTO law). Niš: Faculty of Law, Publication Center.

Cvetković, Predrag. 2009. Izvori prava Svetske trgovinske organizacije i njihov značaj za države u tranziciji (english translation: Sources of WTO law and their importance for transition countries). In: Balkan in Eurointegration Process: 20 years of transition, Book 4, edited by Milorad Božić and Srđan Golubović, 137–161. Niš: Faculty of Philosophy.

Goh, Gavin; Morgan, David. 2007. Political Considerations and Pragmatic Outcomes in WTO Dispute Rulings. *UNSW Law Journal* 30(2): 477–503.

Graewert, Tim. 2008. Conflicting Laws and Juristidictions in the Dispute Settlement Process of Regional Trade Agreements and the WTO. *Contemporary Asia Arbitration Journal* 1(2): 287–334.

Khan, Humayun Rasheed. 2014. Ambitious Quest for Rule- Oriented Dispute Settlement System of WTO. *Asian Journal of Multidisciplinary Studies* 2(10): 89–99.

Lindroos, Anja; Mehling, Michael. 2006. Dispelling the Chimera of 'Self-Contained Regimes' International Law and the WTO. *The European Journal of International Law* 16 (5): 857–877.

Marceau, Gabrielle. 2001. Conflicts of Norms and Conflicts of Jurisdictions The Relationship between the WTO Agreement and MEAs and other Treaties. *Journal of World Trade* 35(6): 1081–1131.

Matsushita, Mitsuo; Shoenbaum, Thomas and Mavroidis, Petros. 2006. The World Trade Organization: Law, Practice and Policy. Oxford: Oxford University Press.

Pauwelyn, Joost. 2003. Conflict of Norms in Public International Law: How WTO Law Relates to Other Rules of International Law. New York: Cambridge University Press.

Pauwelyn, Joost. 2003. How to Win a World Trade Organisation Dispute Based on Non-World Trade Organisation Law? Questions of Jurisdiction and Merits. *Journal of World Trade* 37(6): 997–1030.

Pauwelyn, Joost. 2001. The Role of Public International Law in WTO: How far can we go? *The American Journal of International Law* 95: 535–578.

Sbragia, Alberta. 2009. The EU, the US, and Trade Policy: Competitive Interdependence In the Management of Globalization. Unpublished. Presented at the European Union Studies Association 11th Biennial Conference, Marina Del Rey, California, April 23–25, 2009.

Schoenbaum, Thomas. 1998. WTO Dispute Settlement: Praise and Suggestions for Reform. *International and Comparative Law Quarterly* 47(3): 647–658.

Trachtman, Joel, P. 2004. Recent Books on International Law (reviewing Joost Pauwelyn, Conflict of Norms in Public International Law: How WTO Law Relates to Other Rules of International Law). *American Journal on International Law* 98(4): 855–861.

Trachtman, Joel, P. 1999. The Domain of WTO Dispute Resolution. *Harvard International Law Journal* 40: 333–378.

Adam Szot

The Influence of European Court of Human Rights' Jurisprudence on Public Administration Governance Processes

Abstract

In the modern world of globalisation and integration the question arises as to whether the legal processes (namely law application processes) that occur at the international level may affect the unification of processes and decisions undertaken at the national level by the state authorities. This article is an attempt to answer the question about the potential impact of the jurisprudence of the European Court of Human Rights (ECHR) on public administration discretionary powers in governance processes.

There are at least three important aspects of this phenomenon that correspond with the main questions of the paper. The first one (1) whether the ECHR system is efficient enough to prevent the infringement of human rights at the national level, especially when we consider discretion of public administration bodies. The second one (2) how the jurisprudence of the ECHR may affect said discretion. The last question is the consequence of standards of protection of human rights that are introduced by the ECHR and which are binding on the countries that have signed the Convention of Human Right Protection. That is why it is worth analysing how a supranational court (like the ECHR) can influence the national decision making processes and at the same time whether we can observe unification of those processes in different states. In this context the question is (3) – whether the ECHR can be seen as an institution of global governance and if its jurisprudence does not breach the principle of separation of powers at the national level.

1. Introduction

In the modern world there are newer tasks presented to public administration in governance processes in the state or in specific areas of social life, that are meant to meet the individual and collective needs of its citizens. In order to make the implementation of these tasks possible the legislature grants public authorities a certain range of discretion. At the same time the scope of this discretion can be influenced by a variety of factors of a diverse nature – legal, economic, social, political, etc. Legal factors include national and international legislation and the practical application of law – earlier legal decisions like court rulings or decisions of public administration. These decisions can more or less directly affect the scope and manner of use of the discretionary powers of the administration.

At the same time the influence of extra legal factors on public administration may lead to a decision that violates human rights. Different states introduce in their legal systems specific mechanisms that should prevent this kind of situation. Of course those mechanisms are not always efficient enough to counteract the aforementioned infringements. Therefore there is a functioning international human rights protection system part of which is the system of the Council of Europe in which an important role is being played by the European Court of Human Rights (ECHR). It is worth emphasising whether the jurisdiction of the ECHR can successfully prevent the violation of human rights, especially when we consider decisions undertaken in the scope of discretion.

At the same time, it is worth considering how, in the world of globalisation and integration, decisions of public administration bodies taken within their scope of discretionary powers can be subject to the influence of judgments by international courts (namely the ECHR as an example of a court whose jurisdiction is mandatory for all countries that signed the European Convention of Human Rights). It is worth considering how the processes of application of law (court rulings) at the international level may affect the decisions taken at the national level, not just for individual cases, which have been the subject of adjudication but primarily on the governance processes in the state.

At this point, one can suppose that the case law of the ECHR may have a significant effect on the management processes in the country, becoming an instrument of global governance, unifying the scope and content of decisions and actions taken in each state. At the same time one can formulate another hypothesis that such interactions can violate the principle of separation of powers in the state.

2. Public Administration Activities and its Discretionary Power

Public administration activities can be divided into two groups that correspond with the goals of the administration and the scope of its discretionary power. On the one hand there is a "simple" performance of its duties resulting from binding specific legal provisions or imposed (in the limits set by general legal provisions) by the government. This is the case when the tasks of the public administration body are determined in an unequivocal and categorical way and the public authority has no other option of "behaviour" but to fulfil it. These obligations play an important role in the public administration's activity but they do not exhaust the whole range of its functions.

On the other hand there are actions of public administration that can be seen as independent and creative activity undertaken, within the law, to implement broadly defined state (social) objectives such as, generally speaking, ensuring public order and safety or providing adequate support to citizens; in other words, the implementation of widely understood activities in favour of the public interest. In this sense administrative authorities are fulfilling, generally defined by the law (and within the framework of the law), duties of governance in the state in different areas of social life to the point where a conflict with the public interest occur (and within the limited financial resources).

In those situations, carrying out the affairs of state and seeking to meet the needs of citizens (governance processes), public administration bodies, in the framework of general goals, will need to determine the optimal way of fulfilling them as to the form and method of their implementation. The accomplishment of those goals can include issuing a single decision to a citizen, releasing several decisions of similar content in similar factual circumstances, passing a legal act, or undertaking other imperative or non-imperious actions.

In order to realise governance tasks and to ensure that the activities of public administration take into account the dynamics and specifics of a rapidly changing world and society, public authorities are equipped by the lawmaker with a certain range of freedom – discretionary power. Public administration discretionary power is defined in various ways and its different aspects are highlighted. In my opinion, however, the most scientifically useful aspect is its *sensu largissimo* understanding as a certain range of freedoms of a decisional body that can be identified at every stage of the decision making process (see Galligan, 1986, pp. 46–74; Treves 1947, pp. 276–291).

Such understanding of discretionary power may concern the freedom to choose between action and inaction, between forms and methods of action, ways of collecting the information needed to undertake a decision, freedom of interpretation of the law, or the possibility to choose among potential contents of the final decision, the one that in the intentions of decisional body should fully realise its goals. For example, during the phase of determination of the facts of the case it can be seen as the freedom to determine which facts are subject to its reasoning, how they are going to be determined and, of course, freedom of assessment of the facts of the case. Discretionary power during the phase of validation and interpretation can be seen as the freedom to choose the source of legal norms (from the sources accepted in specific legal order) and its interpretation in order to recessive the normative basis of the decision in the specific case.

Discretionary power of public administration is particularly apparent in two stages of the decision making processes – the initial stage and the final one. In the former, it can be seen as the possibility of deciding to take or not to take any action and the correct selection of legally acceptable forms of this action. In the so-called pre-decisional phase, the authorities shall undertake reasoning to answer the question about the possibility and/or the need to initiate a process leading to changes in the social reality. In the latter one, discretionary power is particularly noticeable when the lawmaker introduces to the law the construct of administrative approval, which generally speaking grants decisional body with the possibility to choose from at least two legally permissible contents of the final decision the one that in its opinion is the right (optimal) one in the specific case (see Jaśkowska, 2010, pp. 292–298).

At the same time in decision making processes one can find also other sources of said discretion that are not the outcome of conscientious legislator's actions (such as imperfections of the legal language, the social context of the law, etc.) (see Leszczyński, 2001, 54). All of this together creates a sphere in which the administration possesses a certain level of freedom in the scope of argumentation and the content of issued decisions.

One needs to remember that public authorities can be affected by a number of factors – legal, organisational, political, and social – and the decision making process may be influenced by many different and sometimes conflicting interests. A variety of factors both within legal norms and outside the scope of the law influence the decisions made by public administrations.

The larger the scope of the discretionary power wielded by the public administration, the bigger the impact of non-legal (extra-legal) factors on the entire decision making process and the shape of the final decisions. At the same time, it should be remembered that the administration is a type of organisation with specific goals that is responsible for their implementation. Its authorities are not independent and function within complex organisational and political structures. *Ipso facto*, the particular characteristics of the administration are the reasons for its being interested in the content of the decisions it makes. This can lead to situations in which the legitimacy of an act may be "sacrificed" due to other criteria such as thrift or the need to act in accordance with political objectives.

3. Judicial Review of Public Administration and Protection of Human Rights

In order to counteract law infringements by the public administration, modern democratic states implement a number of solutions in their legal systems that protect the individual from arbitrary, unwarranted, or illegal decisions made by the administrative authority that violates human rights. An essential and necessary element of control by public authorities in the states providing for the principle of rule of law is the control exercised by independent courts.

The judicial oversight of the legality of decisions made within the scope of the discretion is not just restricted to a declaration of compliance or inconsistency with the content of norms enclosed within the legal provisions of material and procedural law, but it is also confronted with the axiology of a given branch of the law, the entire legal system, or even the legal order. The "legality of the goal" criterion assumes that the action of an administrative authority must not only be in accordance with the text of the legal provision but also with the purpose for which it was established (see Jakimowicz, 2010, 52). In this sense, incompatibility with this goal can be assessed as an action in violation of existing norms. In French doctrine this is found to be a part of "public administration morality" (détournement de pouvoir).

Thus the question is in what manner and how "deeply" and "broadly" may the judicial decision influence the scope and manner of implementation of the discretionary power of the administration. One might say that taking into account the separation of powers principle jurisprudence should not interfere directly with the content of public administration actions especially in the situation when legal norm grants the body with a certain range of discretion. In those situations the court should rather verify whether administrative authorities acted within the scope of legally permissible forms with the use of legally acceptable methods and whether the process of interpretation of law was carried out in a proper way. As well as whether the content of the final decision does not violate legal norms. However as it was mentioned legality and especially the legality of the issued decision must be understood widely. But sometimes it can be seen as a justification for a court to interfere in the governance processes, which can eventually lead to the violation of separation of power principle.

At the same time it is worth emphasising that jurisprudence can affect the discretionary power of public administration in various ways. Besides the direct impact in a situation of verification of a specific actions or decisions there can also be seen other aspects of a court ruling that can be recognised as an example of indirect impact. It can be seen especially in the situation when there is a fixed line of judgements in certain kind of cases. In this sense jurisprudence can influence the reasoning of a decisional body even in governance processes for the pragmatic reasons – administrative body will probably prefer to issue a decision in accordance to previous judgements than accept the consequences of constant repeal of its decisions.

Therefore we can see that the courts that oversee the legality of public administration actions, in a direct or indirect manner, influence the scope of the administrations' discretion in the decision making process, restricting it on the one hand and directing it on the other.

The effective system of national control over public administration, especially over decisions undertaken within the scope of discretion, should prevent aforementioned violations. However in reality many different situations appear in which such breaches happen anyway. As we consider the decisional processes at the national level and the relationship between public administrative bodies and the judiciary, at least three possible situations may occur.

In the first situation, the administrative authorities violate human rights and the court recognises and prevents it. In this situation comes the elimination of the decision from the legal system or its correction (in terms of how competent the courts are in respect to such decisions), because of its incompatibility with human rights.

In the second situation, the administrative decision breaches the rights of its addressee and the court, for various reasons, does not prevent it. In this case, there is a breach of human rights and the national authorities responsible for the review of decisions didn`t oppose it and a faulty (as in it does not comply with law and human rights) legal decision or action remains in force and has certain legal effects.

In the third situation, the administrative body acts in respect to human rights but the court changes the content of the decision in a way that violates those rights. This is perhaps the worst possible situation, as it means the lack of proper preparation of the court (regardless of the reasons and motives for the court to change the decision) and probably in the most severe way infringes on the principles of legal certainty and the confidence of citizens in the state.

The effect of the second and third situation is a legal decision that violates human rights that can be a subject of control of the ECHR. For the state authorities and courts of the countries that have signed the European Convention of Human Rights (Convention for the Protection of Human Rights and Fundamental Freedoms and its additional protocols) the jurisdiction of ECHR is obligatory.

Therefore the question arises whether the supranational system of human rights protection (namely Council of Europe system) can efficiently control decisions and actions of public administration bodies (even those connected with governance processes) and whether the system is sufficient to protect people from arbitrary decisions made by public administration. While trying to answer this question, it is necessary to look at the human rights protection system from two different perspectives: procedural and material.

The first perspective concerns the problem whether the procedure before the ECHR makes it possible to verify decisions of state authorities, especially those undertaken in the scope of discretionary power. Often it can be difficult because the true motivations and reasoning of public administration bodies can by hidden under a well prepared justification of a decision.

However, the contradictory procedure before the ECHR allows each side to present its statement – first in the written version and then oral arguments. It allows individuals to point out to the ECHR issues that were, in their opinion, subject to violation. At the same time the ECHR establishes the facts of the case and tries to answer the question of whether a human rights violation actually took place. The lack of procedural restrictions in this regard in conjunction with the contradictory process provides an opportunity to determine whether the decision of public authorities, even if taken within discretionary powers, have breached human rights.

The second perspective, the material one, is concentrated on the scope of the activity of the ECHR – the scope of its control. One needs to remember that the European Convention of Human Rights introduces general rules that are then developed into detailed and specified by the judicial activity of the ECHR. The ECHR's jurisprudence permanently raises the standards of human rights' protection, which allows it to keep pace with the rapidly changing world and dynamics of social life. In this context we can say that because of the judicial standards of the ECHR the system is effective enough and can prevent further violations even in the situation of decisions made in the scope of discretion of public administration.

4. Influence of the ECHR's Jurisprudence on Public Administration Discretion

The issue of judicial review over the activity of the administration has acquired additional meaning in a globalised world with enhanced legal and social integration. In this context the impact of supranational human rights protection systems on decisions taken at the national level is an important issue. The question is to what extent does the system of human rights' protection within the Council of Europe affect decision making processes of public administration bodies in the governance processes.

It should be pointed out that the subject of ECHR jurisdiction are cases where a violation of human rights has already occurred and the judgement of the ECHR can only compensate the injured individual grievances or his or her losses. At the same time, however, the decisions of the ECHR have to also prevent human rights' violations in the future, thereby accomplishing a preventive function. The consequences of the judgements of the ECHR may consist of a change of the legal provisions in national law or changes in the decision making practice (judgment of the ECHR of 6.11.2007, Bugajny and others v. Poland 22531/05).

While analysing potential impact of judgements of the ECHR on governance processes in the state, we should pay attention to the way in which judgments of the ECHR may influence the public authority actions, the levels of said impact and types of reasoning of the decision maker that are being affected the most.

The case law of the ECHR influences the functioning of public administration and thus the governance processes either directly or indirectly (see Andenas & Bjorge, 2013, pp. 225–234). The direct impact is visible with regard to the specific case (decision passed by an administrative body) that have become the subject of the ECHR ruling and other cases of a similar type (decisions passed by other bodies but in similar state of affairs to the one that is in the range of competences of specific administrative body). Indirect impact is associated with the formation of a specific line of decision making and jurisprudence at the national level based on the standards of the ECHR jurisprudence and mainstreaming judgements of the ECHR as an argument of interpretation or decisionmaking. The indirect impact through judgements of national courts that control actions of a public administration body may concern the practices of the state authorities in which there was a violation of human rights but also other states whose case is not directly concerned.

The judicial decisions of the ECHR may affect the public administration and its activity at different levels.

The first level is associated with direct ways of impact. This is the situation when the authority draws conclusions from its own case or cases carried out by other bodies in similar cases, and in which the ECHR passes judgement stating that a violation of human rights took place. Here a decision passed by a specific administrative body was found to be violating those rights and was eliminated from the legal order. In this case administrative authorities should either act in order to undertake another decision in a given state of affairs in accordance with human rights or take no activity at all because any action in this situation can be seen as a breach of those rights.

At the same time one needs to remember that the content of a specific decision or the reasoning of a decisional body can also be affected by the jurisprudence of the ECHR in other cases similar to the one that are in the competence of an administrative body. For example while recognising a decision of an administrative authority acting in a specific area in the state the judgement of the ECHR can influence the decision making process of other administrative bodies acting in other areas of that state. In this sense one might say that administrative bodies follow the "precedent" (judgement) of the ECHR.

What is more, in some cases public administration authorities of one state follow the content of the ECHR judgement addressed to administrative authorities in other states. So some king of unification of decisional processes can be observed. Moreover even if public administrative authorities from different states do not follow the case law of ECHR that is not addressed to them directly, a certain level of unification can be seen because of the introduction to the jurisprudence of the ECHR human rights' protection standards that are identical for all states and their authorities.

On the second level, the influence of the ECHR jurisprudence on national governance processes involves the public administration taking into account (while undertaking specific actions) judicial decisions (line of jurisprudence) of national courts competent to review the decisions of the administration, the judgements of which are (to a lesser or greater extent) influenced by the judgments of the ECHR. On this level the impact of the Court jurisdiction is less noticeable which does not necessarily mean that it is less instanced.

The third level is the one in which the judicial decisions of a ECHR affects other supranational courts (for example the Court of Justice of the EU) or authorities, and those then become an argument in cases before national courts to verify the functioning of public administration. Benvenisti (1999, 843) puts forward an interesting formula that the ECHR is a court that on an international level can be seen as an authoritative one and its judgments are a source of inspiration not only to national courts but also for judges and members of committees of other international bodies.

The impact of the jurisdictions of the ECHR requires taking into account the standards of human rights protection for decision making processes undertaken by the state authorities. Those standards developed by the ECHR define the absolute limit for the activity of public authorities introducing a certain sphere of personal freedom that in principle cannot be infringed by those authorities (at least without changing the national legislature first).

Thus those standards can affect the reasoning of a public authority both in the decisions related to the exercise of unequivocal obligations as well as on management activities (connected with governance processes) of public administration. In this sense it will affect the discretionary power authority on different stages of the decision making process.

In the pre-decisional phase, it is linked to the question of whether the implementation of tasks set by public administration in the context of human rights protection requires any action. If the answer to that question is positive it may influence the choice of one of the legally permissible methods to accomplish this task. In this context, for example, it is worth mentioning the proportionality principle which is not stated at all in the text of the Convention, but only proclaimed in the case-law of the ECHR (the ECHR judgments: judgment of 25.03.1992 Campbell v. The United Kingdom 13590/88; judgment of 13.06.1979 Marckx v. Belgium 6833/74; judgment of 26.04.1979 Sunday Times v. The United Kingdom 6538/74; judgment of 24.08.1998 Lambert v. France 23618/94; judgment of 07.12.1976, Handyside v. The United Kingdom 5493/72).

The principle of proportionality requires that there should be a reasonable relationship between a particular objective to be achieved and the means used to achieve that objective (see Clayton & Tomlinson, 2000, 278). It is considered one of the most important legal principles under the ECHR (see Kalisz, 2012, pp. 102–103). The proportionality principle means the "fair balance" between the protection of individual freedoms and the interests of the general public (see Aleinkoff, 1986, 943). The test of suitability and necessity (undertaken within aforementioned principle) can restrict the freedom of the decisional body. Thus the jurisprudence of the ECHR can be considered a kind of directive of choice of action.

The ECHR's jurisprudence standards can also play an important role in the interpretation of law. As pointed out by Lizewski (2015, 403), interpretive arguments can help both in the interpretation of national legislation and in gaining a proper understanding of the provisions of the convention. He points also to the legislative nature of the ECHR's standards, because they shape the substantive understanding of individual human rights. In this sense, even in countries of civil law (continental) culture, adjudications become, along with legal provisions, a full-fledged source of law.

Finally, the judgments of the ECHR influence the final shape of decisions, particularly in cases where the authority is granted with the administrative approval construction. Then the ECHR's standards can become one of the directives of choice of the consequences (directives that need or can be taken into account while passing the final decision) that the authority may (it is not legally binding so the body is not obligated to do it) take into account when making a decision. At the same time these standards determine the absolute limit for authority – for example, by eliminating one of the potential contents of the final decision, because it may infringe in some sense standards of protection of human rights. In this context one might say that these standards are limiting the discretionary power of public administration even in the situation in which its actions are in accordance to the law.

In this regard, it is clear that the jurisprudence of the ECHR, on the one hand, limits the discretionary power of public administration in all decision making processes and, on the other hand, directs the reasoning of a public authority.

5. Jurisprudence of the ECHR and Governance Processes

If the jurisprudence of the ECHR can affect the scope of the discretionary power of public administration one more question remains: is it possible that it can lead to the unification of decisional processes of administrative authorities in different states? Is it possible that standards of protection of human rights created by the ECHR will affect administrative bodies and governance processes in the way that will draw closer the decisional processes in different states? If the answer to those questions should be positive it could mean that the ECHR can be seen as an institution of global governance.

At this point one must remember that the introduction of the standard of protection of human rights does not presuppose its immutability, and most importantly does not prevent the autonomy of states that are high contracting parties to the European Convention of Human Rights. On the contrary, the Convention permits, with respect to certain rights, so-called limiting clauses (the concept of "margin of appreciation" – see Yourow H.C. 1996; Arai- Takahashi 2001, the ECHR judgements: judgment of 20.09.1994 Otto Preminger Institute v. Austria 13470/87;. judgment of 22.10.1981, Dudgeon v. UK 7525/76; judgment of 21.02.2002, Ghidotti v. Italy 28272/95). An example are the "freedom rights" which are characterised by being highly "axiologically sensitive" and for which the ECHR cannot work out a uniform or acceptable standard with regard to their reference to morality or religion (see Liżewski, 2015, 281).

The perception of the Convention as a living instrument for the protection of human rights which should be interpreted in relation to the current needs and the specificities of the country allows for the flexible protection of human rights and relieves tension between national authorities and the ECHR (see Brems, 1996, pp. 312–313).

In this respect, it should be argued that the jurisdiction of the ECHR may significantly influence the decisions of public authorities including those which are undertaken in the area of governance. In formulating standards of jurisprudence the ECHR at least to some extent affects the development of uniformity in governance processes in the sphere of public decisions in states that have signed the European Convention on Human Rights. At the same time it does not mean an absolute unification and is associated with certain minimum requirements in a democratic state while maintaining the autonomy and axiological individualism of specific countries and societies (see Kalisz & Szot, 2011, pp. 153–154). This happens regardless of how and on what level the decision of the ECHR affects public administration as well as the stage of the decision making process in which this occurs.

So the answer to the aforementioned question is rather negative – the ECHR cannot be seen as an institution of global governance despite the fact that its jurisprudence can affect governance processes at the national level, sometimes leading even to its unification. This is not a result of a conscious decision or intention of the ECHR and even if it takes place it is caused by similarities of legal systems or decision making policies of different states that reacts to the ECHR judgments in a similar way rather than is it a result of a deliberate activity of the ECHR.

6. Conclusions

The issue of the actual or potential influence of the ECHR's judgements on public administration decisions (especially governance decisions) is very complex. The considerations of this paper are the best example of it. Some problems were only signalised in the text and can be a subject of further research. The main goal of this paper was to answer three questions and for those answers to be clear to the reader they should be highlighted one more time.

Because of the complex procedure before the ECHR and at the same time because of the standards of human rights' protection given by the ECHR that all states that signed the Convention must respect in every action of its authorities the system of protection of human rights within the Council of Europe is efficient enough (1) to prevent the infringement of human rights at national level. It applies also to actions and decisions undertaken by the public administration within the scope of its discretionary power.

The ECHR's jurisprudence may influence administrative authorities' discretion (2) in two different but related ways. First, it restricts the scope of said discretion to the activities, reasoning and decisions that are in accordance with human rights and human rights protection standards. Secondly it can be seen as one of the directives of choice for the national authorities in the sense of it being a guideline for all of the activities, reasonings, and decisions of public administration bodies.

In the current world of globalisation and integration the unification of legal systems and decision making processes (also governance processes) in different states can be seen more clearly. Despite the fact that the jurisprudence of the ECHR can be seen (mainly because of the obligation to come along with standards of protection of human rights that are created by the ECHR) as a mechanism or factor of this unification of governance processes in reality it is not (3). One may observe that because of the rulings of the ECHR some decisional processes of administrative bodies and their outcomes are becoming similar or even identical in different states but it can be seen as an additional (marginal) effect of influence of jurisprudence the ECHR on governance process at the national level.

This paper was created as a result of the research project No. 2013/11/N/HS5/04212 entitled "The influence of judicial decisions on the discretionary power of public administration in the law application processes" funded by the National Science Centre (Poland).

Cases before the European Court Of Human Rights

Judgement of the ECHR of 6.11.2007, Bugajny and others v. Poland 22531/05
Judgement of 25.03.1992 Campbell v. The United Kingdom 13590/88;
Judgement of 13.06.1979 Marckx v. Belgium 6833/74;
Judgement of 26.04.1979 Sunday Times v. The United Kingdom 6538/74;
Judgement of 24.08.1998 Lambert v. France 23618/94;
Judgement of 07.12.1976, Handyside v. The United Kingdom 5493/72
Judgement of 20.09.1994 Otto Preminger Institute v. Austria 13470/87;.
Judgement of 22.10.1981, Dudgeon v. UK 7525/76;
Judgement of 21.02.2002, Ghidotti v. Italy 28272/95

References

Aleinkoff, Alexander T. 1986–87. Constitutional Law in the Age of Balancing, *The Yale Law Journal* 96: 943–1005.

Arai-Takahashi, Yuki. 2001. The Margin of Appreciation Doctrine and the Principle of Proportionality in the Jurisprudence of the ECHR: Intersentia.

Benvenisti, Eyal. 1999. Margin of Appreciation, Consensus and Universal Standards, *International Law and Politics* 31: 843–854.

Brems, Eva. 1996. The Margin of Appreciation Doctrine in the Case-Law of the European Court of Human Rights, *Heidelberg Journal of International Law* 56: 240–315.

Clayton, Richard; Tomlinson Heugh. 2000. The Law of Human Rights, Oxford University Press.

Galligan, Denis J. 1986. Discretionary powers – a Legal Study of Official Discretion, Oxford University Press.

Jakimowicz, Wojciech. 2010. Zewnętrzne granice uznania administracyjnego, *Państwo i Prawo* 5: 42–54.

Jaśkowska, Małgorzata. 2010. Uznanie administracyjne a inne formy władzy dyskrecjonalnej administracji publicznej. In: System prawa administracyjnego, t. 1: Instytucje prawa administracyjnego, edited by Hauser Roman; Niewiadomski Zygmunt; Wróbel Andrzej. 215–305: Beck Publishing.

Kalisz, Anna. 2012. Principle of proportionality as an element stabilizing the diversity of values in democratic societies (in the context of individual freedom). In: Crisis and Quality of Democracy in Eastern Europe, edited by Jovanovic, Miodrag A. 95–108: Eleven International Publishing.

Kalisz, Anna; Szot, Adam. 2011. The General Clause: A Measure of Universalizing the Content of Law or An Expression of its Diversity? On 'Public Interest' and 'Public Moral' Clauses. In: Legal and Political Theory in the Post-National Age, edited by Cserne, Péter; Könczöl, Miklós. 147–158: Peter Lang.

Leszczyński, Leszek. 2001. Zagadnienia teorii stosowania prawa. Doktryna i tezy orzecznictwa, Zakamycze.

Liżewski, Bartosz. 2015. Operacjonalizacja ochrony praw człowieka w porządku Europejskiej Konwencji Praw Człowieka. Wydawnictwo UMCS Lublin.

Mads, Andenas; Eirik, Bjorge. 2013. National implementation of ECHR rights. In: Constituting Europe – The European Court of Human Rights in a National, European and Global Context, edited by Føllesdal Andreas; Peters Birgit and Ulfstein, Geir. 181–263: Cambridge University Press.

Robertson, David. 1997. A Dictionary of Human Rights: Europa Publications Limited London.

Treves G. E. 1947. Administrative discretion and judicial control. *The Modern Law Review* 10: 276–291.

Villiger, Mark E. 2015. Binding Effect and Declaratory Nature of the Judgments of the European Court of Human Rights: An Overview. In: Judgments of the European Court of Human Rights – Effects and Implementation, edited by Seibert-Fohr, Anja; Villiger, Mark E. 33–39: Nomos Verlagsgesellschaft.

Yourow, Howard C. 1996. The Margin of Appreciation Doctrine in the Dynamics of European Human Rights Jurisprudence: Kluwer Academic Publishers.

List of Contributors

Martin Belov (editor) – Senior Assistant Professor in Constitutional and Comparative Constitutional Law, University of Sofia "St. Kliment Ohridski," Faculty of Law, Bulgaria.

Christoph Good – Senior Research Fellow, University of Zurich Centre for Human Rights Studies, Switzerland and Lecturer for International Law, Andrássy University Budapest, Hungary.

Anna Kalisz – Assistant Professor and Lecturer of "Humanitas" University of Sosnowiec, Poland.

Miklós Könczöl – Assistant Professor, Pázmány Péter Catholic University, Faculty of Law and Political Sciences, Department of Legal Philosophy, Hungary; Research Fellow, Hungarian Academy of Sciences, Centre for Social Sciences, Institute for Legal Studies.

Mate Paksy – postdoctoral researcher, University of Liege, BEIPD/COFUND, Belgium.

Axelle Reiter – Adjunct Professor (lecturer) in International Law at the Faculty of Economics of Verona University (Vicenza) Italy.

Michele Saporiti – Research fellow in Philosophy of Law (University of Milano-Bicocca), Italy; Chercheur post-doctorant in Political Philosophy at Groupe Sociétés, Religions, Laïcités: EPHE (Paris-Sorbonne)-CNRS, France.

Saskia Sassen – Robert S. Lynd Professor of Sociology, and co-Chair, The Committee on Global Thought, Columbia University, USA.

Adam Szot – Assistant Professor, Maria Curie-Sklodowska University, Lublin, Poland.

Szilárd Tattay – Assistant Professor, Pázmány Péter Catholic University, Budapest, Hungary; Research Fellow, Institute for Legal Studies, Centre for Social Sciences of the Hungarian Academy of Sciences, Budapest, Hungary.

Alexander Tsekov – Assistant Professor, South-Western University "Neofit Rilski," Blagoevgrad, Bulgaria.

Monika Zalewska – Postdoctoral Researcher, University of Lodz, Poland.

Uroš Zdravković – Assistant Professor, University of Niš, Faculty of Law, Serbia.

Central and Eastern European Forum for Legal, Political, and Social Theory Yearbook

Edited by Jürgen Busch / Péter Cserne / Michael Hein / Miklós Könczöl / Miodrag Jovanović / Marta Soniewicka

Vol. 1 Péter Cserne / Miklós Könczöl (eds.): Legal and Political Theory in the Post-National Age. Selected papers presented at the Second Central and Eastern European Forum for Legal, Political and Social Theorists (Budapest, 21–22 May 2010). 2011.

Vol. 2 Miodrag A. Jovanović / Bojan Spaić (eds.): Jurisprudence and Political Philosophy in the 21st Century. Reassessing Legacies. 2012.

Vol. 3 Péter Cserne / Miklós Könczöl / Marta Soniewicka (eds.): The Rule of Law and the Challenges to Jurisprudence. Selected papers presented at the Fourth Central and Eastern European Forum for Legal, Political and Social Theorists, Celje, 23–24 March 2012. 2014.

Vol. 4 Antonia Geisler / Michael Hein / Siri Hummel (eds.): Law, Politics, and the Constitution. New Perspectives from Legal and Political Theory. 2014.

Vol. 5 Luka Burazin / Đorđe Gardašević / Alessio Sardo (eds.): Law and State. Classical Paradigms and Novel Proposals. 2015.

Vol. 6 Martin Belov (ed.): Global Governance and Its Effects on State and Law. 2016.

www.peterlang.com